P9-CFX-272

THE THING
IN THE BUSHES

Turning Organizational Blind Spots into Competitive Advantage

KEVIN G. FORD AND JAMES P. OSTERHAUS, PH.D.

WITH JIM DENNEY

PIÑON PRESS

P.O. Box 35007, Colorado Springs, Colorado 80935

OUR GUARANTEE TO YOU

We believe so strongly in the message of our books that we are making this quality guarantee to you. If for any reason you are disappointed with the content of this book, return the title page to us with your name and address and we will refund to you the list price of the book. To help us serve you better, please briefly describe why you were disappointed. Mail your refund request to: Piñon Press, P.O. Box 35007, Colorado Springs, CO 80935.

©2001 by Cambria Associates and TAG, LLC
All rights reserved. No part of this publication may be reproduced in any form without written permission from Piñon Press, P. O. Box 35007, Colorado Springs, CO 80935.
Library of Congress Catalog Card Number: 01-065280
ISBN 1-57683-228-7

Cover Design: Steve Eames
Cover Illustration: Steven Adler
Interior Illustrations: Cromwell Communications, Royal Oak, MI
Creative Team: Patricia Klein, Lori Mitchell, Amy Spencer, Glynese Northam

Some of the anecdotal illustrations in this book are true to life and are included with the permission of the persons involved. All other illustrations are composites of real situations, and any resemblance to people living or dead is coincidental.

This publication is designed to provide accurate and authoritative information in regard to the subject matter covered. It is sold with the understanding that the author and the publisher are not engaged in rendering legal, accounting, or other professional service. If legal advice or other expert assistance is required, the services of a competent professional person should be sought. *From a Declaration of Principles jointly adopted by a Committee of the American Bar Association and a Committee of Publishers.*

Ford, Kevin Graham, 1965-
    The thing in the bushes : turning organizational blind spots into competitive advantage / by Kevin G. Ford and James P. Osterhaus with Jim Denney.
      p. cm.
    Includes bibliographical references.
    ISBN 1-57683-228-7
    1. Organizational effectiveness. 2. Corporate turnarounds. 3. Competition. I. Osterhaus, James P. II. Denney, James D. III. Title.

    HD58.9 .F668 2001
    658.4'063--dc21   00-065280

Printed in the United States of America
1 2 3 4 5 6 7 8 9 10 / 05 04 03 02 01

Substantial discounts on bulk quantities are available to corporations, professional associations, and other organizations. For details and discount information, contact the special markets department at Piñon Press at 1-800-955-4432.

Contents

FOREWORD

You hold in your hands a one-of-a-kind experience. The truths in this book aren't found in a standard MBA program. That's because this book is all about what works in practice.

The principles that Kevin Ford and Jim Osterhaus explain so clearly in this book are much more than theory. They provide the framework for people to produce and achieve results. And in the process, those people will grow, develop, and find meaning in their work. They'll become the subjects, not just the objects, of their work.

I know for a fact that any organization—be it a storefront business, an Internet company, a military organization, a nonprofit organization, a club, or a church—will never achieve its full potential until it confronts its own organizational blind spots.

That's why the practical, transformational concepts in this book are *desperately* needed by organizations of all kinds. The business leader, government leader, or business school professor who truly understands the role of relationships and relational networks is all too rare in this world.

So let the standard MBA program develop the theories of competitive behavior and strategic career management. Let them continue to educate business students in the intricacies of pro forma statements, discounted cash-flow valuation, and coherent operating systems-process analysis. Those are all good things to know.

But if you want to build a Relationally Healthy Organization—one that weeds out The Thing in the Bushes—you'll have to read this book. The good news is that this book is a *joy* to read—lively, powerful, engrossing, and even fun.

Prepare to be transformed. This book is going to change you; and through you, it is going to change your organization.

So what are you waiting for? Turn the page and dig in!

C. William Pollard
Chairman and CEO, The ServiceMaster Company,
and author of The Soul of the Firm

ACKNOWLEDGMENTS

First, we are grateful to God for giving us a passion for helping people and organizations move beyond their problems; for giving us partners to help us develop these concepts; and for giving us the chance to make a difference.

Next, we are thankful for Joe Jurkowski, who is one of the best organizational consultants we've ever seen. A good portion of the ideas in this book are his ideas. He is truly a master consultant, and we are privileged to partner with him at TAG. We are also incredibly thankful for the support and concept development from the rest of our partners at TAG. To Gary Hurst, Sue Johnston, and Jeanne Snapp—a big thanks for all your help. Rick Martin and Kathy Elliott have been invaluable. Our consulting affiliates—Bob Wacker, Dan McAllister, Gary Oliver, Chris Elliott, Leighton Ford, Doug Thompson, Doug Rachford, and Earl Pence, just to name a few—have helped us refine these ideas in various industries.

We have both worked with Jim Denney in the past and, as always, have found him to be a first-rate writer and person. He provided incredible editorial assistance and research, and is the one who spent countless hours cutting, pasting, writing, and rewriting. Likewise, Patricia Klein, our editor, was extremely helpful in forcing us to think in a very focused way. The book would have been a shabby piece of work were it not for the assistance of Jim and Patricia.

The Piñon Press staff has been delightful to work with—a huge compliment coming from us. Paul Santhouse and his team received numerous voice mails and e-mails from us—perhaps on a weekly basis. Thanks to them for putting up with us. Their personal touch has separated Piñon from other publishers. Thanks for caring about us as people first, and authors second.

We are thankful for our families and friends for their ongoing support of our work through TAG and our service in life. We owe a huge thanks to John Hunt who has made an indelible mark on corporate America. And lastly, we appreciate our clients who have helped us as we have assisted them. Thanks for letting us shake the bushes.

Kevin G. Ford and
James P. Osterhaus, Ph.D.

The Thing
in the Bushes

EXECUTIVE SUMMARY

This prologue introduces "The Thing in the Bushes," a metaphor to describe the unidentified and often-denied problem that prevents an organization from achieving its goals. Whenever there is dysfunction in a group (such as a family or organization), there are frequently two problems: (1) the Identified Problem and (2) The Thing in the Bushes. The Identified Problem is what people think is wrong. Although it is typically unspoken, it is rarely the real problem. The Thing in the Bushes is the real problem nobody talks about, because it lurks in our collective blind spot.

When we try to "fix" the Identified Problem instead of solving the real problem (The Thing in the Bushes), it only gets worse. In fact, the "solution" becomes the problem. Usually, the problem is not in the parts but in the whole. It is not a single component but the entire relational network of the organization that is dysfunctional.

The business world is a world of relationships. Problems in organizations grow out of complex patterns of interactions that involve most, if not all, of the people within the organization. So we must look at organizational problems not as isolated events but as symptoms within the entire relational network of the organization. The "Relational Performance" of an organization—how it relates to its customers, community, shareholders, and employees—can be assessed in terms of nine Relational Performance Principles:

1. Break the code.

2. Encourage personal excellence.

3. Unleash leadership in everyone.

4. Practice relational network thinking.

5. Create healthy boundaries.

6. Nurture effective communication.

7. Balance trust and cynicism.

8. Proactively manage change.

9. Focus beyond yourself.

These nine principles are the keys to Relational Performance. They are not isolated components. They complement and interact with each other in dynamic ways. Good Relational Performance is the foundation of organizations that are financially successful, productive, innovative, energetic, and enduring.

What makes The Thing in the Bushes so scary is that we don't even know it's there.

It lurks in the shadows. It feeds on human emotion. It destroys everything we've worked for, everything we've sacrificed for. It always emerges when we least expect it, when everything is going well—then it vanishes as soon as we become aware of its presence.

The Thing fills us with a sense of unease, a gnawing dread. Everything seems vaguely *wrong* somehow, but we can't put our finger on *why*. Worst of all, we don't know what to do about it.

The Thing destroys small businesses, large corporations, law firms, medical corporations, retail firms, partnerships, churches, teams, unions, clubs, and military organizations. Any time people come together to accomplish something good or profitable or worthwhile, The Thing is there, lusting and hungering, waiting for an opportunity to pounce and destroy.

The Thing may sound like some specter from a Stephen King novel, but it is real, powerful, and dangerous.

But The Thing is not invincible!

It can be exposed. It can be seen for what it is. And it can be dealt with effectively.

Let us show you how. Let us introduce you to . . . *The Thing in the Bushes.*

Law and Disorder

Whenever there is a problem in any group of people, whether that group is a family or an organization, there are often two problems: (1) the Identified Problem and (2) The Thing in the Bushes. The Identified Problem is what people *think* is wrong. When someone asks, "What's wrong here?" everyone points to the Identified Problem. Sometimes the Identified Problem is the real problem, and it can be solved with a simple technical fix. Often, the Identified Problem is unspoken—giving it even more power and attention. But when we try and try to solve a problem, and we keep getting stuck, then the Identified Problem is *rarely* the real problem. In such cases, the *real* problem is The Thing in the Bushes—and that's the problem nobody talks about.

When we assume that the Identified Problem is the main barrier to reaching our goals as an organization, our tendency is to apply inadequate or misplaced solutions that never address the reality of the situation. We may look for scapegoats. We may keep applying the wrong tool to the problem (like pounding a nail with a screwdriver—and when that doesn't work, pounding harder!). We get nowhere and we get frustrated—and the solution *becomes* the problem.

The real problem is The Thing in the Bushes—the problem that is unidentified and hides in the shadows. It may be known but denied, or it may be something that no one is even aware of. In any case, The Thing in the Bushes lurks in our blind spot, in our denial and evasion, in our fear of facing the truth about ourselves, in the shadow side of ourselves and our organization. But even if The Thing in the Bushes is submerged below the level of our conscious awareness, we can uncover it and expose it. Clues to The Thing's whereabouts can be gained from observing how people interact with each other.

It is crucial not to mistake the Identified Problem for The Thing in the Bushes, not to mistake the *symptom* for the *disorder.* If you only treat a symptom, you may relieve the pain for a time—but you'll miss the deadly cancer at the root of the pain.

The Thing always represents the quiet voice of our organizational system. It sometimes speaks for those who aren't heard. It sometimes represents the important issues that have been squelched by the tyranny of the urgent. The Thing usually reveals itself through problems and dysfunctions. It rarely speaks directly and usually only offers clues to its discovery. It is always avoided and feared.

Not long ago, TAG (formerly The Armstrong Group), our consulting organization, received a call from a large law firm, Oliver, McKenna & Smith (we've changed this name and the names of some client companies and their employees in this book; see appendix 2 for a listing of all fictitious as well as actual client companies). The forty-year-old firm of OM&S was in crisis and had already gone through a number of consultants, to no avail. The issue, according to Matthew Oliver, the senior partner who called us, was that the firm needed help with strategic planning—the task of outlining a broad vision in terms of the organization's values and goals, with regular measurements of progress toward achieving that vision. The firm could not come to agreement over its vision for the future.

We went to OM&S to assess the situation and began by meeting with the senior partners. We hadn't been on-site for more than half an hour before we sensed the presence of The Thing. The problem that we had been brought in to solve—a problem with strategic planning and a coherent vision for the future—was only a symptom of the deeper, hidden problems that plagued the law firm of Oliver, McKenna & Smith. But what were those hidden problems? That's what we had to find out.

We began by conducting a Culture Type Indicator (CTI) with the whole staff. CTI is a diagnostic tool we use to determine the culture type of organizations. (You may want to take the sample individual CTI in appendix 3 before reading further so that you can assess your own organizational type. Just remember that the CTI was intended for large groups rather than individuals.) From the deviation in results, it became clear that there was an issue in the firm that nobody talked about—perhaps a values clash, a generational clash, or an old-guard-versus-new-guard conflict. When there is an unspoken issue (the Identified Problem)—whether in a dysfunctional family or a dysfunctional organization—the issue remains unspoken because people assume nothing can be done about it. They believe the problem is unsolvable, so they repress it and talk about something else.

Next, we asked to see what the firm had done in the past in the way of strategic planning. We were led to a bookshelf that groaned under the weight of past plans. You had to give Oliver, McKenna & Smith credit: those people knew how to plan. The latest plan was a beautifully bound, gold-embossed volume some 150-odd pages long, illustrated with beautiful color graphs. It had been methodically formulated, meticulously enshrined—but never implemented.

Questioning further, we discovered that the firm was in the advanced stages of an internal crisis. Conducting interviews with everyone from the senior partners to the office staff, we detected simmering fears and resentments. Over the past few months, a number of consultants had been brought in to help OM&S solve its strategic planning problems, but to no avail. OM&S could plan all the strategies it wanted, but the strategies would never be implemented as planned.

It was a clear case of law—and disorder. There was a serious, scary, *hidden* disorder lurking in the corridors of Oliver, McKenna & Smith. We had seen it many times before. Once again, The Thing in the Bushes had reared its ugly head. We had to find it—and stop it.

Relational Network Thinking

Our first clue that The Thing was lurking in the law offices of OM&S was the finger pointing we encountered in our interviews with the partners and staff. Sometimes it was politely phrased, sometimes it was blunt and hostile, but again and again we heard people say, "So-and-so is the problem," or "The process always breaks down in Such-and-such Department."

We've seen it many times in many organizations. There is a full-blown crisis going on. People know that something is terribly wrong and needs to be changed—but what? Human nature being what it is, when something goes wrong, people immediately start looking for a scapegoat—someone or something on which to hang the blame. It might be an individual, a department, or a division within the organization. The thinking goes, "If only we could get rid of Jason . . . " or "If only we'd never hired Lori . . . " or "If Marketing would only pull its weight . . . " or "If we could just spin off the overseas division, everything would be fine!" So we give Jason and Lori the axe, we rattle the cages over in Marketing, we dump the overseas division, and everything is solved, right? Wrong. Things get *worse.* The "solution" doesn't solve the problem—the "solution" *becomes* the problem.

As human beings, we're used to solving problems by breaking them down into their component parts. Car won't start? Here's your problem: dead battery. Just take it out, put in a new one, and the car runs fine. Simple. But organizations are not so simple. Often, the problem is not in the *parts,* it's in the *whole.* The problem is embedded and entrenched within the entire organizational system. It is rooted in the way people relate to each other. And that makes the problem harder to see, harder to isolate, and harder to fix. You can't just take out the bad part and put in a good one. The whole relational network of the organization is dysfunctional and in need of realignment.

In our own consulting practice, we devote our attention to the entire relational network, not just to the individual components. We call this "relational network thinking"—a way of thinking that focuses on the connections and relationships between people rather than on isolated parts and problems within an organization. Again and again, we have seen that the health of an organization can only be assessed in the context of the whole. A change in one part affects every other part. The organization regulates itself through feedback loops, in which information travels throughout the organization, giving it life, organic integrity, and stability. When that relational network malfunctions, the health of the entire organization is threatened.

You cannot sum up any organization by reciting the roster of its members. Every organization, from Disney and GM and Hewlett-Packard down to the real estate agency or church or retailer down the street, is made up of systems, patterns, traditions, attitudes, beliefs, and habits that—more than any *single* individual or *collection* of individuals—define and constitute that organization. Every organization has its own unique cultural type, and that cultural type is always more than the sum of the individual personalities who inhabit that organization (which is why the CTI should be administered to the entire organization).

Seeing a chronic relational problem as residing in *only* one person or *only* one department almost *always* misses the point. Problems in organizations grow out of complex patterns of interactions that involve most, if not all, of the people within the organization. The person who is identified as "the problem" is usually the one who expresses the symptoms of the deeper relational difficulty and is often the one attempting to call attention to the real problem so that it can be solved. Tragically, these people are often punished as troublemakers when they are actually trying to save the organization from its own dysfunction.

Unfortunately, most of us have a hard time recognizing the hidden, distorted, dysfunctional patterns in our relationships. We are too close to the trouble to see our own enmeshment in the overall problem. So we try to sort out the situation by separating people into categories. We look for perpetrators and victims, good guys and bad guys. When we frame things in such stark terms, everything *seems* so much clearer. But it is *not* clearer. We have simply reduced our perception of reality to high-contrast black and white. We are not *viewing* reality. We are *filtering* reality.

And we may be filtering out the very information our organization needs in order to survive and prosper.

The world is too complex for simplistic, linear ways of looking at things. The business world is too complex. The world of human relationships is too complex. More and more, we are finding that the business and relational worlds are not separate worlds at all. They overlap and intermesh. The world of business *is* a world of relationships.

Driving The Thing Out of the Bushes

As we analyzed the situation at OM&S, we knew our first order of business was to find out where The Thing was hiding. Where were the bushes at OM&S?

In this book, our goal is to help your organization—no matter what kind of organization it is—to become successful by identifying and dealing with The Thing in the Bushes. The Thing is usually found lurking as the shadow side of one or more of nine ingredients or principles that we will explore in the course of this book: (1) a clear *code;* (2) the development of *personal excellence;* (3) a healthy *leadership* style; (4) a clear understanding of *relational network thinking;* (5) clear and dynamic *boundaries;* (6) healthy *communication;* (7) the ability to create an atmosphere of *trust;* (8) the ability to manage *change* positively; and (9) a willingness to *focus beyond yourself,* beyond the organization, and to invest in the wider community. When these ingredients are absent or distorted, the organization is unhealthy—and it is in these unhealthy aspects of the organization that The Thing hides and does its destructive work.

Don't expect The Thing to reveal itself directly. Rather, these principles provide the clues for discovering its hiding place. In contrast, when these ingredients are strong and healthy, the organization has a high level of "Relational Performance," a term that we'll use throughout the book.

Here's the success equation that we've found in organizations: Identifying and dealing with The Thing in the Bushes leads to Relational Performance. Relational Performance creates a strong and healthy culture. A healthy culture attracts and retains superior employees. Superior employees create better products, services, and experiences for customers. Better products, services, and experiences lead to customer retention, which is cheaper than marketing to new customers. In fact, your retained customers become your most effective marketers. Cost savings as a result of customer retention are then reinvested in the organization (either in new markets, new initiatives, or continuous improvement in organizational development). This keeps the organization always ahead of the pack.

The key is starting at the right point: finding and dealing with The Thing in the Bushes. This is how you can turn organizational blind spots into competitive advantage.

So these are the "bushes" where we began our search for The Thing that haunted the law office:

1. LIVE OUT YOUR CODE

A healthy, productive, and successful organization is built upon a clear guiding code. Every organization has a code, but many don't understand the code. By code, we mean the essence or soul of that organization, comprised of its culture, values, mission, and goals. It is crucial that the code of the organization be a healthy one (for example, "We are committed to making obscene profits no matter who we hurt" would be an unhealthy code). And it is crucial that all the people in the organization be committed to that healthy code.

The code sets the direction for all the members of the organization. It is the group's lodestar or compass point. The code keeps everyone in the boat, rowing in sync and in the same direction. When the code is clear and every member buys into it, allying himself or herself with that code, then the entire organization pulls together. When a few people lack commitment to the code—either because they don't grasp it or because they actively disagree with it—you have people rowing out of sync and in the wrong direction. Before long, the boat is going around in circles instead of moving forward. The Thing in the Bushes loves to get organizations off course.

2. ENCOURAGE PERSONAL EXCELLENCE

An organization with good Relational Performance is composed of healthy, positive members who know how to relate to each other in healthy, positive ways. Have you ever asked yourself, "How can we unleash the imagination and energy of our people? How can we make work enjoyable? How can we reduce turnover?" In order to have healthy members, an organization must hire the right people and have a plan for their ongoing growth and development as individuals.

We define "healthy" as having a good work attitude, emotional maturity, and strong relational skills. Healthy members are committed to the success of the organization, yet they also have an active life outside of the organization. Healthy members maintain physical, emotional, and relational balance, and they contribute that glow of good health to a healthy, balanced organization. The Thing fears healthy members and can often use a small number of unhealthy, unbalanced individuals to infect and destabilize an entire organization, throwing the entire relational network out of whack.

3. UNLEASH LEADERSHIP IN EVERYONE

An organization with good Relational Performance is built around strong, wise, inspiring leadership at every level of the organization. The Thing stalks wherever dysfunctional leadership styles are found. Dysfunctional leadership can take many forms: weakness and indecision; intrusive micromanagement; rigid and inflexible bureaucracy; intimidating, hypercritical dictatorship; mercurial, unstable, and unpredictable chaos-ocracy; and on and on. The Thing takes advantage of dysfunctional leadership styles, creating discord, fear, vacillation, frustration, and paralysis.

4. PRACTICE RELATIONAL NETWORK THINKING

The principles of relational network thinking are basic to the Relational Performance of any organization or group: (1) learn to focus on the whole, not just the parts; (2) learn to focus on relationships, not just individuals; (3) recognize that organizations seek to maintain organizational balance (homeostasis), which is often unhealthy; and (4) learn to set appropriate boundaries. The Thing in the Bushes often lurks where people attempt to apply simplistic, linear solutions to complex, network-wide problems.

5. CREATE DYNAMIC BOUNDARIES

An organization with good Relational Performance is composed of individuals, divisions, and teams that maintain healthy boundaries. Boundaries act as "fences" determining what a person or group is and is not responsible for.

Boundaries become unhealthy and inappropriate when they are either too rigid (which constricts the free flow of vital information) or too vague and ill defined (which generates confusion when people can't figure out what their responsibilities and expectations are). When boundaries are not clear and healthy, The Thing stirs up conflict and frustration. Tasks don't get done; deadlines get missed; and valuable time is wasted dealing with finger pointing and scapegoating.

6. NURTURE AUTHENTIC COMMUNICATION

An organization with good Relational Performance is alive and abuzz with open, free-flowing communication. In a healthy organization, people feel free to say what they mean and mean what they say. Vital information and important opinions travel freely from top to bottom, bottom to top, and end to end—all throughout a healthy organization. When communication is stifled, for whatever reason, The Thing is free to feed and grow and even *kill* the organization.

7. BALANCE TRUST AND CYNICISM

An organization with good Relational Performance is built on trust. In fact, all relationships are built on trust—relationships between family members, among employees, between employer and employee, among club and union members, between pastor and parishioner. Without trust, there is no relationship. There is only suspicion.

The Thing lurks in the shadows of suspicion, in the bushes of distrust. The Thing will use the fruit of distrust—discord, rumors, cynicism, fear, pessimism, discouragement—to defeat your business, your organization, your club, your church, your family. Relationships must have trust in order to be healthy.

8. PROACTIVELY MANAGE CHANGE

An organization with good Relational Performance navigates transitions and responds effectively to changing conditions. Transitions are constantly occurring within organizations—people come and people go. Relationships change. Boundaries, leadership, and communication styles are affected. Members of the organization must negotiate new ways of dealing with each other. Outside the walls of the organization, market conditions are constantly shifting and evolving.

The danger of changing times is that some individuals, and often the relational network as a whole, resist or ignore the transitions that must be made. Resistance to change often creates crisis within the organization—and The Thing often lurks within that crisis atmosphere, looking to destabilize and scuttle the organization as it navigates the rocky shoals and foaming white water of change.

9. Focus Beyond Yourself

An organization should have a higher purpose than merely making money. Profits are a means to an end—not the end itself. The goal of all organizations should involve a focus on making the world a better place. When an organization sees itself as a stakeholder in the wider community, the community itself becomes a stakeholder in the organization.

Companies should not merely consume; they should give back. But sometimes The Thing in the Bushes rears its head, trying to divert our attention from the organization's higher purpose. It whispers to us, slyly suggesting, "This organization exists to maximize earnings for shareholders. Sure, bettering the world is important—but later! We'll work on that when we have more time, more resources, more profits to play with! But right now, we need to focus on maximizing profits, ROI, and ROE!"

Assume that your organization has a blind spot. The Thing is lurking there somewhere. These nine principles are the map to finding it. They are the keys to a high level of Relational Performance. They are not isolated components. They are complementary—and they build on each other.

Once an organization deciphers its own code, it attracts people who have a matching personal code (personal excellence)—and people without a matching personal code depart. Personal excellence fosters an atmosphere where everyone is a leader. When everyone exercises leadership, they see the big picture and begin to practice relational network thinking. Relational network thinking raises the importance of dynamic boundaries that, in turn, foster healthy communication. Healthy boundaries and good communication contribute to an atmosphere of trust. When people trust each other, they are more able to navigate the tides of change. An atmosphere of positive change begins to raise deeper questions of why a company exists—and this helps an organization focus beyond itself.

So you can see how these nine principles work together to produce Relational Performance. When there are problems with any one of these nine principles, there are usually problems in several of them at once.

For example, an organization has an unpredictable, tempestuous CEO named Richard. He has poor leadership skills, and he oscillates from moody and withdrawn to hostile and intimidating (a failure of principle 3: leadership). When he is in his moody-withdrawn mode, Richard's second-in-command, Joyce, steps into the leadership void and takes over the CEO duties, countermanding many of Richard's previous edicts and yanking the organization in a different direction (a failure of principle 5: boundaries). This produces a cynicism and lack of trust in the organization's leadership (a failure of principle 7: trust). But nobody dares address the problem openly, for fear of reprisal on the part of the unpredictable CEO (a failure of principle 6: communication). All of these principles interact and intermesh within the relational network of the organization. That is why the organization must be viewed not as a machine made up of individual parts, but as an organism, dynamic and living, an orchestrated whole that is greater than the sum of any individual parts, any individual principles.

When problems occur within the relational network of an organization, they may be triggered by external circumstances (such as a hostile corporate takeover or an industry-wide economic downturn), or by internal events (a CEO retires, a dysfunctional employee is hired, a division is phased out). When these problems arise, old ways of coping may no longer work. It's time to step back and take a look at the entire organizational picture, the entire relational network.

It's time to hunt down The Thing in the Bushes.

The Thing in the Bushes at OM&S

As we assessed the crisis at Oliver, McKenna & Smith, we quickly grasped that the problem affected the entire relational network of the law firm. OM&S was an old firm with a rich tradition, but it was undergoing changes. Thomas McKenna Sr. was retiring from the firm, and his thirty-six-year-old son, Thomas "Tommy" McKenna Jr., had recently been made a full partner. Brash, conceited, and not nearly as scrupulous as his father and the other senior partners, Tommy had little use for the honorable traditions and principled values that formed the *code* of OM&S. He openly boasted of his ability to squeeze two billable hours out of every hour on the clock—a boast that scandalized the graying old-liners of the firm.

Tommy's *leadership* style was chaotic and often at odds with the leadership style of the other partners in the firm. Though they resented Tommy's egotistical ways and his ethical corner cutting, the senior partners avoided talking about the problem out of deference to their longtime friend, Thomas McKenna Sr. As a result, there was no *communication* about the problems and resentments festering at OM&S.

Privately, the old-guard partners and employees complained to us that Tommy had no respect for long-established procedural, ethical, and relational *boundaries,* and that *trust* had broken down both inside and outside the firm. This clash of values threatened to rattle the forty-year-old firm apart—unless all the members of the firm learned how to *navigate the changes* that were taking place within the offices and corridors of Oliver, McKenna & Smith.

No wonder OM&S couldn't formulate and execute its strategic plan! It was being torn in half, pulled in opposite directions—and no one at the firm would even talk openly about the problem. In such a closed and stifling relational atmosphere, The Thing in the Bushes could roam at will, feeding and destroying. Left unchallenged and unchecked, The Thing would ultimately kill a law firm with a long and respected history. We weren't about to let that happen. Now that we had caught sight of The Thing in the Bushes, we weren't going to let it get away.

The first order of business for the esteemed law firm was a weekend retreat in a relaxed and comfortable conference center in the Blue Ridge Mountains. We crafted a plan for the OM&S Strategic Planning Retreat, with an agenda designed to produce candid responses from all members of the organization. Themes to be dealt with included such issues as the firm's code, values, vision, and mission; roles, responsibilities, and boundaries; dealing with change and challenges; leadership and followership; and more.

The crucial weekend arrived, beginning with a Friday evening session. We entered the rustic conference room where a warm fire crackled in the stone fireplace. That fireplace was the only source of warmth in the room. The entire OM&S organization—senior partners, junior attorneys, managers, and office staff—sat in their chairs, cold, silent, and stony-faced. Tommy McKenna was there, and so was Thomas McKenna Sr., despite the fact that he was edging toward retirement and only devoting one or two days a week to the firm.

And something else was in the room. We both felt it. The Thing was there, too.

We began by projecting the results of the Culture Type Survey (CTI) up on a screen and explaining the findings to the group. Then we invited the people in the room to respond. As the discussions began, we noted a tacit avoidance of the core problems of the firm. People talked, but skirted the real issues that were hurting the relational health of the organization. A few small fixes were suggested—what we call "first order changes":

Why don't we retool the compensation package for the office staff? And shouldn't we install a copier on the second floor? Perhaps we could ditch the P&R account. Maybe we need to relocate to a newer office building with a brighter décor. All superficial stuff. The Thing was there, and they all felt it glaring at them from the shadows—but no one would openly acknowledge its presence.

We didn't get very far during that first evening session—but then, we didn't expect to. We knew it would take time for the real issues to emerge, and we were willing to wait it out.

After a good night's sleep and a satisfying breakfast, we all gathered for the Saturday morning session. It began where the previous night's session had left off. Again, the discussion was superficial. The issues raised were superficial. The atmosphere was edgy. The body language of the participants was tense and wary. A secret hovered over the room. Everyone knew it, though no one acknowledged it openly. For two or three hours, a number of people offered various simplistic, first order suggestions. Finally, the room lapsed into silence.

We allowed the silence to go on. Time dilated. "There's an unspoken truth in this room," a senior partner finally observed.

No one responded.

"Everyone here knows the unspoken truth she's talking about," we added. "We've interviewed all of you individually, and many of you have acknowledged a deep problem in the organization. But no one wants to put it on the table for everyone to see."

The seconds ticked by. People counted the threads in the carpet at their feet. We waited out the silence.

"Okay," Tommy McKenna said at last. All eyes snapped in his direction. "Look," he continued, "we all know what's going on here. Cards on the table, shall we? This firm is always talking about its *tradition.*" He said it as though it were a dirty word. "Well, 'tradition' is just another word for 'too rigid to adapt.' I'm trying to drag this firm, kicking and screaming, into a new millennium. OM&S has been around for almost a century, and if we're going to continue to be profitable for another century, we can't keep doing things the way they were done in 1950. This law firm has to change or die."

"Tommy," growled Old Man McKenna in a stentorian voice, "I thought I taught you better than that. Tradition doesn't mean rigidity; it means *solidity*—a solid foundation upon which to build trust and a respected reputation. This firm has never gone for the quick and easy buck, and I pray I never see the day it does."

"That's it!" Matthew Oliver interjected. He was the youngest of the senior partners, an athletic-looking man in his early sixties. He turned to us. "That's the real issue that's hanging us up, isn't it? The old guard versus new. The rich tradition of the past versus an open-throttle future, eh? It's an issue that draws a line right down the middle of this law firm—and we've never even talked about it before. That's got to be it!"

Matthew Oliver's insight opened a whole new round of communication in the group. It got loud at times—sometimes with laughter, sometimes with anger. But the important thing is that there was a candid exchange of ideas and feelings about issues that had never been opened up before. And yet . . .

After only an hour or so of discussion, the group again reached a point of "stuckness." The Thing in the Bushes was still there, still lurking, felt but unseen. The old-guard-versus-new-guard issue was a *real* issue, but it wasn't *the* issue. It was the Identified Problem. There was still something else, something that no one had dared put on the table. As important as this issue was, it was still a superficial matter compared to the unspoken problem that kept the entire group stuck.

After a couple full minutes of silence, we asked, "Have we gotten to the core problem yet?"

No one answered. More silence ensued.

"Everyone in this room assumed that the old-guard-versus-new-guard issue was the real problem, but it's not, is it?" we queried.

"Then what is?" asked Matthew Oliver.

"We think we know," we said. "But we don't want to presume. Who wants to articulate it, put it out in the open so we can all deal with it?"

Seconds passed, then a soft voice gently invaded the silence. "I know," said a young woman who had hardly spoken during the entire session. She was in her twenties, fresh out of law school. She looked pale and scared. "I knew something was terribly wrong at this firm my second day here," she said. "By the end of my first week, I knew what it was. It's father versus son."

There was a deathly silence in the room. The tension was greater than ever. The group was about to become "unstuck."

"Is that true?" asked Thomas McKenna Sr. "Is it Tommy and me? Are we the problem?" He looked around the room. Heads nodded their reluctant agreement.

We turned to Old Man McKenna. "How does it make you feel when your son wants to go in a new direction—a different direction than you have taken this firm all these years?"

McKenna's eyes glistened. "I thought I had raised him differently . . . "

"Maybe that's part of the problem," we said.

"What do you mean?" asked McKenna.

"To answer your question," we said, "let's put a question to the entire group: Who is Tommy McKenna?"

All eyes turned toward the junior McKenna.

"He's Mr. McKenna's son, of course," answered one of the junior attorneys. Several others in the group nodded.

"Exactly," we said. "Looks like we've arrived at the core of the problem. There's confusion here: Is Tommy a full partner or is he the son of the founder? He's both—and no one knows when to treat him like a partner and when to treat him like a family member. There is a powerful father-son relationship here that has distorted the business relationships in this firm. The family dynamics have infected the way everyone interacts with each other at OM&S."

A light came on in everyone's eyes. It was clear that we had put a finger on the truth. The people at OM&S could never be sure if they were dealing with Tommy the partner or Tommy the son of the most powerful man in the firm. Equally important, Tommy and Thomas Sr. didn't know the difference, either. The result: confusion over the organization's code, leadership roles, boundaries, communication, trust, response to change, and on and on. The entire relational network was out of whack because of this confusion of roles between a father and his son.

When the boundary confusion was exposed, The Thing in the Bushes was out in the open for everyone to see. At that point, it became a relatively simple matter to solve the problem. We defined clear lines of leadership responsibility and institutional boundaries (see chapter 5 for a complete discussion of boundaries). To reinforce the businesslike nature of their roles within the firm, the two McKennas agreed to call each other "Thomas"—never "Dad" or "Son" (or even the juvenile-sounding "Tommy")—while at work. As boundaries became clearer, so did the lines of communication. Trust improved. The major transition, which had once threatened the existence of OM&S, was navigated smoothly and safely.

The problem had once seemed unsolvable by the very fact that it was unspeakable. Now that problem was laid to rest—and the law firm of Oliver, McKenna & Smith was ready to begin healing and planning for the future.

The New Bottom Line

This is the kind of case in which TAG specializes. TAG is a group of consultants from a variety of backgrounds and disciplines who have joined forces to solve problems in organizations. TAG was founded by a combination of seasoned business executives and psychotherapists from a family therapy background. This gave us all a fresh look at organizational challenges. The resulting synergy is an unusual yet powerfully effective approach to organizational development.

We have brought these experienced, knowledgeable professionals together with one focus: to identify and expose The Thing in the Bushes, and in the process to resolve the most significant issues — Relational Performance issues — that underlie most of the problems that threaten organizations and mire them down. We help businesses, nonprofits, and other organizations learn to relate to their customers, communities, and one another in productive ways. Over and over, we have seen that good workers find a healthy work environment, good work relationships, and equitable treatment to be more attractive and advantageous than higher pay. In other words, people would rather be in an organization with good Relational Performance than make more money in a dysfunctional organization.

Also, we find again and again that when organizations struggle financially, it is usually not because they lack good technologies or processes, but because they have not done a good job of managing the organization's Relational Performance. Relational Performance — how an organization relates to its customers, community, shareholders, and employees — is the new bottom line.

In our research, we have uncovered a clear cause-and-effect relationship between the Relational Performance of companies and the success and profitability of those companies. Organizations with good Relational Performance have lower rates of employee turnover and absenteeism, and experience higher client satisfaction than unhealthy organizations. Those factors lead to greater effectiveness and higher profits. But in organizations where The Thing in the Bushes lurks, Relational Performance is low, dragging down morale, client satisfaction, and profitability.

For example, a recent *Harvard Business Review* article showed that companies that had mastered these nine Relational Performance principles experienced up to 25-percent greater growth and profit and about 10-percent greater return on investment to stockholders than companies with poor Relational Performance.

When American Express Financial Advisors (AEFA) wanted to know why so few clients bought life insurance, their research revealed surprising results. Clients were as influenced by relational factors in making their purchase decisions as they were by financial concerns.

Salespeople who focused on communicating the financial benefits of the life insurance purchase were missing the boat . . . and the sale!

What employees failed to understand was the importance of relational skills to their success. With follow-up research, AEFA discovered that Relational Performance of salespeople predicts their success, and it can be taught. Employees who were trained for relational skills increased their sales by 18 percent. Eighty-eight percent of those who were trained said the training was important to their job performance. The majority also reported improvement in their personal lives as a direct result of the training.[1]

Sweeping changes in society have created new relational needs that didn't exist only a decade ago. "Virtual organizations" don't have the "face time" required to build trust. Younger employees are more concerned with relational issues than previous generations of workers. The Internet, technological innovations, the information explosion, global competition, the transition from mass production to mass customization—all of these factors have combined to create an unusual set of relational needs which companies have never had to address before. Even though the business world is in flux, the Relational Performance model gives business leaders the timeless principles and practical tools for navigating change and maintaining the relational health and stability of their organizations.

The nine principles are the foundation of organizations that are financially successful, productive, innovative, energetic, and enduring. Organizations that master them are able to create and thrive in the midst of the ever-increasing pace of technology in a networked world where workers innovate at 3:00 A.M., half a planet away. Research indicates that these organizations demonstrate increased productivity and employee commitment levels, enhanced creativity, lower turnover, greater initiative, clearer communication, and a stronger sense of shared responsibility. Understanding the building blocks of Relational Performance provides a framework for spotting trouble when it occurs and moving toward a successful solution.

The Top Ten Challenges of the Information Age

Like an electron making a sudden, discontinuous quantum leap from one orbital shell to another as it whirls around the nucleus of an atom, the business world made a quantum leap as it crossed the threshold of Y2K. Here is a brief survey of the top ten *changes*—and the top ten *challenges*—that organizations face in the Information Age, largely as a result of the rise of e-commerce (we will examine these conditions in greater depth in chapter 8: "Proactively Manage Change"):

TOP TEN CHANGES CAUSED BY THE RISE OF E-BUSINESS

1. The change from mass markets to markets of one. The world economy has evolved from an economy of mass production (Henry Ford) to continuous improvement (Japanese electronics in the 1970s) to mass customization in the twenty-first century. Instead of marketing to the masses, organizations must cater to markets of one.

2. The rise of the experience economy. The world has evolved from an agrarian economy (pre-industrial) to a production economy (the Industrial Revolution) to a service economy (post-World War II) to the experience economy of today. In the twenty-first century, customers look for the experience rather than the service—and employees will be as experience-conscious as they are conscious of salary and benefits.

3. Hiring and paying for competencies instead of skills. The old economy rewarded specific skills and tenure on the job. In the new economy, where people flow in and out of organizations according to changing conditions, hiring and pay are based on the ability to adapt, think, change, flex, and innovate. In short, hiring and compensation must be based on competencies (see chapter 2: "Encourage Personal Excellence").

4. The elimination of geographical boundaries. Technology is creating a world without geographical boundaries. Old geographical allegiances no longer hold an organization together. Replacing the old geographical boundaries are new "virtual boundaries" such as mission, values, common focus, and vision.

5. The rise of automation. Technology is automating everything that can possibly be automated. Successful organizations differentiate themselves by focusing on the intangibles that can't be automated, such as emotional experiences and relational health.

6. Employee mobility replaces employee loyalty. With U.S. unemployment at its lowest level in three decades, employees can pick and choose jobs. If compensation and job interest are basically the same, they will choose the better environment. Even if compensation and job interest are slightly lacking, they will choose the relationally healthy environment.

7. Management authority gives way to employee leverage. Managers used to have authority over employees. They could threaten to fire an employee or dock the employee's pay. But today's pool of available talent is small and employees know they have leverage. In the twenty-first century, managers must treat employees like volunteers who can quit at will and find a job as good or better right down the street.

8. The spread of short-term thinking. Every day another tech start-up has an IPO that jumps on average 80 percent the first day. This creates an elite class of young entrepreneurs whose penny-a-share stock has split four times and is valued at fifty dollars a share. Implication: this generation, the instant gratification generation, is not thinking long term, but organizations with good Relational Performance *must* focus on the long term as part of a healthy code.

9. The information explosion. The amount of information in the world doubles every eighteen months. This is a problem—and an opportunity. Information overload creates a niche for companies that can help people locate, sort, sift, organize, and analyze pertinent information.

10. Face time is shifting to virtual time. Traditionally, face-to-face contact helped establish trust; the transition away from personal contact to virtual contact makes it more difficult to establish trust—at the very time that trust and relationships are becoming all the more crucial in conducting business. From telecommuters to virtual offices, employers must pay special attention to going the extra mile in communicating expectations, achievements, affirmation, and other relational information. Even in a virtual organization, time must be set aside for face-to-face relationship-building events, such as retreats, no-agenda meetings, and so forth.

Clearly, the business world of the twenty-first century is profoundly different from that of the twentieth century. As we write these words, the business world is experiencing continuing economic growth, despite nervousness in the tech sector. By the time this book is published, we could see even greater growth—or an economic downturn. Regardless of which way the economy goes, one thing is certain: There will always be rapid change, which tends to produce chaos and uncertainty. So the principles in this book will remain valid and crucial to your organization no matter which direction the economy moves.

The key to surviving and thriving as an organization in the twenty-first century is to develop good Relational Performance. Only an organization built on healthy Relational Performance has the focus, vitality, and flexibility to navigate the rapidly changing conditions that are already upon us *and* to maneuver among future conditions that can't even be imagined, much less foreseen, at this time. In the chapters that follow, we will show you, through practical concepts and real-life success stories, how to enhance your organization's Relational Performance. We'll lead you through the process of

- deciphering, formulating, and implementing your organization's code;

- encouraging the growth and excellence of all your members;

- developing strong, effective leadership in your organization;

- establishing and maintaining clear, healthy boundaries;

- maintaining open lines of communication throughout your organization;

- building trust, both within your organization and in the community at large;

- navigating internal transitions and external change;

- and more.

That's your road map of the journey ahead. So turn the page, come along with us, and discover how to spot The Thing in the Bushes, expose it, and deal with it effectively. The adventure begins . . .
Now!

1

BREAK

THE CODE

EXECUTIVE SUMMARY

Every organization has its own code—an underlying ideology that defines the essence and soul of that organization. A code is the corporate life force, the heartbeat of everything that occurs in and around the organization. Code shapes the face an organization displays to itself and to the world. It should answer these questions:

- *Our identity:* Who are we?
- *Our tradition:* Who are our heroes and how did we get here?
- *Our values:* What do we believe in?
- *Our mission:* What do we do and why are we here?
- *Our vision:* Where are we going?
- *Our strategy:* How will we get there?
- *Our rituals, symbols, and style:* How do we reflect our code?

Code consists of five interlocking pieces:

1. Values: These are our deep-seated beliefs about what is important to us. It is not enough to say, "We believe in honesty, integrity,

31

quality, and service." Every organization says that. But an organization must define its values in more-controversial areas, such as empowerment (whom do we trust to show initiative, creativity, and decisiveness?); leadership (hierarchical or decentralized?); innovation (trendsetter or trend-follower?); and tradition (treasure the past—or scuttle the past to seize the future?).

2. Mission: The mission (purpose) of an organization flows directly from its values. It is an organization's reason for existing. A mission serves as a set of guardrails to keep the organization focused and on course. A mission also gives members a sense of meaning and fulfillment in the performance of their duties so that they can reach a point where they can say, "Mission . . . accomplished!"

3. Vision: An organization's vision for the future should be bold and visual. It should engage the imagination and the senses. A powerful vision motivates, excites, and energizes people. We call vision a "Champagne Moment." It conveys a future goal when everyone can crack open a bottle of bubbly and say, "We did it!" A Champagne Moment should be daring and challenging, requiring both luck and energy to achieve.

4. Strategy: A strategy is the integration of values, mission, and vision with specific practices. Strategy answers the "how" questions: How do we take advantage of opportunities and conditions? How do we maximize our strengths? How do we deal with problems and meet challenges? How should we allocate our resources?

5. Symbolism: An organization's symbols may take many forms, including vocabulary, architecture, visual design, corporate myths, rituals, and more.

These five ingredients of a healthy code help to focus the vision of the organization and keep all the members on the right path toward the organization's goals.

It was the fall of 1999. We had spent nearly thirty consecutive days on the road or in the air: Washington to Calgary to Denver to Las Vegas to Phoenix to Sacramento, back to Denver—and now we were driving with TAG's chief financial officer, Rick Martin, to follow up on a Relationally Healthy Organization (RHO) Survey we'd conducted at Sturman Industries in Woodland Park, Colorado. All the airports we had walked through these past few weeks were a blur in our memory. We could never remember from day to day what color our rental car was. Exhausted as we were, we would have much rather been home—or possibly at a resort somewhere. We just needed some downtime to let our souls catch up to our bodies.

As the car approached the front gate of Sturman Industries, we perked up. The Sturman corporate site looked exactly like the kind of restful resort our weary bodies craved. It was a corporate Shangri-La—a sixty-thousand-square-foot headquarters, R&D center, and manufacturing facility tucked away in an evergreen forest, and it truly did look more like a five-star vacation lodge than a plant for manufacturing digital valves for the automotive industry. Passing through the gate, we saw the tennis courts and, beyond the facility, a blue mountain lake. In the distance, Pike's Peak kept watch over the well-manicured grounds.

This was an unusual consultation for TAG, in that Sturman Industries did not come to us for help. Instead, we had read about what a radically different kind of company it was. So we had contacted Sturman and asked if we could visit and conduct research to determine the roots of its success.

Stepping over a wooden bridge that crossed a gentle stream, we were greeted at the front door by Carol North—one of the hundred or so employees with no formal title. She ushered us into a huge atrium with tall windows that displayed Pike's Peak in all its frosty grandeur. The office complex was tastefully adorned with overstuffed leather couches, rustic stonework, vaulted ceilings, pine beams, and a massive fireplace. A tour of the plant showed us that the large windows, natural light, and resort-like atmosphere was not just to impress visitors in the atrium; the architectural style extended even into the R&D labs and manufacturing plant, where the public rarely ventured. The resort-like ambience was not just for show—it reflected the soul of the organization.

As we settled into one of the plush leather couches, we felt the last shreds of weariness leave our minds. The tension dissipated completely. We didn't feel like we were on a business trip at all. We felt like we were on vacation!

Yet Sturman Industries is not a vacation spot. Located (appropriately enough) at One Innovation Way in Woodland Park, it is an innovation leader not just in the design and manufacture of digital valve technology, but in the way business is done. No one else in America does it like

Sturman, and no one does it better. But why shouldn't Sturman be an innovative company? It was founded by two of the most enterprising and innovative people you'll ever meet: Eddie and Carol Sturman.

And the Sturmans have created by far the healthiest code we have ever seen in an organization.

A Benchmark Organization

Eddie Sturman doesn't believe in Murphy's Law. His philosophy of life is "If anything can go right it will, and at the best possible moment." His uniquely optimistic approach to business has produced what we call "the Fantasy Island of corporate America."

Sturman Industries has enjoyed an average of 85-percent sales growth from 1989 to 1999 with only a 1-percent turnover rate—unheard of in an age of recruiting and retention battles. Many employees set their own schedules, and all employees luxuriate in a level of freedom and job satisfaction unheard of in most businesses. The company regularly beats out much larger and older firms, winning major engineering contracts, such as providing engine systems to Navistar International for Ford Motor Company so that Ford can meet the government's stringent Corporate Average Fuel Economy standards for vehicles with large engines.

The Sturman story begins when Eddie was just a teenager, playing goalie on the Israeli national soccer team. He never intended to move to the United States and was actually tricked into moving from Tel Aviv to America by his parents! They bought him a ticket on the *Queen Mary* to New York—and they conveniently failed to mention that it was a one-way ticket.

As a boy, Eddie had never been challenged by school, but he craved the excitement of the soccer field. What did he need school for? He knew he was bright enough and savvy enough to make his way in the world—and he proved it by finishing two years worth of American high school in a semester of exams. After that, Eddie obtained a degree in engineering and pursued a career in engineering, but as he got into the corporate world, he took an immediate dislike to the way most companies were managed. Workplaces tended to be drab and uninspiring. Innovative thinking was discouraged. People were regimented and had no freedom. Worst of all, no one in the corporate world showed any vision, any sense that there might be a *better* way to do business.

An honest-to-gosh whiz kid, Eddie applied his creative mind to the task of digitizing the controls of various mechanical systems. He invented the Sturman Valve, a digitally controlled valve system for NASA, which replaced old power-hungry valve systems with economical, magnetically latched valves. The Sturman system was smaller, lighter, safer, faster, and more efficient than the old system. During the Apollo program, Eddie's electronic valves helped put men on the moon.

When he wasn't working for the space program, Eddie was busy inventing other innovative designs, such as the first automobile safety bumper, new refrigeration technologies, wireless irrigation systems for agriculture, and more. During those busy years, Eddie found time to meet and marry his soul mate, Carol. Carol was a former schoolteacher and leading sales vice president for a large real estate company, and she had a passion for leadership, coaching, and developing people. It was a match made in corporate heaven. Eddie and Carol complemented each other perfectly—not only with their shared passion for putting people and the environment above profits, but also with their interlocking skills. Eddie brought his engineering brilliance to the marriage, while Carol supplied the business acumen. Together, they formed Sturman Industries in 1989, operating out of a small industrial park in Camarillo, California.

As Eddie continued with his inventions, Carol marketed Sturman technology to the world. As with any company producing state-of-the-art technology, it took time for the world to discover what Sturman Industries had to offer. But with Eddie's optimism and Carol's dare-to-dream boldness, they knew that Sturman Industries would someday be known worldwide.

As the company grew, they realized that they wanted out of the stifling, monotonous environment of industrial parks. They wanted to build a new home for Sturman Industries—a pleasing, relaxed environment where employees would feel energized and inspired, and where the company's families would grow up strong and healthy. In 1995, after conducting a nationwide search for a new corporate setting, they settled on a wooded six-hundred-acre plot in Woodland Park.

In late 1999, TAG—which keeps a watchful eye on companies across the nation—realized that Sturman Industries was going places. We suspected that the reasons for its success was its high Relational Performance. So we administered the RHO Factor Survey to Sturman's employees. The RHO Factor Survey measures the nine principles in this book and provides a comparative view against our national database of participants. Expecting positive results, our researchers were shocked to see just how positively Sturman's people did: their scores were off the charts! As a result, TAG named Sturman Industries the recipient of the 1999 Relational Performance Award — the benchmark among all organizations studied.

When we arrived in the fall of 1999 for our first on-site consulting visit at Sturman, we interviewed people in the organization, from founders Eddie and Carol Sturman to the rank and file in the shops. In the course of our study of this amazing company, we began to unpack the secrets of Sturman's success.

The Sturman Code

It quickly became apparent that one of the keys to Sturman's success was its *code.* Every organization has its own particular code — a story that defines the essence and soul of that organization. The code of an organization is reflected in its values, beliefs, norms, rituals, symbols, heroes, and even (as so brilliantly exemplified at Sturman) in its architecture, setting, and décor. An organization's code is reflected in the way its members dress, talk, and comport themselves. It is reflected in the facial expressions, the body language, and the conversations echoing in the halls. Ask anyone their first thought of McDonald's and you get words like "uniformity" and "consistency"—part of their code. Talk to a Hewlett-Packard employee and they immediately speak of their code — the HP Way. The Marines have long been characterized by their code.

An organization's code is the corporate life force, the heartbeat of everything that occurs in and around the organization. It determines how people within the organization are treated, how employees see themselves, and how the company relates to its clientele. Employees gauge the appropriateness of their thoughts, behaviors, and actions according to the code. It shapes the face that the company displays to itself and to the world.

Clearly, an organization's code should be carefully, thoughtfully formulated and then instilled into the workforce at every opportunity. An organization's code should answer these questions:

- *Our identity:* Who are we?
- *Our tradition:* Who are our heroes and how did we get here?
- *Our values:* What do we believe in?
- *Our mission:* What do we do and why are we here?
- *Our vision:* Where are we going?

- *Our strategy:* How will we get there?
- *Our rituals, symbols, and style:* How do we reflect our code?

In the beginning, the code of the organization reflects the founders' personalities—either for good or ill, whether the code is consciously or unconsciously adopted. Over time, the code takes on a life of its own, shaping all who come into the organization. The code becomes a way of organizational life, a complete set of attitudes. Business people often talk of an organization's "culture," and a code is all that—and much more.

Eddie Sturman explained the Sturman code to us:

> I have two visions. First, I want Sturman Industries to make the best products in order to make the world better. At this company, we want to be stewards of the environment, to conserve resources, to make safe products. And second, I want Sturman Industries to serve as an example of a better way to run a company.
>
> My background is in engineering, but the industry has missed the boat. Most companies around the world are built on a top-down hierarchical structure. They don't let people think. In today's world, people are better educated and better able to lead and make decisions, so why not let people use their brains? Let them determine what to do. Companies that don't let people think only kill motivation. Some people might ask, "Well, what about the risk? If we give our employees a lot of freedom, they may fail!" Fine, let 'em make mistakes. Mistakes are part of the process— we encourage mistakes. We don't like to see people make the same mistakes again and again, but we want people to know they are free to fail as long as they are using their brains. Around here, I say, "Everyone is a teacher and everyone is a student." This is very much a learning environment.
>
> At Sturman, we believe if we first envision where we want to go, we then find a way to get there and it will become a reality. Carol and I based this company on an ideal. Our intention was that members of our team would be able to experience the reality of this dream through their own

innovative ideas and actions. We encourage our members to be visionaries, just as we are visionaries. We give them a great environment to inspire them, and we expect them to provide the initiative and skills to dream and innovate. We give them a lot of freedom—freedom from oppressive bureaucracy, complicated rules, and inane policies—but along with that freedom comes the responsibility that they have to meet team objectives.

We have a very low turnover rate here. In an age of low unemployment, we still have a long waiting list of applicants. We don't need a recruiter anymore. Most of our employees bring in their friends and family to work here because they are so proud of this company.

"We have a great company and a great environment," added Carol Sturman,

but don't expect perfection. This is a lot like a family, and every family has its share of problems. There's no such thing as a perfect family and no such thing as a perfect company. But our employees love it here—they have tons of freedom.

When I interview people, I begin by asking, "What is your dream?" If their dreams aren't congruent with Sturman's vision, we don't hire them. We look carefully at tech skills, of course. Obviously, we want to hire the most talented people in the world. But the cultural fit is more important than anything else, even skill level. We look for people who fit the code of our company. We look for attitude. We want to put people where they want to be, where they can fulfill their own dreams, and match their dreams to our dreams. We want them to be fulfilled. We respect them and want them to succeed. This respect is what helps us move through conflict as well as the good times.

Eddie agrees. "There's a business power in that sense of employer-employee respect that is unmatchable," he says.

In this environment, people end up doing what they want—and succeeding. And their success is our success. People who come here say there is an atmosphere at Sturman that just can't be found anywhere else. We had a senior exec from a European engine company come here for a meeting. He came here to do business with us, but when he left, he said, "This wasn't a business meeting. This was an *experience.*"

You can tell a lot about a company's code, culture, and values by simply walking through the front door and looking around. You may see a dingy, depressing sweatshop. Or you may see what we saw at Sturman Industries: a place of light and inspiration. Whatever you see when you look at the building that houses an organization, you can be sure of one thing: you have seen the *soul* of that organization.

When Carol talks about their company's facility, her eyes light up. The soul of Eddie and Carol is reflected in the walls and windows and tasteful appointments of the workplace they have created. "This building and these facilities were a one-time investment," she says, "and they appreciate in value!"

They are a fraction of the cost of salaries and other expenses, yet most companies only think of cost cutting when it comes to their physical plant. Many executives would look at our vaulted ceilings and fireplaces and view of Pike's Peak and think, *What extravagant waste! They could save millions by operating from a warehouse in some industrial park!* Maybe so, but we believe that the environment we create reinforces the attitude we want—the positive energy, creativity, and teamwork that are vital to our success. We believe this beautiful environment communicates to our team that we value them and we want them to have a great work environment. I don't understand companies that cut corners and cram two or three people in one ugly little office. That devalues the employees.

"No doubt in my mind," adds Eddie, "our environment has made us more profitable. But we don't do it for the dollar return. We do it because it's *right.*"

"Our industry is old and stodgy," Carol continues. "We wanted to be who we are, regardless of what anyone else does or says. This environment has made people more relaxed. And the more relaxed people are, the more creative and innovative they are."

That is the Sturman code—to make the world better through better products and to set an example of Relational Performance to the world. A code is the foundation upon which a company is built. A sound code is the key to Sturman Industries' success. The company's code shapes the attitudes, creativity, and work ethic of the company, just as it shapes the company's idyllic physical site. It determines what kinds of people are hired, and it focuses the creative energies of those people. A healthy code is one of the essential ingredients of good Relational Performance.

What Is a Code Made Of?

We have seen every kind of code imaginable. We consulted at one high-tech computer firm in Washington, D.C., whose code was obvious at first glance. The company motto, posted on the wall, was "Have fun. Make money. Do good work." The receptionist, Katie, had a diamond stud in her tongue. Company attire was blue jeans and T-shirts. By outward appearance, you could not tell the two owners from anyone else in the company. One sported a ponytail down his back and ran a used bookstore on the side. The other was a guitarist in an alternative-rock band. Though they hardly fit the stereotype of wealthy capitalists, both were worth millions. "Laid back" doesn't begin to describe the code of this company.

Another company in the South where we consulted was at the opposite end of the spectrum. The interior looked like the set of the beautiful mansion in *Gone with the Wind*. Rich dark wood paneled the walls. Dentil molding and carved scrollwork adorned the magnificent spiral staircase that dominated the foyer. The waiting room was a library filled with leather-bound books. Original oils by recognized artists graced the walls. This was a place of dignity and refinement, catering to an upscale, genteel clientele.

An organization's code molds the face that it shows to the public. But sometimes, the face shown to the public is not the real story—and The Thing lurks in the incongruence. For example, a well-known department store chain publicly communicates how it invests an uncommon degree of trust and responsibility in its employees, with a goal of providing customer service that astonishes and pleases. The stated message is "we trust you and we value employees as much as we do customers."

But many of these employees leave disillusioned. The underlying message is spelled out in the company's two Golden Rules: "(1) the customer is always right and (2) if the customer is wrong, see rule number 1." The culture promotes one consistent message: sell, sell, sell. So trust and responsibility are undermined by the tacit message. The stated code doesn't match the real code. The real code is more closely linked to "profit at all costs—even if it requires sacrificing your health." So the focus on trust in the written statement actually creates distrust as the stated values collide with the underlying values. The result: a cynical environment.

It's not enough to *have* a healthy code. It's not enough to *proclaim* a healthy code. The entire organization—all of the members—must understand and buy into that code. They must be immersed in it. They must live it on a daily basis.

One company that epitomizes a workforce steeped in a healthy code is Southwest Airlines. Company founder Herb Kelleher reinvented air travel when he put his fleet of planes, painted to resemble killer whales, in the air. Southwest is a maverick organization in an industry largely committed to generic sameness and conformity. The people of Southwest are zany, flashy, outrageous. They have fun on the job. They are committed to each other as family and committed to serving the public.

They don't serve meals on Southwest flights, only bags of salted nuts—hence the title of a book about Southwest Airlines: *Nuts!* But "nuts" could also describe the company itself. As a result of its craziness, employee freedom, and commitment to low-cost, high-quality service, Southwest has enjoyed phenomenal success. The company's stock tripled in value during the 1990s; its turnover rate is the lowest in the industry; its safety rate, profitability, on-time rate, and customer service rank highest in the industry.

There are many reasons for Southwest Airlines' astounding success, and one of the most important reasons is that everyone in the Southwest organization understands the company's code and is committed to it. The Southwest code was no fluke. The company has carefully, deliberately shaped its code and inculcated that code into its workforce. As authors Kevin and Jackie Freiberg observed in *Nuts!,* "Southwest's corporate persona is a maverick personality that has determination, a flair for being positively outrageous, the courage to be different, the vulnerability to love, the creativity to be resourceful, and an esprit de corps that bonds people."[1] The result is an airline company that is "nutty, flashy and very hip when the competition was conventional, businesslike and very bland."[2]

Relational Performance is built on the foundation of a healthy code. What, then, are the ingredients of a healthy code? What is a code made of? We can picture code as a jigsaw puzzle built from five interlocking pieces: values, mission, vision, strategy, and symbols. Let's look at each of these in turn.

The First Piece of the Puzzle: Values

Values are deep-seated beliefs about what is important and about the organization's place in the world. Values outline the organization's worldview, its sense of ethics, its view of people both within the organization and beyond, and its sense of responsibility toward the community and the world. Values determine the organization's purpose, shape its vision, and guide its decisions—especially on personnel issues, the hiring and development of people.

What do we believe in as an organization? We believe in our values. That is our faith. That is our worldview. That is the source of meaning in everything we do. Values connect us to the larger purposes and meaning in the universe. Without values, the work of our organization becomes a meaningless grind. With a framework of values, our work is a joy, a high calling, an adventure.

Many organizations will say, "Oh, sure, we have a values statement. It says we believe in honesty, integrity, quality, and service." Well, duh! Who doesn't? And if they don't really believe in these values, will they ever admit it? Conflict in an organization never arises out of bland and universal values such as these. When resentment seethes or a fight breaks out in an organization, it is over more-controversial values— the values that differentiate one organization from another, one professional from another, one employee from another. The controversial values include such issues as

- vertical versus horizontal (Do we need a clearly identified chain of command or is flexibility and fluidity of decision making more helpful?);

- innovation versus efficiency (Do we tolerate mistakes for the sake of creativity or are standardization and efficiency more important for the bottom line?);

- solo versus team (Do we set people free to work at their

own pace, or do we need a collaborative work environment?); and

■ destination versus journey (Are we more concerned with the process of how we make decisions and impact others or with hitting deadlines and producing results on a regular basis?).

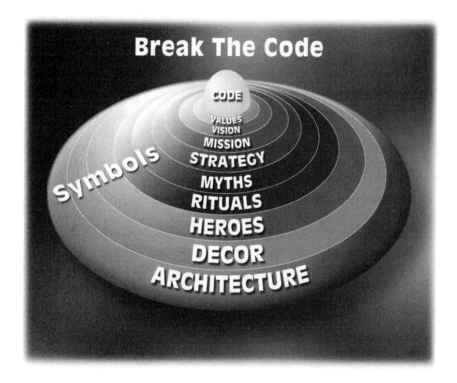

Conflicts don't arise from values we all hold in common. They arise from the areas of difference in our values. That difficult and controversial cluster of values is where organizations most need to focus their attention. Tragically, it is also the area of values that most organizations avoid. (The four quadrants above form the basis of the Culture Type Indicator (CTI); see appendix 3.)

It is important that we distinguish between an organization's core values (the four or five cornerstone ideals that are unquestioned) and an organization's operating values (the prioritization of, say, twenty or thirty operating principles that guide day-to-day decision making). Experience shows that most conflict in organizations arises around operating values, not organizational core values. The Thing in the Bushes often lurks in these differences over operating values. People in organizations generally assume that when conflict arises, it is focused on differences in personality—that becomes the Identified Problem. Usually, however, the conflict has to do with differences in operating values—and that is The Thing in the Bushes we must expose and deal with.

Values come straight from the heart of the people who have created, guided, and maintained the organization. Our values cannot be manufactured, trumped up, or faked. Our values are *who we are.* They shape the choices we make as an organization about how we will spend our time and our money. If you want to see what your personal values really are, just look at your schedule organizer and your check stubs. Similarly, if you want to understand your organizational values, take a look at your books and observe where employees invest their time.

Eddie and Carol Sturman clearly articulated the values of their company when we visited their Colorado facility. The Sturman core values are a respect and caring for the environment coupled with a respect and caring for the people who work there. These values serve to anchor and shape the Sturman code, which in turn is the foundation for all the company is or does. You not only hear these values articulated by the company's founders, but you also see them lived out in the company's daily activities. The values even give shape and form to the headquarters that house Sturman Industries.

All great companies are built upon a foundation of healthy, positive values. As he was building his pharmaceutical company many years ago, George Merck II stated the values of his organization: "We try never to forget that medicine is for the people. It is not for the profits. The profits follow, and if we have remembered that, they have never failed to appear."[3] Values echo down through the years of an organization, defining who the people are within it.

James C. Collins and Jerry I. Porras, authors of *Built to Last: Successful Habits of Visionary Companies,* observe that values "are the essential and enduring tenets of an organization. A small set of timeless guiding principles, core values require no external justification; they have intrinsic value and importance to those inside the organization." They go on to cite a number of examples of organizations with strong, enduring values: Disney's reputation for imagination and wholesomeness reflect not a mere marketing strategy, but an inner conviction on the part of Walt Disney himself that imagination and wholesomeness are core values to be prized. William Procter and James Gamble preached product excellence at Proctor & Gamble not merely as a formula for success, but "as an almost religious tenet." For Bill Hewlett and David Packard, the so-called "HP Way" of Hewlett-Packard—a respect for the individual employee and the individual client first and foremost—was not something they read in a book on management; it sprang from the inner core of the founders themselves. As Ralph S. Larsen, CEO of Johnson & Johnson, reflects,

> The core values embodied in our credo might be a competitive advantage, but that is not why we have them. We have them because they define for us what we stand for, and we would hold them even if they became a competitive disadvantage in certain situations.[4]

An organization always has values, even if those values have never been consciously analyzed or formally stated. For some organizations, a statement of values might read, "Screw the employee, the customer, the competition, the environment, and society as a whole. We don't care about getting repeat business or high employee turnover or being good corporate citizens. All we care about is making a fast buck." No company would state its negative values so bluntly, and it's unlikely that a company with such a set of values would last long in our free-market economy. The point is that, for good or ill, every organization has values; it cannot *not* have values. So it is important that we, as leaders and members of our organizations, pull those values out into the sunlight so that we can inspect them and, if need be, adjust them. Values are a key aspect of an organization's code.

The Second Piece of the Puzzle: Mission

The mission (or purpose) of an organization flows directly from its values. A company's values are the moral, ethical, and even spiritual principles that it believes in. A mission is a company's reason for existing. In a healthy organization, that mission or purpose is usually stated in terms of a commitment to carry out the values. As David Packard, cofounder of Hewlett-Packard, told his employees during a training speech on March 8, 1960,

Why are we here? I think many people assume, wrongly, that a company exists simply to make money. While this is an important result of a company's existence, we have to go deeper and find the real reasons for our being. As we investigate this, we inevitably come to the conclusion that a group of people get together and exist as an institution that we call a company so they are able to accomplish something collectively that they could not accomplish separately—they make a contribution to society, a phrase which sounds trite but is fundamental.[5]

An organization's mission is a broad, fundamental, enduring sense of purpose. It is what we do—and it clearly defines what we don't do. You might even think of it as a sense of calling, a spiritual and sanctified reason for existing. Just as a clergyperson feels called to minister to God and to human souls, just as a doctor feels called to minister to the health needs of patients, just as a performer feels called to minister to the world through music or drama, in the same way an organization should have a sense of being called to minister in the community and the world.

A mission serves as a guidepost, a lodestar, a compass heading, a set of guardrails to keep us focused and on course. An organization's mission sets its ethical boundary lines, demarking what is right for the company to do—and what it must not do. General Electric states that its mission is to improve the quality of life through technology and innovation. Motorola's mission: to honorably serve the community by providing products and services of superior quality at a fair price. For Marriott, it is making people away from home feel that they are welcome and among friends. But for too many organizations, the mission statement is ambiguous and meaningless. It neither guides nor directs.

An organization's mission is a guide to the behavior of all members. A mission also gives people in the organization a sense of meaning and fulfillment in the performance of their duties. There is nothing quite as satisfying and fulfilling to a member of an organization than these words: Mission . . . *accomplished!*

Mission is a key component of your organization's code.

The Third Piece of the Puzzle: Vision

The word "vision" has become watered down through overuse as a metaphor to suggest mere understanding, foresight, or perception.

What we mean by "vision" is much more powerful and profound. We are suggesting here a return to a realization that a vision is *visual*—it is an image, a bold and startling picture of a possible future.

In 1935, Walt Disney assembled his top animators in a meeting room at his Burbank studios and told them of a vision he had for a totally new kind of motion picture: the animated feature-length film. He not only described the story in words, but he also acted it out, playing all the different characters, using exaggerated gestures and facial expressions, pacing back and forth as he spoke, reeling off all the dialogue in a variety of character voices: a falsetto for Snow White, a bumpkinish burble for a dwarf, a malevolent sneer for the queen.

For over an hour, he held his animators spellbound as he filled their minds with sounds and images for his big dream, *Snow White and the Seven Dwarfs*. When he had finished, he had created such a concrete, graphic image of his vision that his artists did not have to imagine what the film would look like and sound like. They simply had to recreate the images that Disney had already planted in their minds. When the film was released in 1937, it was the same story that Walt Disney had so brilliantly visualized for them two years earlier—and it was a huge success.

Your organization's vision for the future should be bold and visual—in fact, it should be *more* than visual, engaging as many senses as possible: the warm glow of accomplishment, the sound of applause, the sweet smell of success. When the members of an organization can *see* and *feel* a brighter future in clear, tangible images, those images become a magnet that draws them toward that future. A powerful vision motivates, excites, and energizes people. It gives the members of the organization a common and exalted purpose to reach for.

Several years ago, one of our client companies was struggling with developing a vision statement. They just couldn't put their desired future into a coherent statement. So we asked them to represent their desired future symbolically. "How will you know you've arrived," we asked, "without telling us in words?" Immediately, several of them yelled out, "We'll be on the cover of *Fortune!*" And a new vision was born.

An organization that lacks a clear and tangible vision for the future cannot unify and inspire its people. Such an organization risks disunity and chaos among the ranks. But when everyone in the organization unites behind a common vision, there is less room for the kinds of conflict and friction that can disrupt or destroy an organization.

A strong, clear corporate vision is imperative in today's world, where organizations operate as teams of mutual empowerment rather than as yesterday's top-down hierarchies. We must treat employees as volunteers in today's work world. Most employees can work at a job down the street that offers a better compensation package and perhaps a better career path. Today's executive cannot use compensation or position as an exclusive way to motivate, and the threat of losing a job is powerless. Today, a workforce cannot and should not be bullied into action; instead, people must be empowered and motivated to fly in formation toward a common vision of the future. Again and again, in organization after organization, we see that people will align themselves together when they are given a higher purpose, a sense of calling, in highly visual, emotional terms.

Early in the history of his company, pioneering automaker Henry Ford gave his workforce a vision of a better future they were helping to build. These are his vivid words:

> I will build a motor car for the great multitude. It will be large enough for the family, but small enough for the individual to run and care for. It will be constructed of the best materials, by the best men to be hired, after the simplest designs that modern engineering can devise. But it will be low in price so that no man making a good salary will be unable to own one and enjoy with his family the blessing of hours of pleasure in God's great open spaces.[6]

Vision is not an analytical, calculated, left-brain enterprise. It is an exercise of our emotional, intuitive, heart-felt, right-brain inner being. It touches and moves people at the deepest level of their being. When a leader's vision becomes the shared vision of the entire organization, that vision is magnified ten-fold, a hundred-fold, a thousand-fold. A vision becomes a dynamic force for change, because it enables people to believe that, as members of the organization, they have something unique and irreplaceable to contribute. They really *can* help shape the future.

A vision consists of two parts: first, a ten-to-thirty-year "daring goal" and second, a clear, bold description of what it will be like and feel like and look like to attain that goal. Such a vision (what we call a "Champagne Moment") conveys a concrete, vivid, visible reality that takes place in a time as yet unrealized. It is, in effect, a dream that is made to seem so real that people can see it, feel it, taste it. And it lends itself to celebration—to one day being able to crack open a bottle of bubbly to say, "Look! We did it!" (Celebration is a vital aspect of organizational life—and a component that many organizations forget.)

In our research, we find that visionary organizations often stimulate progress through the use of Champagne Moments. While any organization can set a goal of climbing this hill or that mountain over there, a visionary organization commits itself to climbing Mount Everest. A Champagne Moment is powerful, compelling, energizing, and daunting. It is simple enough that every member of the organization can grasp it and articulate it. A Champagne Moment is never vague; it is concrete and tangible (like the goal of getting on the cover of *Fortune*). It provides a clear, focused picture of what success looks like so that the members of the organization will know and celebrate when they have achieved it.

A Champagne Moment should be daring and challenging enough to have only about a 10-percent probability of happening. It should require favorable market conditions, some luck, and a ton of focused energy. An excellent example of a Champagne Moment is the goal President John F. Kennedy gave the nation in a speech to Congress on May 25, 1961.

> I believe that this nation should commit itself to achieving the goal, before this decade is out, of landing a man on the moon and returning him safely to the earth. No single space project in this period will be more impressive to mankind, or more important for the long-range exploration of space; and none will be so difficult or expensive to accomplish. . . . But in a very real sense, it will not be one man going to the moon—if we make this judgment affirmatively, it will be an entire nation. For all of us must work to put him there.[7]

Now, *that's* a Champagne Moment! It's visual, it's audacious, it's difficult to the point of seeming well-nigh impossible—and when Kennedy articulated that vision, Congress and the nation responded. Even though Kennedy did not live to see it fulfilled, his grand, audacious vision became a reality.

All great achievements begin with a vision—including the great achievements of *your* organization. Vision is an indispensable component of your organization's code.

The Fourth Piece of the Puzzle: Strategy

Strategy is the integration of values, mission, and vision with specific practices. It is what makes an organization unique. It should be virtually impossible to replicate from one organization to the next. Strategy is determined and affected by conditions, contexts, and external forces, but it adheres to the enduring tenets of the organization. In short, our strategy is our general schematic or system for achieving our desired future. Strategy consists of eight dimensions: our market context; our level of investment; our core competencies; our competitive advantages; the strategic initiatives that guide our operational decisions; our guiding policies; the allocation of our resources; and the cross-functional synergy between our departments, divisions, or business units.

One timeless strategy is to get "close to the customer." In early 2000, Blackboard, Inc., a high-tech online learning company in the Washington, D.C., area, hired us for executive coaching with their CEO, Lou Pugliese. Arriving at the Blackboard headquarters, we found an organization that had achieved the ultimate in getting close to the customer. As we researched the company, we began to uncover their remarkable strategy. In the mid-1990s, distance learning was primarily focused on taking an academic course and putting it online. A few companies had ventured into collaborative technologies, which would allow students and professors to simultaneously create and edit online. But virtually no online learning company considered the fact that American scholars are mavericks — they don't want anyone else messing with their stuff.

Blackboard began to realize that the best strategy was not merely to put classroom courses online, but to develop a universal, user-friendly platform that would allow professors to build their own courses online. In a period of six months, Blackboard went from one to ninety employees, reached a market penetration of over 30 percent, and was listed by *Washingtonian* magazine as one of the fifty best places to work in D.C.

Strategy answers the "how" questions: How do we take advantage of this opportunity or that condition? How do we maximize the competencies and strengths of our organization? How do we deal with this or that internal problem? How do we meet this or that external challenge? How do we best allocate our resources? How do we gain the competitive upper hand in this market? Strategy positions us against competitors and aligns us with allies. It is the sum total of what makes our organization uniquely *us*.

The Fifth Piece of the Puzzle: Symbols

Symbolism is an important part of any organization's code. Symbols take many forms. Some are intangible and almost unconsciously adopted and used, such as a particular style of body language, gestures, vocabulary, phrases, and jargon employed within the culture of an organization. Others are solid, tangible, and prominent, like the buildings that house the organization. Some symbols have meaning only for the members of the organization, while other symbols are used to represent the organization in the wider community and the marketplace. As an organization evolves over time, some symbols remain timeless and unchanged, some old symbols disappear, and other new symbols arise to take their place. Here are several categories of symbols that characterize the code of an organization:

MYTHS

Myths symbolize the storyline and historic meaning of an organization. They explain, in story form, what an organization is all about. Myths may be historically true or apocryphal, but they are always meaningful and symbolic. Typically, a myth will tell the story of the founding of the organization or the story of key passages in the organization's growth and development.

An oft-heard slogan around the Disney organization is "It all started with a mouse." The story is told that, after his original creation, Oswald the Rabbit, was stolen from him by an unscrupulous distributor, a broke and despondent Walter Elias Disney took a train trip from New York to Los Angeles, where he planned to start over. Along the way, Walt recalled a family of mice that used to live in the wastebasket by his sketch board. One particularly tame mouse would climb onto the sketch board where Walt would feed it food scraps. Inspired, Walt pulled out a sketchbook and created the lovable mouse right there on the train. He wanted to call it Mortimer, but his wife, Lillian, gave him the name that has endured: Mickey Mouse. The historical accuracy of this account has been questioned, but the charm and appeal of that myth lives on in Disney lore.

Historical accuracy is not important in myth making. What matters is not the substance but the symbolism it conveys. While there is usually a kernel of truth at the base of an organizational myth, that kernel is often embellished to some degree. Myths have a way of ignoring ambiguities and slanting organizational stories in particular directions to make a point and an emotional impact. The unfolding myth sets the tone of the organizational story. Sometimes the myth is related as a tragedy, at other times as a comedy or even a romance. Though myths may play fast and loose with the facts, they always point to deeper truths in the organizational story.

Rituals

Rituals symbolize the beliefs, archetypes, behavior patterns, and ideals of an organization. Rituals are collective activities that do not serve a pragmatic purpose, but that the organization considers socially and even spiritually essential. Rituals are carried out for their own sake.

Examples of rituals in an organization include traditional events, ceremonies, and gatherings; ceremonial ways of recognizing individual achievements and milestones; and traditional ways of greeting and paying respect to one another. Some rituals are formalized and intentional. Others are practiced in an unconscious way. For example, a business meeting is ostensibly held for business reasons, but often the real (if unconscious) reason is ritualistic—it's a time when certain individuals receive their recognition or a time when the boss receives his quarterly dose of accolades from his loyal minions. The more thoughtful and intentional we are in devising and maintaining rituals in our organization, the more healthy and worthwhile those rituals are likely to be.

Heroes

Heroes symbolize the personality of an organization. The hero of Microsoft is Bill Gates, whose intensely driven personality has left an indelible mark on the company he founded. In a related way, the hero of Wal-Mart is Sam Walton; the hero of IBM is Thomas J. Watson Sr.; the hero of MacDonald's is Ray Kroc; and the hero of Disney is, well, Disney. Heroes can be living legends or departed saints. They can even be imaginary creations, such as Mickey Mouse. A hero is any personality who possesses highly prized characteristics that symbolize the organization. Heroes populate the myths and give meaning and emotional power to the story of an organization.

Visual Style

Visual style is the symbolic face an organization shows to the world. An organization's visual style is reflected in its logos, brochures, advertising, company cars, signage, and the architecture and décor of its physical site. We have consulted at one bank that is all dark wood, polished brass, and plush leather seating; we have been in another bank that is constructed and decorated to look like a kindergarten classroom. Each reflects a very different visual style and a very different code, but both have carefully crafted their visual image for a deliberate effect. While offering similar products and services, these two organizations reflect very different organizational codes and appeal to very different clientele.

Visual style extends from the exterior to the interior, from the artwork hanging on the walls to the apparel and grooming styles of the members. All aspects of the visual style of a healthy organization are coordinated and mutually complementary, reflecting that the members are in sync with, and immersed in, the organizational code.

These, then, are the ingredients of a healthy organizational code: values, mission, vision, strategy, and symbols. When these five pieces of the puzzle come together, they form a picture of a code that every member of the organization can buy into, live out, and reflect to the community.

Thomas Watson Jr., former CEO of IBM, understood the importance of a healthy code. In his book *A Business and Its Beliefs,* he made this observation:

> This, then, is my thesis: I firmly believe that any organization, in order to survive and achieve success, must have a sound set of beliefs on which it premises all its policies and actions.
>
> Next, I believe that the most important single factor in corporate success is faithful adherence to those beliefs.
>
> And finally, I believe that if an organization is to meet the challenges of a changing world, it must be prepared to change everything about itself except those beliefs as it moves through corporate life.[8]

The Power of a Healthy Code

To sum it all up, a healthy code is . . .

A corrective lens. A healthy code focuses our vision and helps us to clearly see the past and the future. It corrects such vision problems as myopia (short-sightedness), cataracts (cloudy vision), and astigmatism (warped vision).

A barometer. A healthy code enables us to measure the climate within our organization as well as how external forces are shaping us.

A game plan. A healthy code keeps us on the right path and enables us to safely reach our destination, while allowing us flexibility in how we reach our destination.

A magnet. A healthy code attracts people who fit that code and who are eager to buy into and exemplify the code.

A strainer. A healthy code screens and filters, keeping out ideas and people who do not fit the code. Those who resonate with the code tend to stay in the organization; those who don't, leave—or never apply in the first place.

All organizations have a code, for good or ill, whether conscious or unconscious. When it is unconscious, it feeds The Thing in the Bushes. When an organization breaks its code, however, it can become a powerful catalyst for growth. Accordingly, every organization must make a decision about its code:

> *Option 1:* We will cogently, deliberately decide what our code will be, and then we will actively work to shape our organization accordingly.

> *Option 2:* We choose to drift along, passively and ignorantly.

Code is too important an issue to ignore. Later in this book, we will reveal active, practical steps that you can take in your own organization to design and construct a healthy code. The healthiest, most visionary organizations are those that have consciously, carefully, and deliberately constructed their code—companies like Sturman Industries.

Heading Home . . .

The next day, as we flew back to D.C., we reflected on our visit to Sturman Industries—a place that was more a mountain retreat than a factory site. We came to Colorado for a business meeting, feeling exhausted, depleted, spent. We left feeling refreshed, invigorated, like we could conquer the world! If this is how we felt after one day, what must it be like to work in such an environment every day? No wonder Sturman's RHO Factor Survey is off the charts!

And it all began with a healthy code.

2
ENCOURAGE PERSONAL EXCELLENCE

EXECUTIVE SUMMARY

Relational Performance makes the workplace a more humane and human environment so that people don't have to choose between having a career and having a life. The Relational Performance model enables people to have healthy boundaries and margin in their lives. (Margin is the space that should exist between ourselves and our physical and emotional limits.)

Operating an organization with a relationally unhealthy workforce can be hazardous to the organization's financial health. On average, corporations spend nearly one-quarter of after-tax profits on medical bills. Stress-related compensation claims threaten to strangle the liability system. Fifteen percent of all employees engage in alcohol or drug abuse. In relationally unhealthy organizations, morale nosedives, commitment decreases, turnover rises, absenteeism and lateness increase, communication is strangled, quality and productivity suffer, and profits edge downward. But healthy organizations are marked by a sense of fun, caring, individual growth and progress, and mutual respect.

Healthy organizations hire and reward people on the basis of *competencies*, not merely on the basis of skills or tenure. Competencies are the demonstrable attributes that make an employee valuable to the organization (for a comprehensive list of competencies, see appendix 1). By assessing employees in terms of their competencies (as measured by tangible behaviors), you are able to make the appraisal and coaching processes simpler and more objective. You can assess people in terms of an objective 360-Degree Performance Appraisal using observable behaviors as key indicators of success.

"The situation here is desperate," said Heloise Jenkins, executive vice president of The National Association of Occupational and Environmental Physicians (NAOEP; its employees pronounce it "nay-op"). "Our staff is overworked and overstressed. Annual turnover is at 30 percent a year and rising. People don't communicate with each other. The tension is in the air."

We sat across from Heloise in her office and knew that she wasn't exaggerating. We had felt the tension when we walked into the NAOEP building, having been greeted with suspicious stares from office workers who obviously lived their professional lives in a climate of pressure, stress, and insecurity.

"What have you done in the past to address the problem?" we asked.

"Well, we did a one-day team-building program last year," Heloise replied.

"How did it go?" we asked.

"Great! Everyone loved it. For a day, we all thought we had really turned a corner, but the following Monday, we all came to work; the usual pressures and deadlines got dumped on everybody; and all of that beautiful team building went right out the window. Everyone seemed to forget what we had said and done the previous week. Now things are worse than ever."

"How about the executive director?" we asked. "How is he perceived by the staff?"

"Jack Conroy?" said Heloise. "Everyone loves him. The problem here isn't personality clashes. It's something else. It's something—something I can't put my finger on. If we knew what it was, maybe we could solve it ourselves. But we just don't know what to do."

This was an organization that was truly stuck. The Thing was present—and it kept itself well camouflaged. Flushing The Thing out into the open would not be an easy task.

"Well," we said, "we think the first thing we should do is tour the building."

"A tour?" Heloise blinked. "We've only got a couple hours for the focus groups."

"We can tell a lot from walking through a workplace," we replied. "A tour tells us about the architecture and space, and the architecture and space tells us a lot about an organization's code."

So Heloise took us on a tour of the premises. The first thing we noticed was that the entire space was functional, utilitarian, and impersonal—the building reflected the unimaginative name of the organization. The sparsely appointed reception area was not ugly, but not attractive or inviting either; the décor was perfunctory, Motel Six-ish.

And that was the high point of the tour. Beyond the reception area, the aesthetic values of the office space went decidedly downhill. Walls were painted that same shade of pale, neutral green you might find in a warehouse or a prison. Paper supplies and cardboard boxes were stacked and stashed, creating a visual sense of chaos and claustrophobia. There were no cubicle partitions. In each room, three to five people shared a stuffy, windowless space. It was a wonder anyone could think, much less work, in such a noisy, distraction-filled environment. The worst room of all had a hand-lettered sign on the door that read:

THE VAULT
Abandon hope all ye who enter here.

Upon entering the room, however, we realized the sign was no joke. The gray concrete walls and dreary furnishings made the room feel more like solitary confinement than an office.

After the tour, we followed up with some focus-group interviews, working our way through the entire staff of thirty-eight people. Each member of the NAOEP staff felt that the products and services the organization provided to the clients (mainly physician practices) were outstanding. Turnaround time was good and quality was high. Several times in these focus groups, we heard the comment, "We've been really working on TQM initiatives—we're building a quality culture."

TQM—Total Quality Management. Yes, we could see that. NAOEP had TQM written all over it, and the organization was clearly delivering the products and services to its clients according to the precepts of TQM. But there was no Relational Performance in the organization, which was why there was such a mood of angst in the air, such low morale, and such high employee turnover. Despite NAOEP's high productivity, the organization's operating overhead was eating away at the bottom line, in no small part because of the high cost of recruiting and training new workers and the overuse of temporary workers. TQM was delivering what it promised: increased efficiency and total physician satisfaction. But all the short-term gains were creating long-term woes as low morale and high turnover ate into the bottom line like a cancer.

TQM had failed, and the patient was in critical condition. What was needed now was an emergency transfusion of Relational Performance.

WHAT IS TQM?

Total Quality Management is the systematic integration of all roles, tasks, and functions in an organization in order to build a culture that continually improves products, services, and processes. The interest in TQM caught fire in the late 1980s and became a way of corporate life by the mid-1990s. The ultimate objective of TQM is total customer satisfaction.

Seems like every day there's a new TQM success story in the pages of the *Wall Street Journal, Fast Company,* or *Harvard Business Review.* The story goes something like this one that made headlines after the introduction of TQM:

> Doctor's Hospital in Detroit learned from their Michigan
> neighbor, Domino's Pizza. They promised to see ER patients
> within 20 minutes or the care was free. The initial three
> week phase of the project saw no patients free of charge—
> and the number of patients increased by over 30 percent.

These kinds of stories fire up our imagination with possibilities. But we rarely read the stories of TQM's downside. And yes, there is a downside.

Process reengineering, continuous improvement, quality culture, reduced cycle times, empowerment—these have become the buzzwords of American management in the era of TQM. Many organizations have restructured their entire operations around these concepts. Companies have rushed to TQM without really questioning the basic assumptions. TQM is a business philosophy that undeniably produces success at one level—but also has the capacity to cripple an organization over the long haul.

In a period of six months, we were called in to solve the problems created by TQM "solutions" in three organizations: A financial institution reduces consumer loan turnaround time to four minutes, but wastes hundreds of thousands of dollars each year due to turnover on the teller line. A medical practice with eight physicians sees 1,120 ambulatory patients per week, but can't keep an office manager or executive director for more than a few months. A well-established newspaper cranks out the best product in the Midwest, but internally, the company lurches from crisis to crisis because of employee dissatisfaction, stress, and burnout. Each of these organizations faced the same dilemma: they had implemented various forms of TQM, and despite outward success, they were rattling apart from the inside.

Are we saying you should avoid the TQM approach? No. TQM has a definite upside. It serves its purpose. But we want you to be aware that TQM does not produce Relational Performance. It is not designed to. What's more, it has inherent dangers. Here are the three primary dangers of TQM that we have identified:

Danger No. 1: Focus Inversion

TQM turns the focus upside down, putting quality above all else, even ahead of the needs of people. TQM defines "quality" more in terms of outward products and services, less in terms of employee well-being and Relational Performance. This one-dimensional approach to quality becomes the central focus—and the members of the organization pay the price. In a healthy organization, quality is not the focus; it's the byproduct of healthy members working together in a healthy environment. When quality is the be-all and end-all, an organization begins digging its own grave.

We helped IBEW Plus Credit Union in Las Vegas for several years during a time of incredible difficulty and external challenges. The credit union suffered several setbacks outside of its control: a spate of robberies, the loss of most of its experienced senior managers, and the competitive threat posed by recent mega-bank mergers—all within a twelve-month period. Despite these costly threats to its viability, IBEW Plus not only survived—it thrived! Because CEO Rita Alleyne focused her employees on maintaining Relational Performance rather than Total Quality Management, IBEW weathered the storms. Over a three-year period from 1996 to 1999, the credit union experienced phenomenal growth, with assets increasing from fifty-nine million to ninety-five million dollars.

We believe that if you focus on Relational Performance, the quality of products, customer satisfaction, and increased profits will naturally follow as a consequence of organizational good health. And we've seen that belief confirmed again and again.

Danger No. 2: Quality Above All Else

The gurus of the TQM movement preach that an organization's culture must be totally structured around quality. In other words, quality above all else. This assumes, however, that a culture consumed with quality is the right culture to build. Certainly quality should be a significant part of an organization's culture, but should it be the organization's obsession? Robert Frost once observed, "Beware when you wall something in; you're also walling something out." A commitment to quality as an exclusive culture is a commitment to walling out other commitments.

As you consider TQM in your organization, have you considered what you're walling out? Often a commitment to reduced cycle time walls out creativity. A commitment to increased efficiency often requires workforce cuts, which demolish workplace morale and motivation. A commitment to a comprehensive measurement system can stifle synergy. And a commitment to only one type of competitive advantage can blind us to new approaches and paradigm shifts.

Dan McAllister, Ph.D., professor at Georgetown Business School and a research affiliate with TAG, observes, "The problem with TQM is that there is an obsession with one way of thinking. As a result, people pave roads over cow paths. TQM inhibits the development of new ways of thinking and ignores the relational needs of employees and leaders." TQM can be integrated into the larger Relational Performance system, but it should never be the total focus or obsession of the culture.

DANGER NO. 3: QUALITY AT ALL COSTS

The business magazine *Fast Company* devoted an entire issue to a single question: "How Much Is Enough?" In that issue, Tom Morris wrote, "The only way most people recognize their limits is by trespassing on them—by going so far in pursuit . . . that they finally realize that they've gone over the line."[1] Herein lies one of the dangers of Total Quality Management: it allows no room for reflection, creativity, solitude, mistakes, synergistic interactions, or *aha!* moments. By contrast, the principles of Relational Performance incorporate the best of quality, relational health, and customer focus in a systematic approach to organizational success.

Most executives know the value of margin—and they usually try to maintain margin in their own lives. But what about our employees? They need margin in their lives in order to perform at the top of their game. Do we encourage margin in the lives of our members? Or do we drive them into stress-out and burnout with an obsessive attitude of quality at all costs?

Quality is not the bull's-eye. It's the by-product. The most progressive industries—such as the high-tech industry—understand that. Throughout Silicon Valley and other geographical hubs of high technology, you see companies that are thriving, not by obsessing over quality, but by focusing on relational health throughout the organization. When those companies are relationally healthy, the creativity, energy, and enthusiasm of their members propel those companies into stratospheric realms of profitability—and quality.

Again and again, we have seen that what organizations need today is not TQM but Relational Performance. An obsession with quality buys short-term success. A focus on Relational Performance buys long-term wholeness and a long-term reputation for quality.

The Rocky Rhodes Story

Charles "Rocky" Rhodes is a great example of what it means to set boundaries in your life and your profession. The story of Rocky Rhodes has been told in the *Wall Street Journal* and *Industry Week.* He told us his story during a personal interview in his home.

In 1982, Rocky cofounded Silicon Graphics, Inc. (SGI) in Mountain View, California. It quickly grew to become a two-billion-dollar-plus company employing over eleven thousand people. Rocky, a hands-on engineer, was heavily involved in the creation of 3D graphics software for SGI's innovative workstations. While building the company, eighty-hour workweeks were the norm in his life—and hundred-hour weeks were not unheard of. His wife, Diane, a product manager at Apple, seemed to be as much a workaholic as Rocky—until 1987, when she gave birth to Dustin, the first of their three children. Diane quit her job, and Rocky was thrown into a struggle that was not only mental and emotional, but also spiritual. He recalls,

> When Dustin was born, everything in my life was changed.
> For years, I had been immersed in my work, yet I knew my
> spiritual life and my family were more important. I didn't
> want my professional life to consume the things that were
> more important. Five years later, after Bianca and Gabriel
> were born, I knew I had to do something about my priorities.

Rocky and Diane began by jotting down their priorities on a yellow Post-It note. Both agreed on these four priorities in this specific order:

1. God (They believe that if they put God first, then everything else falls into place.);

2. *Family* (Next to their relationship with God, nothing is more important than their marriage relationship and their relationship to their children.);

3. *Exercise* (Rocky and Diane are passionate triathletes.); and

4. *Career* (Work and financial security are important—but a distant fourth to the importance of faith, family, and health.).

Rocky slapped that note on the refrigerator door of his Los Altos home and looked at those four priorities, shaking his head. He realized that the way he lived his life was in the reverse order from what he and his wife had just outlined. "My priorities," he relates today, "were upside down."

He started by rearranging his schedule. He cut back nights and weekends, and moved into an advisory role instead of a key engineering role in new-product development. He even tried working at home, but struggled with the interruptions that are inevitable in a house with young children.

In 1994, he was offered a tantalizing prospect by his SGI partner, Jim Clark, to get in on the ground floor of a new Internet company, Netscape Communications. Saying no to that offer was one of the most expensive decisions of his life, but Rocky never looked back and never regretted his decision. He knew what was important to him, what his priorities were: God and family, not career and money.

The following year, in September 1995, Rocky astonished his peers by cutting back to a part-time, twenty-hours-per-week schedule at SGI. He compares the feeling of cutting back his hours to "jumping off a cliff."

He had jumped off the high-tech fast track completely, but that's not to say that Rocky spends his time loafing around the house. Hardly! He's as busy as ever, but he spends his time and energy in accordance with the priorities he has set for his life. He allocates time to his personal spiritual growth, his church, volunteer work for a children's museum, and most of all, to his three children.

As this book goes to press, he has just signed on with a new start-up company, MyCFO, Inc., where he plans to take the lessons from the past and manage his priorities differently this time around. Once again, he is partnering with Jim Clark. But this time, he has set boundaries around his schedule. He will be there when the kids leave for school. He takes time to journal and pray after dropping them off for school. He'll see them for dinner. He won't work weekends. Rocky is one of a growing number of career downshifters who are realigning their lives to values and priorities rather than to the often-excessive demands of a busy career. Though still fully engaged in the e-commerce world, he has left the rat race to rejoin the human race.

A survey conducted by *U.S. News & World Report* and Bozell Worldwide showed that 48 percent of Americans have simplified their lives in the preceding five years by either turning down a promotion or cutting back their working hours. And a DuPont survey found that 21 percent of its employees have declined overtime hours or a more pressure-filled job during the preceding decade.[2]

Unfortunately, most people in the workforce today have not amassed the kind of wherewithal that Rocky Rhodes has to make downshifting possible. Nor would it be in the best interests of the global economy for everyone in the workforce to become part-timers. But organizations that incorporate the principles of Relational Performance make the workplace a more humane and human environment so that people don't have to choose between having a career and having a life. The Relational Performance model is designed to make it possible for people in organizations to have healthy boundaries and margin in their lives.

Margin is the space that should exist between ourselves and our limits. The term was coined by a medical doctor, Richard A. Swenson, in his book *Margin: How to Create the Emotional, Physical, Financial, and Time Reserves You Need* (NavPress, 1995). When we reach the limits of our physical strength, emotional strength, spiritual resources, and abilities, then we have run out of margin in our lives. When we squeeze the last millimeter of margin out of our lives, when we operate right on the outer edges of our human capacity, we set ourselves up to crash and burn.

Many organizations, unfortunately, have no conscience about squeezing the margin from the lives of their workers. Total Quality Management, for example, can often be a margin-killer in organizations. It makes no allowances for a member's need for reflection, creativity, or synergistic interactions. When workers are driven to deliver quality at warp speed, there are often short-term gains followed by a long-term loss of both speed and quality due to worker burnout and high turnover rates. Leaders need to recognize that both the individual worker and the organization will be much better served when allowances are made for members to live meaningful lives with a comfortable boundary of margin.

The loss of margin in people's lives today is a direct consequence of technological changes and advances. A hundred years ago, it was a cultural given that people work in the daytime and sleep at night. The electric light bulb has given us cities that never sleep. Fifty years ago, it was a cultural given that Sunday was a day of rest, that every business was closed that day and on Thanksgiving and Christmas. Today, many businesses operate full tilt, 24-7, 365 days a year. The boundaries that once existed between career life and private life, between office and home, have become smudged and blurred. Pagers and cellular phones make workers available anytime, anyplace. The result is a workforce of marginless lives—people on the edge of implosion.

From our vantage point, having toured many workplaces across the country and having interviewed hundreds of workers, we have seen the high cost of marginless living: people who are stressed to the breaking point, physically overloaded, emotionally drained, spiritually depleted, feeling unfulfilled, isolated, and angry. Though no conclusive study has yet been reported, it is easy to imagine that the loss of margin in the workplace might well have to do with increasing incidences of violence in the workplace.

The amount of time in a day is finite and non-negotiable. The amount of physical and emotional energy that a human being has to expend is also finite. These time and energy resources should not be carelessly, ruthlessly squeezed out of people by their organizations. The human requirement for margin—a boundary space between oneself and one's absolute limits—must be respected. Organizations should encourage good, healthy margin in the lives of their members: plenty of sleep and exercise, good nutrition, reasonable workload, and an active life outside of the workplace (volunteer work, community involvement, church or synagogue attendance). Members should not only be permitted but also encouraged to maintain a vital social, spiritual, and family support network.

Margin is not a luxury. It is a necessity. It is one of the crucial boundaries for building your organization's Relational Performance.

A Culture of Fun

Operating an organization with a relationally unhealthy workforce can be hazardous to the organization's financial health. As this book was being written, we were interviewed by *Management Review*. We told that publication that the cost of running a relationally unhealthy organization includes the following deleterious factors:

■ On average, corporations spend nearly one-quarter of after-tax profits on medical bills.

- Stress-related compensation claims threaten to strangle the liability system.

- Fifteen percent of all employees engage in alcohol or drug abuse.

- Industrial injuries have tripled since 1950, with an average annual loss of seventeen workdays per employee (at an expense of around ten thousand dollars per employee).

- Eighty percent of employees do not work to their full potential.

- Morale nosedives, commitment decreases, turnover rises, absenteeism and lateness increase, communication is strangled, quality and productivity suffer, and profits edge downward.

Have you ever asked yourself, *How can we unleash the imagination and energy of our people? How can we make work enjoyable? How can we reduce turnover?* In order to have healthy members, an organization must hire the right people and have a plan for their ongoing growth and development as individuals. We define "healthy" as having a good work attitude, emotional maturity, personal leadership growth, teachability, and strong relational skills.

Healthy members can separate office problems and home problems; they don't arrive at work after an argument or problem with their spouse or kids and start lashing out at colleagues. Healthy members are committed to the success of the organization, yet they also have an active life outside of the organization. Healthy members maintain physical, emotional, and relational balance, and they contribute that glow of good health to a healthy, balanced organization.

"Is it fun to work here?" That's a good question. When the answer is no, we assume The Thing is skulking nearby. Members of an organization with good Relational Performance will answer yes without hesitating. A person can't feel stressed at the same time he or she is having fun. So when there is a sense of fun in the workplace, we put more margin in the lives of our people and they are able to work to their greatest potential.

Imagine a company where the COO challenges the CEO to a game of foursquare, while an administrative assistant is working on breaking the Hula Hoop record at the same time members of the design team are competing in a heated game of hopscotch. Would you say that the members of this organization have lost their minds? Not if the company is the Gymboree Corporation of Burlingame, California. You see, it's Thursday afternoon recess, and everybody in the company is out on the playground. That's right, the playground. If you had come yesterday, you would have gotten to see the entire company partaking in a kindergarten-style snack time. *Play* is part of Gymboree's code.

Gymboree is one of a number of innovative, new-thinking companies that have made the transition from a stiff, gray, all-business demeanor to a warm, friendly, fun culture. Ken Meyers, senior vice president of human resources at Gymboree, says, "Employees certainly have a positive feeling about the organization." Small wonder!

Sometimes it takes a little while to win over newcomers to the organization—occasionally as long as twenty minutes! One skeptical new vice president was on her first midday recess, along with several other members of her department. *I haven't had recess since the sixth grade!* she thought as she strolled out of the building and onto the park-like grounds. *What am I supposed to get out of this?*

But as she walked the paths with her group, the conversation was lively and full of new ideas. "It was great!" she later recalled. "It really boosted our energy level." Those twenty-minute breaks (which often stretch out longer) give people a chance to get to know one another on a more personal, friendly level, and the relaxed, fun nature of the conversations helps to stimulate ideas and creativity. Relationship building during recess also helps build bonds of loyalty. Many employees state that the reason they stay with the company is because of the culture—a culture of fun.

There is even evidence to suggest that a culture of fun can save a company from bankruptcy. In 1987, when John Amerman took the reins of Mattel Toys, the company had just posted a stunning 113-million-dollar loss—due, in large part, to several new toy lines that had flopped big-time. A black and funereal mood had settled over a company whose stated mission was to manufacture fun. Amerman knew that a depressed and somber company could not survive long in the fun business.

So, during his first week as CEO at Mattel, Amerman called his employees together and announced a new policy: from now on, he said, Mattel is going to be a fun place! He reorganized the company into teams, issued orders to everyone to relax and enjoy themselves, ate lunch in the cafeteria with the rank and file, and made sure he was out on the floor every day so that he was accessible to everyone in the organization. Amerman was an immediate hit, and morale soared. Soon, so did profits. Within three years, Mattel had rebounded from a 113-million-dollar loss to a record 91-million-dollar profit in 1990. The board okayed a company-wide bonus to every employee equivalent to two weeks' pay.

In 1989, Amerman called the Mattel workforce together to announce the company's stunning turnaround. The style with which he delivered his message was pure fun—a rap routine with a chorus of Mattel secretaries, "The Rappettes." Mattel employees howled and applauded when they saw their white-haired CEO hip-hopping:

> Yo! Supersonic motivatin' toys we're creatin'!
> Everybody knows that Mattel is devastatin'!

Afterward, Amerman found himself being high-fived and hugged by his workforce. "It was like I hit the home run in the ninth inning of the seventh game of the World Series!" he later recalled. That's the power of fun![3]

Sure, every organization has its ups and downs, and work can't be fun all the time. But laughter, optimism, and a sense of fun are basic to good Relational Performance.

A Culture of Caring

When Mr. Martinez finishes his late-night shift as an inspector at a national-brand turkey processing plant in Arkansas, he doesn't have to get on the freeway for the long commute home. His "commute" is a stroll across the parking lot to the home he rents from the company that employs him. It's a dormitory-style, furnished apartment equipped with cable TV, a complete kitchen, housekeeping services, and a washer and dryer. It even has a picnic area out back. Mr. Martinez says it's the nicest place he's ever lived in.

It was, in fact, the lure of employer-subsidized housing that motivated him to leave California for his present job in Arkansas. "There is nothing more to ask God for," he says, "because here I have it all." Today, more and more employers are providing housing for employees as a recruitment and retention device—and as part of building a culture of caring.

Most people have an honest desire to do something well, and they deserve the opportunity to demonstrate their abilities. An organization with healthy Relational Performance gives people that opportunity, because they know:

- why they are doing what they are doing;

- where they fit into the overall picture;

- that they are an integral part of the team;

- that they are equipped and confident to do their job;

- that their contributions are valued by the organization;

- that they have permission to take risks—and even to fail;

- that they have the immediate and full support of the organization in difficult times;

- that the organization cares about them as people; and

- that they have an opportunity to learn and grow in their careers.

In short, a Relationally Healthy Organization is made up of members who are confident, eager to be productive, satisfied in their work, and ready to go the extra mile to ensure the success of the team. They feel a strong sense of belonging within a community. They feel cared for and empowered, and that knowledge generates motivation and enthusiasm. The physical, emotional, and relational health of each individual is a key factor in good Relational Performance.

In today's culture of caring, companies recognize that in order to hire and retain good people, they need to be concerned with employee welfare around the clock, not just from 8:00 to 6:00. Organizations must pay attention to employees' minds, bodies, relationships, and families. Whereas it was once enough to simply provide health insurance, now many companies are offering comprehensive wellness programs, fitness centers, employee assistance programs, and support for dependents. Employees are demanding that employers recognize the human side of business, not just the profit side. Forward-looking companies are not just asking, "How can we sell more widgets?" but also, "How can we unleash the imagination and energy of our people? How can we make work enjoyable? How can we respond to the needs of our members? Is The Thing in the Bushes related to the way we treat employees?"

This is a definite change for the better.

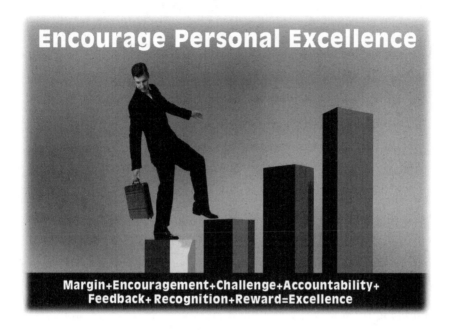

Encourage Personal Excellence

Margin+Encouragement+Challenge+Accountability+
Feedback+ Recognition+Reward=Excellence

Retooling the Workplace for the New Millennium

The workplace is changing rapidly. Old assumptions no longer apply. We must look at the shape and structure of our organizations with new eyes.

The fastest-growing segment of working people is those not even employed by the organizations they work for. Outsourcing firms employ them. They are "temps" or part-timers. Often they work on retainer for a specific period of time. In Washington, D.C., they've even developed their own moniker—Beltway Bandits—because their skills are in such high demand around the Beltway that they contract with the company that pays the most.

These people do not come in as subordinates, but as experts and contractors. They are "knowledge workers," hired with specific skills that make them highly prized. These contractors usually know more about their jobs than their bosses know. Old ways of relating to employees don't work with knowledge workers—they have to be managed as if they were volunteers. They are highly mobile, and they can leave at any time. The source of their productivity is their knowledge.

In addition to knowledge workers, traditional employees will no longer be managed in a traditional manner. Opportunities for advancement and better pay abound in an era of incredibly low unemployment. Both knowledge workers and employees will be motivated by the same factors that motivate volunteers:

■ *A sense of challenge.* They need to know the organization's mission and believe in it.

■ *A sense of growth.* They want and need continuous training—continuous upgrading of their skills.

■ *A sense of progress.* They need to see results.

■ *A sense of respect.* They need to be managed as partners, not underlings.

Both knowledge workers and employees need to be persuaded. Managing them is really more of a marketing job than an administrative job. Instead of asking, "What do *we* want?" managers must ask, "What do *they* want?"

One of the paradoxes of the new economy is that workers want to be treated the same—and they want to be treated differently. In other words, they don't want to see unfair preferences because of racial or gender discrimination; they don't want the reinstatement of the "old boy network." But they want to be treated as individuals, with individual human needs and abilities.

Tony DiCicco, the highly successful coach of the U.S. Women's World Cup soccer team, understands this paradox. He knows how to treat people the same and differently at the same time. When asked about his success, he replied that male and female athletes respond differently to many factors: criticism, separation from families, relationships within the team. Women, he discovered, don't respond well to more than a month away from their families. Women would rather sever ties to the team than strain family relationships; men, on the other hand, are frequently willing to sacrifice almost everything for their team—the team becomes all-encompassing.

While it is true that there are more similarities than differences between the sexes, Tony is sensitive to the special needs of the women on his team. He believes men and women should be trained and worked similarly, but managed differently. He tries to be sensitive to the women athletes' feelings and relationships with their families.

He has also learned that, in general, men and women respond differently to constructive criticism. After one defeat, Tony commented on some mistakes made by two of the women on his team—the same kind of comment that is routinely made to male players without ill effects. But when he made these comments to the women, they thought he was saying that the loss was their fault. Tony reflected,

> That [kind of critique] can work on a men's team, because you are dealing with egos so much more, but that doesn't work on a women's team. The way [to work with women players] is to create a relationship with them that they trust, and together set standards to reach, and help them meet those standards. If you just get on the critical side of it, they don't respond.

Diversity begins within each of us, with the recognition that the world is a diverse and wonderful place, and that the workplace should reflect that diversity. Creativity is best nurtured in an environment of diversity, flexibility, and understanding. When you bring people from diverse backgrounds into an organization, you must treat them the same (fairly and equally) and you must treat them differently (as unique individuals with individual capabilities, personalities, and needs).

Though some organizations have to be dragged kicking and screaming into the new millennium, many are discovering that diversity is good for business. The Ford Motor Company, for example, made this discovery in a big way with its Windstar minivans. Sales and market share for the Windstar have climbed steadily since Ford turned much of the engineering over to the people who generally use them: moms. Out of two hundred engineers on the program from 1996 to 1998, fifty were women, including the thirty Windstar moms (all engineers, ten of whom were expecting or gave birth during the time of van development).

Though just 7.9 percent of engineers are women nationwide, Ford saw the wisdom of including the end user in the actual design and refinement of the product. Thanks to the input of actual moms, the Windstar now includes such features as sliding doors on both sides, a back-up beeper, a special low-wattage "baby mode" setting for the dome light so that it doesn't glare in baby's eyes, an "oops" guard to keep French fries and other foods from slipping into seat crevices, bins with diaper spaces, and a switch to keep the driver's door from locking when the key is in the ignition, in case the driver has to get out to tend to children.

Would a man have thought of such innovation? Doubtful. Perhaps that is why a study by the Business and Professional Women Foundation and the American Management Association found that firms with a majority of women on their senior management teams experienced a 22.9-percent growth in sales, compared with 12.6-percent growth in firms with male-only teams. Organizations that had some women on their management teams experienced a 5.6-percent growth in market share, more than twice the 2.6-percent increase of male-only teams.

And gender diversity is just one example of the ways we must encourage diversity in the workplace. True diversity also includes ethnic diversity, personality diversity, talent diversity, generational diversity, work preference diversity, cultural diversity, and on and on. Ensuring diversity in the workplace is not only right and moral; it also makes good business sense. Diversity allows senior managers to focus on populations or markets they might otherwise overlook. Managers of different genders and ethnic backgrounds bring a broader perspective to the table, enabling companies to widen the range of products and services they offer. This is especially important in today's global market.

Many corporations offer women such family-friendly options as flextime, telecommuting, and maternity leave. (Unfortunately, many women hesitate to avail themselves of these options, fearing an adverse effect on their careers.) Savvy firms understand that diversity at the top is in the corporate self-interest—but merely recognizing this fact doesn't make it happen. True diversity takes place when companies take active steps to attract and retain top women and people of diverse ethnicity.

Working Mother magazine published a survey of "family-friendly companies" in October 1998. According to that survey, here's what matters most to women in the workplace:

■ Companies that meet workers' dependent-care needs.
   Women want to know their children are well cared for.

■ Companies that offer flexible schedules.

■ Companies where opportunities for advancement abound
   and women can get ahead.

■ Companies that keep morale high with various incentives.

Women at the top are good for business, but organizations need to alter the culture at the top so that women feel as welcome as men. This means developing a corporate culture that is committed to supporting them in balancing work and family life. For many women, having to trade marriage and children for a career in senior management is not an appealing compromise. The most successful companies are those that recognize this fact and make it possible for women to soar in their careers without compromising their families.

Competencies for Personal Excellence

Developing members with good Relational Performance begins when we ask ourselves a fundamental question: *What kind of person do we want around here?* In other words, what kinds of competencies do our employees need to have in order to be effective members of our organization? Competencies are the demonstrable attributes that make an employee valuable to the organization. We can generally divide competencies into the categories of knowledge, skills, values, traits, and motives. So as we ask ourselves what kind of person we want in our organization, we are really asking what kinds of competencies we need to see in people we hire. That question is not as simple as it sounds. Too often, the way we think about this question is subjective and ill defined. To arrive at a more objective and well-defined answer, follow these steps:

Step 1. Ask yourself: What are the competencies required by this organization to sustain and reinforce its code? *Define these competencies in writing.* Most organizations make the mistake of linking compensation to job title, experience, or tenure—yet a person's title doesn't guarantee his or her performance nor does the length of that person's time on the job. These criteria can be a good *starting point* for determining a compensation range, because past experience helps to predict future success. But compensation should be linked to performance. In other words, those who truly contribute to the success of the organization should be rewarded—and that means we must look beyond title, beyond time served. We must evaluate our members according to their competencies. (For a detailed list of competencies and how they contribute to the goals of an organization, see appendix 1.)

Step 2. Ask yourself: What are the observable behaviors associated with those competencies? *Define those behaviors in writing.* Competencies are sometimes hard to quantify. Concepts like integrity, teamwork, leadership—these easily become mere buzzwords that mean different things to different people. So we need to be very concrete and specific about the competencies we are looking for in the members of the organization. We need to make them tangible. The way we do that is to assign visible, tangible behaviors to each competency, as we have done in the list of competencies in appendix 1. By assessing employee competencies in terms of tangible behaviors, you make the appraisal and coaching process much simpler and more objective. You no longer have to assess employees in terms of subjective impressions and personal opinion. You have the objective yardstick of observed behavior to guide you.

Step 3. Recruit, hire, and train according to the desired competencies. In the early days of our consulting work, we researched a bank in North Carolina that was experiencing tremendous success in employee retention. Park Meridian Bank was a country club bank. It had a wealthy clientele and required a hefty minimum deposit. There were no teller lines. Rather, tellers had private offices adorned with greenery and red leather chairs. This elite atmosphere provided a culture that required certain high-order competencies among the employees. Bank employees had to look and act like their clients. In fact, many of the employees came from the social circles of the customers.

When we asked about retention and hiring, we were told about the bank's rigorous selection process. Each employee went through seven interviews, including interviews with the members of the board. While most other banks are hustling just to fill slots with warm bodies, Park Meridian Bank hires a tiny fraction of those who apply. Why? Because few have the select competencies required to fit into Park Meridian's culture.

Southwest Airlines hires for competencies that most companies don't even think to look for. The hiring motto at Southwest is "Hire for attitude. Train for skills." Skills are easy to teach—but did you ever try to teach a good attitude? So when Southwest hires, the company looks at attitude first: Are you unselfish? Are you a team player? Do you like to have fun? It's an unusual set of competencies, but Southwest proves it works.

Every organization has a unique code, a unique culture, and therefore, unique competency requirements. But our research indicates that there are approximately fifty competencies that translate to every industry. You must fill in the blanks yourself, determine your own list of necessary competencies and the behaviors that define those competencies, then use those clearly defined competencies as a guide to recruiting, hiring, and training your people.

Step 4. Construct a 360-Degree Performance Appraisal around those competencies, using the observable behaviors as key indicators of success. Once your organization has identified the competencies, it is important to build an awareness of them into the culture. Most performance appraisals are subjective at best and attempt to measure generic buzzwords such as "teamwork" and "initiative." They sometimes measure punctuality and dress code compliance. But they almost never measure the most important attribute of all: *contribution to organizational performance.* By turning the competencies of your culture into a performance appraisal system, your organization is one step closer to good Relational Performance.

It is important that these performance appraisals be conducted in an objective manner. True, there is no such thing as a *completely* objective performance appraisal, but multiple points of input certainly help to reduce subjectivity and unfairness. Cultural change and relational health are doomed if you leave the task of assessment in the hands of a few managers. Such assessments are invariably subjective and frequently distorted.

A 360-Degree Performance Appraisal is designed to take subjectivity and distortion out of the picture. It begins with the employee conducting a self-appraisal using the clear competencies and behaviors that your organization has formally identified and adopted. Next is another level of appraisal conducted by a supervisor, several peers, and several subordinates, again measuring the individual's performance against the established competencies and behaviors. By employing multiple sources of input, this level of appraisal reduces the level of subjectivity in the assessment. It also forces each employee to begin looking at the organizational system—rather than at himself or herself alone—when it comes to expected competencies. This clarifies expectations for the entire organization so that employees can begin making significant changes.

Step 5. Link compensation to performance appraisal scores. Although most employees are motivated by more than salary, we believe that linking compensation to competencies sends an important message to each employee: this is what the organization expects of every individual. Superior performers are rated more highly—and rewarded more generously. As a result, motivation and morale increase. Quality improves. Unwanted turnover plummets. Slackers leave. Profits soar.

Step 6. Provide coaching and feedback based on strong competencies and weak competencies. In subjective performance appraisals, a manager is required to determine what categories and behaviors to look for. But in the Relational Performance model, an objective 360-Degree Performance Appraisal provides clarity for the manager who knows something is great about an employee, but struggles to quantify it.

The 360-Degree Performance Appraisal also provides feedback to the employee who is eager to improve his or her performance in order to better advance both personal career goals and the organization's goals. People naturally crave feedback. Human nature being what it is, we all want to hear how we are doing—and an annual performance appraisal, based on one person's subjective opinion, just doesn't cut it. Performance appraisals should be objective, regular, frequent, and accompanied by incentives such as public recognition or tangible rewards.

Younger employees, in particular, are eager to have a gauge on their progress and performance so that they can advance their careers. Invest in them as people and you'll get greater performance out of them.

Organizations Change When People Change

Back to the National Association of Occupational and Environmental Physicians.

We conducted an RHO Factor Survey on the organization, identifying boundaries and communication as some of the major organizational challenges. We quickly uncovered the fact that employees were excited about the direction of the organization and that they respected the leadership. The Identified Problems were centered on boundaries. There were such rigid boundaries in worker attitudes and job descriptions that the members of NAOEP did not cooperate with each other. Turf wars and antagonisms abounded. If there was a crumpled paper on the floor, no one would pick it up because "it's not my job." There was no sense of teamwork or esprit de corps. Each person did his or her job in a self-contained bubble, with no concept or concern for the larger picture.

The Thing in the Bushes emerged as the survey pointed to the fact that everyone in the organization knew something was wrong, but no one took personal responsibility for the problem or the solution. The boundaries had become so rigid that it was easy for each employee to point the finger and say, "It's your fault, your problem, your job—not mine." NAOEP had done nothing to promote personal excellence. Rigid boundaries kept the organization from encouraging personal growth, outside-the-box thinking, and initiative.

The Thing in the Bushes lurked in the processes of relationships at NAOEP—processes that require constant monitoring in order for good

Relational Performance to take place. We set up a getaway for the entire staff at a retreat center in the mountains overlooking the Shenandoah River. All it took was one day. We spent the first couple of hours discussing the Relational Performance principles and the survey results. Except for that aborted attempt at team-building a year earlier, these people had never spent time discussing their organization in a group setting. We were determined to do things differently and to create lasting results.

Over the course of the day, the members met in groups, discussed how they could improve communication and boundaries, and came up with action plans. Because the traditions at NAOEP had proved counterproductive, we worked aggressively to break those traditions. The previous year's retreat had amounted to little more than a few team-building games and some warm-fuzzy discussions. There were no commitments to change, no accountabilities established, and no sense of what to do next. Most of the employees had never worked with someone from a different department—boundaries were very rigid. So our first step was to create cross-functional teams. This simple exercise began to create energy and momentum.

We brought the cross-functional teams together in a group and built consensus around the next step: what the entire organization needed to do to create change. Then we assigned accountability: who was responsible for these new strategic initiatives? We had people volunteer to implement these initiatives, and the volunteers wrote their names on flip charts. This created secure lines of accountability. Once that was done, we took things in a new direction.

All day long we had been hammering a theme: organizations change only when people change, not the other way around. We repeated that slogan throughout the day. After we designed the organizational changes with lines of accountability, we sent the group out on a retreat of silence. This was quite a change from all the hustle, bustle, pressure, and stress these people normally experienced together. We gave them an assignment: "Determine what you want to change about yourself and write it down. Don't talk to anyone else; don't read; don't interact. Just quietly listen to what the voice inside you is saying." Everyone did the exercise, though some were visibly uncomfortable with it.

Because the people at NAOEP had a hard time communicating with each other, we decided to have them verbally share their commitments to change. Some volunteered readily and articulated their changes. Others were reticent. Most of the participants liked such exercises as the retreat of silence and the communication of commitments time—but a few hated it. (Some people won't like everything you do, even if it's the right thing to do.)

All in all, the exercises did get people to communicate and relate to each other. The entire retreat moved people out of their comfort zones, and that was exactly the point: to get people to move out of isolation and into relating with each other and communicating with each other. As a result, the organization has changed dramatically. We check back with Heloise Jenkins, the executive vice president, every so often to make sure it continues to move forward, and she assures us that it's a totally new place. They've even remodeled the whole office, from the reception room to "The Vault."

If you want to change an organization, you must begin with the members of that organization. Organizations change when people change.

3

UNLEASH **L**EADERSHIP **I**N **E**VERYONE

EXECUTIVE SUMMARY

Relational Performance requires healthy leadership. Most people regard leadership as an elusive, intangible quality—you are either a born leader or you are not. But the Relational Performance model shows that (1) leadership is for every member of the organization and (2) leadership can be taught and learned. The key is to differentiate between the concepts of *leader* and *leadership*. A leader is a person endowed with certain characteristics, attributes, or positions; leadership is based on a set of skills that can be developed throughout an organization. The Thing in the Bushes is often found in the failure to distinguish between these concepts.

Relational Performance means that *every member exercises leadership*. Today, new forms of leadership are replacing the old pyramid-shaped hierarchy. Power has faded in importance compared with qualities of character, influence, and relational ability. Leadership is decentralized and leadership roles are apportioned throughout the organization. While old-style hierarchy is rigid and slow to adapt to change, relational networks are fluid and resilient.

Today's leadership is found in the center of relational webs, anchoring the information network and maintaining direct contact with employees from all levels of the organization. People who occupy leadership positions do not "boss" their subordinates; they encourage the exercise of leadership abilities at every level of the organization.

There are essentially two forms of leadership: transactional and transformational. Transactional leadership achieves its end by mutual exchanges or transactions: "If you perform these duties, I will pay you X dollars." Transformational leadership seeks to align the inner life of the follower—his or her emotions, motives, goals, desires, and values—with the organizational goals and code. Transformational leadership is visionary and proactive; it connects through communication. Transformational leadership doesn't grasp power; it shares power. Transformational leaders "walk the talk" by demonstrating character traits of integrity, honor, self-discipline, caring, commitment, and good humor. They don't just serve themselves; they serve others and they serve the organization. Wise leadership tolerates a dynamic, horizontal networking process while maintaining enough hierarchy to ensure focus and accountability.

In 1998, we got a call from Don Larsen, president and CEO of the Greenlake Savings Bank in Greenlake, Minnesota. When Don called, we could tell that he had thoroughly researched our firm. He knew more about TAG than we did! His company had just undergone a conversion from an educational employees credit union to a savings bank.

In the course of that change, Greenlake Bank's entire customer base had expanded. Whereas it had once served only teachers and a few select employee groups (SEGs), Greenlake Bank now served the community at large. Greenlake had made the change in order to keep its present customer base in the face of a legal action launched by state-chartered banks, attempting to strip credit unions of their customers who were part of SEGs. So Greenlake had skirted one threat to its existence, only to find that the company faced new and equally threatening problems. It no longer enjoyed the advantages of being a cooperative-based credit union—advantages such as not-for-profit status and a loyal membership base.

Already, some of Don's customers were beginning to defect, because they were losing that sense of member ownership found in a credit union. "If I'd wanted my money in a *bank*," said some customers as they closed their accounts, "I'd have *put* it in a bank." Don's company needed to make some important decisions—fast.

Don had a lot to consider: How do we meet the needs of an entire rural community? What should our niche be? Should we move to online banking? Should we continue courting educational employees, or should we redefine our target clientele? Don asked us to help Greenlake conduct a demographic study and formulate a business plan.

We agreed to do focus groups and a quantitative survey. We looked at the service needs of the community. Would it be more appropriate to offer banking from home PCs, more ATMs, or kiosk sites, or should Greenlake simply build more brick-and-mortar branches? We segmented the Greenlake community by age, income, spending habits, travel patterns, and so forth. It was a very thorough survey.

But as we were conducting our survey, a problem emerged. Don would call our office, sometimes several calls a day. He gave us advice at every turn. He didn't merely offer ideas or suggestions or information—he seemed to be trying to do our job for us. Understand, Don is a very nice, warm, cordial man, but as time went on, his intrusions became seriously annoying. After all, he hired us to do this job, and he had selected us because (as he himself put it) he had checked every consultant group in the book and he thought we were the best suited to meet his needs. So why, if he had such a high opinion of us, was he trying to micromanage our every move? It was The Thing in the Bushes again.

Don had come to us with an Identified Problem, but the Identified Problem was not the *real* problem. The real problem, The Thing in the Bushes, was the unidentified, unspoken, denied problem that lurked in Don's blind spot, in the shadow side of the Greenlake Bank organization. We sensed that The Thing in the Bushes at Greenlake had something to do with the way Don kept intruding into our business, our attempt to help him. We decided that the best way to flush The Thing out into the open was to simply present Don with the problem and ask him what gives. So at our next face-to-face meeting in Minnesota, we asked him why he was micromanaging the survey process.

His eyebrows went up in astonishment. "Micromanaging? Me? I'm not a meddlesome sort of person. Fact is, I can't stand that kind of person!"

"Well," we said, "that's what we feel has been going on. You've been calling every day, checking on every detail . . . "

"Oh, that!" Don laughed. "I just wanted to be helpful. I mean, you're out there in the Washington, D.C., area and I'm here on-site in Minnesota. I think I know a little bit about my own community, after all. I just wanted to help you fellas any way I could."

"We appreciate your good intentions," we replied, "But you know, *every* executive who micromanages his business is trying to be helpful, but sometimes well-meaning executives can help their organizations right into bankruptcy."

"Well, I certainly don't want to do that," Don said jovially. "Tell you what. I'll back off a bit, let you and your people do your job, and I'm sure everything's going to work out fine."

So Don's calls dropped off to about two or three a week, and we finished the demographic study and the business plan. The Thing in the Bushes had reared its ugly head—but we had met it face-on, and it turned tail and skedaddled.

A few months passed, and we moved on to other consultations with other companies. One day our phone rang, and it was Don. He sounded worried. "We've got some problems here," he said. "The state examiner told us that we've got the best business plan he's ever seen. Trouble is, we've never been able to implement it."

"What do you think is wrong?"

"Well, I think maybe it's me," Don said. "Maybe I'm the one holding up the show."

It was The Thing in the Bushes—and it was back again at Greenlake Bank. Or more likely, it never left. We had chased The Thing into hiding, but it was still alive and lurking in the leadership style of Greenlake's CEO.

New Leadership for a New Millennium

Relational Performance requires healthy leadership.

Most people regard leadership as an elusive, intangible quality: "either you got it or you ain't." Few people could articulate the specific reasons why this person has leadership and that one doesn't. Yet we all know a leader when we see one. A leader is that person we just trust and respect, and often even a person we just *like* so much that we would follow him or her anywhere. That person describes a vision, and immediately it becomes *our* vision. That person articulates a plan, and we instantly buy into it. That person sets a goal, and we want to reach it.

Can we analyze a person's ability to reach us and move us and inspire our greatest effort? Yes, we can. The key is to differentiate between the two concepts "leader" and "leadership." A *leader* is a person endowed with certain characteristics, attributes, or positions. These are often linked to personality traits or offices held. And let's face it, many people lack these attributes or have never been appointed to special positions of power. But *leadership* is different. It is based on a set of skills that can be developed throughout an organization.

Yes, leadership is a mysterious and elusive concept—*until we learn what makes leadership effective.* Leadership *can* be demystified; it *can* be understood; and it *can* be learned. In fact, it must be, because the success of organizations in the twenty-first century depends on their ability to develop leadership at all levels of the organization. In the thriving organizations of the new millennium, *every member exercises leadership.* Organizations that fail to grasp this all-important truth are doomed to mediocrity and decline.

The world has profoundly changed with the arrival of the Information Age and the virtual organization. New forms of leadership are replacing the old top-down model in organizational structures. In the past, power and authority were the requisite traits of an effective leader. It was always assumed that power should be exercised (often through fear and domination) in a pyramid-shaped hierarchy. Today, power has faded in importance compared with qualities of character, influence, and relational ability.

Organizations that thrive today treat the workforce as human beings rather than cogs in a machine. Leadership is decentralized and leadership roles are apportioned throughout the organization. Hierarchy is rigid and slow to respond to change; relational networks are fluid and resilient. When every member is able to exercise leadership in his or her own sphere of operation, the organization as a whole becomes flexible and agile enough to navigate the white-water rapids of change.

Hierarchy has been replaced by a web-like network of interlocking relationships. Whereas the leader in an old-style hierarchy used to sit atop the Mount Olympus of the organization, with information flowing up and orders flowing down the chain of command, today's leadership is found in the center of relational webs, anchoring the information network and maintaining direct contact with employees from all levels of the organization. People who occupy leadership positions do not micromanage or "boss" their subordinates; they encourage the development and exercise of leadership abilities *at every level of the organization,* from veeps and managers all the way down through the ranks. Wise leadership is able to tolerate a dynamic, horizontal networking process while maintaining enough hierarchy to ensure focus and accountability.

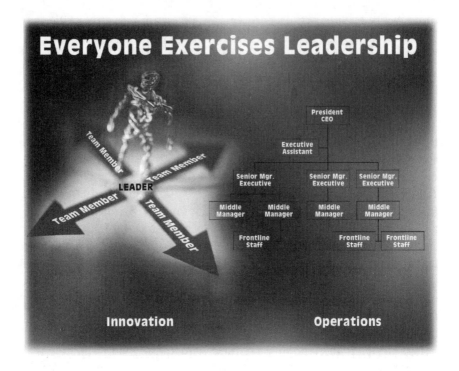

The Greenlake Bank Story, Continued . . .

We went to Minnesota to resolve the leadership problem that threatened Greenlake's future. We began by interviewing various people in the organization. "I feel like I can never do anything right," the vice president of lending told us. She seemed very competent, but stressed and distraught. "Don's always suggesting better ways to run the loan department or new ideas for marketing consumer loans. He's always in my office, looking over my shoulder, hanging around when I'm on the phone or trying to work. If I hint around that he's making it hard for me to get my work done, he just says, 'Don't mind me; I'm just here to help.' I'm very good at what I do, but when Don's around, I feel he thinks of me as a hopeless screw-up who can't do anything without being watched all the time."

Next was the CFO. He came to work every morning and shut his door until lunchtime. Why? "Don always likes to remind me of his background in accounting," he explained. "If I leave my door open, he just walks right in and starts going over the current financials. After he leaves, it takes me an hour to put everything back the way it was. He always tells me he's just trying to be helpful, and he's a nice guy and all—but I just can't get anything done when Don's around."

As we went from office to office, interviewing the top people in the Greenlake organization, we heard variations on the same theme. They all shut their office doors just to keep Don out. They lived in mortal fear that he would stroll in with a few more of his helpful suggestions. The well-intentioned president and CEO of Greenlake had created a climate of fear: No one interacted with anyone else in the organization. Everyone lived behind a shut door, furiously trying to get as much work done as possible before Don stuck his head in the door. Every person dreaded coming to work in the morning and left as soon as the clock struck five. Morale was in the tank.

Finally, we sat down with Don—and he repeated the same question he had asked us on the phone. "So tell me," he said, "what's wrong with this company? Is it me? Am I holding up the show?"

The Thing in the Bushes had been treed.

Leveling the Pyramid

Top-down pyramidal hierarchies are predominantly yesterday's leadership model. They work well in environments where tasks rarely change and where conformity is critical. But in most businesses in the new economy, such hierarchies, even in the hands of a benevolent and caring dictator like Don Larsen, are flawed by their inflexibility and their tendency to stifle creativity and initiative. In the hands of an uncaring despot, such hierarchies are downright dehumanizing and destructive.

In the slower-paced world of the past few centuries, hierarchical leadership survived because organizations didn't need to be flexible and fluid; they didn't need to adapt quickly to changing situations. But in today's world, where the volume of information doubles every eighteen months, the inability to respond to changing situations with creativity, imagination, and ingenuity can be fatal. An organization must be able to draw upon the full energies and abilities of all its members, and it must be able to adjust to evolving circumstances. Instead of dictating from the top of the pyramid, today's leaders must lead within a *relational network,* from the center of a web of relationships.

The old military-style hierarchical leadership model was about attaining rank and status, issuing orders to underlings, and inflicting penalties on those underlings when they failed or disobeyed. This military model was commonly in use even in civilian organizations until very recently. Today, however, employees have more leverage, freedom, and career mobility. If they don't like the way they are treated by Organization A, they can just move down the street to Organization B. So effective leadership today does not mean being a boss—it means building good relationships. Leadership is the product of good character plus good people skills.

Are some people born leaders? No question. But can leadership be learned by those who are *not* born leaders? Absolutely. We now know that leadership can be *learned* and that means it can be *taught*. Leadership ability is an acquired skill, and the effective organization is the one that has learned to teach that skill to *all* its members at *every* level of the organization. Leadership at the center of the relational web means that the person at the center of relationships is exercising a leadership role *even if the organizational chart doesn't reflect it.* Organizations that refuse to recognize this shift to a new leadership paradigm will not be able to compete. They will collapse due to the sheer weight and inflexibility of their hierarchical structures.

We often work with organizations where the CEO tries to hold on to power through position, while another senior exec or mid-level manager is the person who truly interacts with the members of the organization all day long. The CEO may have the brass plate on his or her office door and he or she may have the big window overlooking the city. But the people in the organization don't look to him or her for leadership and guidance; in fact, they tend to look upon him or her with cynicism. They see him or her as a figurehead, not as their leader. They look to that senior exec or mid-level manager who is the actual leader in most day-to-day situations.

So who leads? *Everyone* leads. Sounds like a prescription for chaos, you say? No, it's a prescription for Relational Performance.

Even in the military culture, where the tradition of top-down pyramidal leadership has held sway for thousands of years, there is a growing understanding that this is a new era with new imperatives for effective leadership. *The Washington Post* documented this paradigm shift in a front-page story headlined "Point Men for the Revolution: Can the Marines survive a shift from hierarchies to networks."[1] The story described the amazing shift now occurring in today's military leadership—a shift brought about by new communication technologies.

Strapped to the chest of the Marine squad leader is a small computer that can be activated and linked via satellite to a global communications network. Instantly, that Marine's position and status can be known by his leaders anywhere on the globe. They know everything he is doing and facing in the field. That information can be added to input from hundreds of other squad leaders, giving Marine commanders unprecedented information flow, flexibility, and adaptability. Generals now have a God's-eye view of the entire battle situation, lifting that age-old nemesis "the fog of war," so that leaders can see the overall patterns of a battle as it unfolds in real time.

Meanwhile, the flow of power and decision making has been forever altered. The Marine on the ground has much more responsibility than his counterparts in past eras. One nineteen-year-old soldier with a field computer at his fingertips can call down an incredible amount of firepower.

The final result of this technology-driven transition from hierarchy to network leadership patterns remains to be seen. What happens to the mid-level management personnel—the sergeants and majors of the corps? Will they be needed in the future, or will the new communication technologies replace an entire layer of battle-zone bureaucracy? Will the Marines make a successful transition from a rigid structure of hierarchical roles to an adaptive, self-organizing network that can react swiftly and change with changing situations? Only time will tell.

But it is clear that the new communication technology is transforming the way the Marines carry out their mission. The Information Age is leveling pyramids, destroying hierarchies, and ushering in the age of relational networks. As we write this book, TAG is leading the U.S. Army staff through a similar transformation.

Organizations today are being transformed by communication network technologies: cellular phones, the Internet, e-mail, satellite communication, video conferencing, interactive television, and more. These technologies are linking people together in new ways, and organizational leaders must learn to respond to these changes and lead in new ways.

Relational networks are vastly superior to hierarchies in satisfying customer needs and responding to market demands. There are things about your business or organization that you, as a leader, will not know. You can't know, because you're in the corner office, not on the frontlines. The frontline workers look the public in the eye every day. They listen to the public's complaints and compliments. They hear the reaction when you change a price or remove an item from the shelves or cut back on a service. That's vital information. Your survival depends on that piece of knowledge. Information does not flow easily or rapidly through the layers of a chain of command; in fact, hierarchies tend to *block* the flow of vital information.

The network mentality of the Information Age is changing all of this. The term "Internet time" has entered the language, signifying the blinding rate of speed at which change occurs. Just as electronic networks speed the flow of electronic information, informal, flexible *human* networks speed the flow of vital information within an organization. Informal human networks are not about processing speed and baud rates; they are about trust, healthy boundaries, relational network thinking, and above all, healthy leadership. These are the keys to surviving and thriving in a fast-moving, fast-changing knowledge economy. Informal human networks, bound together by trust, are the pathways that keep vital information flowing—and it is that vital information that propels the organization forward.

The Toughest Task of Leadership

One of the toughest challenges that leaders face is responding to change—change in personnel, in markets, in competition, in technology, and in the regulatory environment. Equally challenging is the task of initiating change when it is needed. Whether leaders seek to bring about change or respond to change, the mere fact of change calls for them to effectively mobilize the people, energies, and resources of an organization.

TECHNICAL AND ADAPTIVE CHANGE

There are different orders of change, of course, and the different orders of change demand different responses. The task of leadership is to differentiate between the different orders of change and to select the appropriate response. Change comes in essentially two "flavors": adaptive and technical. *Adaptive change* refers to changes in values, attitudes, and behaviors—an approach that says, "This situation won't change, so I must change." *Technical change* refers to fixes, such as altering techniques or acquiring new equipment or reshuffling personnel in an attempt to change the situation. Technical solutions in organizations involve simply providing a new or better resource for an existing problem, while adaptive solutions involve a deeper level of change; they often require us to alter deeply held beliefs and modify established habits and patterns of behavior.

The leadership failure that afflicts all too many organizations is the tendency to treat adaptive problems with technical solutions. When companies merge or restructure or reengineer, when communication and cooperation break down between crossfunctional teams, or when organizations get stuck in their inability to develop and implement a strategic plan, you generally have a major adaptive problem that needs far-reaching adaptive solutions. Mere technical patches and fixes will never work.

To make the point even clearer, let's transpose these principles to a different human arena. Instead of organizations, let's look at counseling. Let's say an individual comes to a counselor with severe depression. To treat his depression, it is important to find out the cause of his depression. It may be that this person has a chemical imbalance in the brain that produces his moods. In that case, the cure is a technical change; we simply prescribe an appropriate medication, such as lithium or Prozac, to adjust and compensate for his chemical imbalance.

But what if he has a different sort of problem altogether? What if his depression is due to the fact that he is grieving the loss of his wife of forty years, or that he has just been diagnosed with an incurable and progressive disease? In such a case, a technical solution such as a prescription drug would not address the problem. The patient would need to learn how to apply adaptive change to his situation. He cannot change the situation, so he is going to have to change and adapt to the situation he now finds himself in. This means a change in his attitude and his behavior.

This principle is just as true of organizations as it is of individuals. Let's say that communication between offices in your organization seems to break down too often. Typical technical solution: install a better e-mail system or Wide Area Network (WAN). Or perhaps marketing is not getting its job done. Technical solution: fire the old marketing manager and hire a new one. Or maybe the employees seem to lack motivation. Technical solution: implement a new incentive program. Maybe a technical fix will solve the problem—maybe not.

If you have an adaptive problem on your hands, you need an adaptive change—a change in attitude, values, and behavior. Suppose communication between offices is continually breaking down, and the new e-mail system hasn't worked, nor has the new voice mail system, nor has the new WAN. Now what? Clearly, an adaptive change is demanded. What sort of change? Perhaps a change in attitude between the two offices.

We've consulted in organizations where one office feels like a stepchild. Communication is stifled not because of lack of resources, but because of alienating activities. We don't need new gadgets; we need people to begin relating to each other in a healthy way.

Or suppose marketing isn't getting the job done. Replacing and reshuffling personnel hasn't worked. Time for an adaptive change: The whole organization needs to understand that *everyone* is involved in marketing and that it can't be left up to one person (the marketing manager). The old system, in which only the marketing manager is accountable for results, is a prescription for failure. A new system must be put into place that holds everyone accountable for results. A new attitude must be instilled that says, "Marketing is not an add-on. It's not an option. It's everyone's responsibility."

Or suppose the employees lack motivation. Incentives haven't worked. Motivational pep talks haven't worked. Scoldings haven't worked. Clearly, a deeper order of change is needed—an adaptive change. Employees will be authentically, intrinsically, enthusiastically motivated only if they buy into the vision and direction of the organization. Solution: Empower them. Include them in the planning process. Give them decision-making responsibilities. Allow them to feel a sense of ownership in the goals and direction of the organization.

So how do we know which order of change is required: technical or adaptive? The key question we have to ask ourselves when faced with a need for change is this: can we solve this problem with resources, or does the only solution lie in changing people's values, attitudes, and habits? If it is the latter, then we must boldly shoulder the task of producing adaptive change.

One reason this is such a difficult challenge for leaders is that before we can encourage adaptive change in others, we must accept adaptive change within ourselves. Like the people who work in our organization, we are creatures of fixed attitudes, beliefs, habits, and behavior patterns. We don't enjoy change any more than the people who work around us do. But that is the burden of leadership: to face facts, to accept the truth about ourselves and our situation, to make internal adaptations of our own mind and emotions, and then to mobilize the people around us to adapt as well.

Adaptive change is not easy for anyone. In fact, it is extremely stressful and painful for everyone—for leaders and followers alike. It means releasing old beliefs, while adopting new beliefs, roles, relationships, attitudes, and behaviors. There is always resistance to adaptive change. *Always*. Old traditions, attitudes, habits, and comfort zones die hard. Disorientation and confusion is a frequent by-product of adaptive change. Conflicts easily arise—and leadership must resist the temptation to merely suppress conflict instead of allowing those conflicts to bring important issues to the fore (conflict and collective pain can actually be useful in underscoring the need for adaptive change).

During times of adaptive change, it is crucial for leaders to maintain poise, exude confidence, quell fears, and hold a steady course. This means leaders need to possess a high tolerance for uncertainty, frustration, and distress, both his or her own and that of other people. During times of adaptive change, leaders will be scrutinized by followers, who will watch for both verbal and nonverbal signs of security and steadiness. Leaders must continually communicate assurance and confidence that the change is manageable, healthy, and for the betterment of everyone involved.

Transactional Versus Transformational Leadership

There are essentially two kinds of leadership in the organizational world today. The oldest and most common form of leadership is *transactional*. This form achieves its end by mutual exchanges or transactions: "If you perform these duties, I will pay you X dollars. If you increase your performance, I will give you a promotion and a raise." Transactions are basic human interactions, characterized by the phrase "You scratch my back, and I'll scratch yours."

The type of leadership now emerging is *transformational*. This form seeks a deeper order of change in the life of the follower rather than simply giving a transactional incentive. Transformational leadership seeks to align the inner life of the follower—his or her emotions, motives, goals, desires, and values—with organizational goals and code. Whereas transactional leadership can be viewed as leading a donkey by holding a carrot in front of his nose, transformational leadership is more like nurturing a fast, spirited thoroughbred horse that *wants* to run, *wants* to win, *wants* to compete with every fiber of its being.

When we say that transformational leadership is the new and emerging form of leadership in the organizational world, we are not saying that there have never been transformational leaders in the past. Fact is, human history has been shaped by transformational leaders, by people who could reach inside the minds and hearts of followers, seize their emotions, energize their wills, and expand their imaginations. People like Jesus Christ, Thomas Jefferson, Gandhi, Winston Churchill, Franklin D. Roosevelt, John F. Kennedy, Martin Luther King Jr., Lee Iacocca, Ronald Reagan, and Mother Teresa are all brilliant examples of transformational leaders.

It is widely assumed that such leaders are born, not made—but that is not true. More and more, we are discovering that transformational leadership can be taught—and learned. Employees at all levels of an organization can be taught how to impact the beliefs, needs, values, and goals of the people they influence. We are not talking here about manipulation or some sort of Hitlerian mind control. Transformational leadership is not about taking advantage of people. It's about making people aware of what they *really* want in life—and motivating them to go after it.

Many people *think* they would like a life of ease, sitting at the beach, drinking mai-tais, but transformational leadership helps others realize that true satisfaction in life comes from achieving worthwhile goals. In World War II, many English and American citizens no doubt wished to hide and isolate themselves from the terrors of war, but leaders like Churchill and Roosevelt inspired their people to fight—or aid in the fight—by showing them that victory over Nazism was more important than personal safety or comfort.

How does transformational leadership work? How do transformational leaders manage to transform the inner selves of their followers? Here's a short course in transformational leadership:

Transformational Leadership Is Visionary

People who exercise transformational leadership don't just see the world as it is. They see the world as it could be. One of the most visionary organizational leaders of our time is Microsoft's Bill Gates. In the early 1980s, when hardly anyone had heard of personal computers, Gates set a goal of placing a personal computer in every home by the year 2000. At the time, few others in the computer industry could imagine why *anyone* would want an expensive, sophisticated business tool like a computer in the family room. But Gates knew. He saw what no one else could see, and he went about creating the world he envisioned. Compared with that achievement, the fact that he became a multibillionaire in the process is little more than a footnote.

A person who exercises visionary leadership is not deterred by those who say, "That's impossible!" or "We could never do that!" Transformational leadership involves dreaming big, bold dreams, then enabling everyone in the organization to dream it with them. Most of all, transformational leadership is the process of motivating members to make those dreams come true.

Transformational Leadership Is Proactive

People who practice transformational leadership don't react; they *act*. They don't worry about the future; they *shape* it.

Bob Woods learned that kind of leadership. In 1993, as head of Zeneca Ag Products, an American division of Britain's Imperial Chemical Industries (ICI), he faced an enormous challenge when the British parent company announced its decision to deconglomerate and spin off the Zeneca division, effective January 1, 1995. Zeneca (or North American Ag, as the division was known while it was part of ICI) was a stodgy, tradition-bound bureaucracy headquartered in Wilmington, Delaware. The heads of the various departments—manufacturing, sales, and so forth—were loyal to their own departments, not to the company as a whole. The sales department, for example, was structured to reward volume, not profitability.

The spin-off posed a number of problems for Zeneca Ag. For one thing, the division's poor performance could no longer be concealed by the general profitability of the parent corporation. Zeneca would be forced to stand—or fall—on its own. Also, Zeneca would soon lose access to many of ICI's resources, including computer systems. Some of Zeneca's operating processes would have to be rebuilt from the ground up.

Taking a hard look at Zeneca, Woods saw a company that was not only struggling, it was unlikely to survive the major changes that would take place when the division was spun off on its own. There was no time or money for reorganization. Resistance to change was enormous, particularly among the department heads, all of whom were committed to the status quo. Woods tried to convince them that if the prospects of the company didn't improve, they would all be out of a job. But their response was invariably "It's not my department's fault—it's those guys over there," or "This isn't a real problem, just an anomaly. These things have a way of straightening themselves out."

But Woods knew that these things were not going to straighten themselves out. The company was facing extinction.

The biggest problem Zeneca faced was a lack of operating capital. Realizing that the department heads would be of no help, Woods went *under* their heads for a solution. He formed a crossfunctional team of mid-level managers and told them it was their job to get the company's cash problems under control. "What about the department heads?" someone asked. "They're out of the loop," Woods replied. Some of those senior execs might have been unhappy, but Woods didn't care. Applying the principles of transformational leadership, he leveled the hierarchy at Zeneca—not by going *over* anybody's head, but by going *under* the heads of the bosses. The senior execs had their chance to save the company, Woods reasoned, and they had laid a goose egg. Now he was empowering a whole new level of leaders to solve the problem. One way or another, Bob Woods was going to save the company.

In the process of putting these mid-level managers onto the problem of solving the operating capital crunch, Woods found that he had created a nucleus of leaders to implement the company's transformation from a division of an overseas corporation to a stand-alone company. Once the cash problem was fixed, he ordered the group to take apart Zeneca's entire process structure—from product development to order fulfillment—then put it all back together in a way that was focused on customer demand. A dozen new process teams, all led by middle managers personally recruited by Woods, leaped into the task of rebuilding a tired old division into a lean, energetic new company. He personally spent a great deal of time visiting the teams and cheering them on, telling them to take risks, to think outside the lines, to imagine possibilities, and to innovate. His proactive efforts paid off.

By 1995, profits at Zeneca Ag were up 68 percent. Return on assets had jumped by 178 percent in two years. Cycle time on product development had been cut by a full year. Productivity had climbed by 77 percent. Inventory had been reduced by fifty-four million dollars. Thanks to Bob Woods, the future at Zeneca Ag—which had once been clouded at best, nonexistent at worst—was assured.

Transformational leaders like Woods are proactive. They don't wait for transformation to occur, they *create* transformation.[2]

Transformational Leadership
Connects Through Communication

We've all seen people who demonstrate this skill. Their conversational style is confident, vivid, energetic, exuberant, and persuasive. It reaches people at an emotional level. Good eye communication builds empathy and rapport. Confident gestures and a bright smile convey that this is a likable person who can be trusted. Those who cannot make an emotional connection when they communicate are not perceived and received as leaders.

On October 13, 1988, Massachusetts Governor Michael Dukakis squared off against Vice President George Bush in a live television debate. Dukakis's campaign had spent sixty million dollars to get him elected, and he was widely perceived as a man of ideas and perception. He led Bush by a commanding margin of 17 percentage points.

During the course of the evening, Dukakis was confident and mentally agile as he fielded questions from journalists and jabs from his opponent. Then, midway through the debate, CNN anchorman Bernard Shaw asked him, "Governor, if your wife, Kitty Dukakis, were raped and murdered, would you favor an irrevocable death penalty for the killer?"

"No, I wouldn't, Bernard," Dukakis replied without any apparent emotion. "And I think you know that I've opposed the death penalty all of my life." He proceeded to give a lengthy, dry, emotionless lecture about his position on federal drug policy, concluding with a call for a "hemispheric summit" to address the problem of drugs and crime.

Viewers were aghast. He had just been asked to consider the possibility of the rape and death of his own wife—and his answer had been utterly aloof, detached, and canned. Immediately after that debate, Dukakis's seventeen-point advantage turned to a 21-percent deficit. A post-debate profile in *Time* magazine labeled him "The Man Who Seals Off Emotion." Michael Dukakis lacked the ability to make an emotional connection with his audience, and as a result, he was denied the opportunity to lead.

When a transformational leader communicates, he or she does more than communicate mere verbal content. Such leaders know they must communicate trust, feeling, empathy, humanity, enthusiasm, and confidence—or they cannot lead.

Transformational Leadership Shares Power
Instead of seizing power and taking control, transformational leadership is about empowering others. The word "empowerment" is not just a management buzzword. It is an essential tool in the hand of the person practicing leadership.

Rachel Hubka started as a dispatcher with Chicago's Stewart Bus Company in 1978. A voracious learner, she wanted to know everything there was to know about running a bus company. She learned all the complexities of routing and scheduling school buses. She studied the procedures for hiring and training drivers. She cleaned out buses and watched the mechanics maintain the diesel engines. She even developed and implemented a safety program that was adopted by the company. No one at the Stewart Bus Company knew more about running a bus company than Rachel Hubka—not even the people who owned it.

A few years later, when the owners decided to get out of the bus business, Rachel bought the company. Suddenly, she found herself competing against fifty other bus companies for contracts to bus public school students. She won a contract to bus kids from the crime-ridden, poverty-ridden North Lawndale area, but the contract was contingent on her commitment to hire drivers who lived in North Lawndale.

Hubka knew the risks of hiring people with bad employment histories—and in poverty-prone North Lawndale, the workforce would be marginal at best. But she believed she could make it work if she could empower her drivers and build into them an attitude of pride and professionalism. She took in drivers with no experience whatsoever, and put them through a comprehensive driver-training program. She issued professional-looking uniforms with white shirts, dark slacks, ties, and ID badges. To underscore the professionalism of their role, each driver was given personalized business cards to hand out. The result: she gave opportunities to people who had never before made anything of their lives — and she got a stable, motivated, professional workforce in return.

Hubka has been so successful in instilling leadership skills in her employees that several of them have left the firm to start businesses of their own — a fact that she is very proud of. She empowers her workers by teaching them and being available to them. As the business publication *Organizational Dynamics* explains, Hubka's "door is always open. There is no chain of command. She's a great listener who is able to engage others in meaningful conversations. Because of her own thorough knowledge of her job, Hubka was able to see the possibilities in a situation and create the learning environment she desired."[3]

Lao-tzu, the Chinese Taoist leader-philosopher who lived some six centuries before Christ, put it this way:

> A leader is best when people barely know that he exists; not
> so good when people obey and acclaim him; worse when
> they despise him. Fail to honor people and they will fail to
> honor you. But of a good leader, when his work is done, his
> aim fulfilled, they will all say, "Look! We did it ourselves!"

Spoken like a true transformational leader.

Transformational Leadership Walks the Talk

The stated values of leadership must equal the demonstrated results. People who walk the talk daily demonstrate character traits of integrity, honor, self-discipline, caring, commitment — and a good sense of humor and good fun. Transformational leadership means being willing to sacrifice personal interests at times in order to achieve a greater good and set a good example. It is about serving others and serving the organization — not just serving yourself.

Doug Cahill exemplifies that kind of leadership. He heads the swimming pool products division at Olin, the two-billion-dollar chemical giant. Some years ago, Olin went through an innovative restructuring. All the old position titles were done away with; in their place were only two titles: coach and teammate.

When the new employee directory came out, Cahill got a call from the Olin factory in Livonia, Michigan. Seems one of the employees had opened the book and found he was listed not as a teammate, like the rest of his colleagues, but under his old title, accounting manager. The changes at Olin had been stressful for many in the organization, and this employee was shaken by that listing. "Are they trying to send me a message?" the man frantically asked. "Are they telling me I'm not on the team?"

Cahill—an executive who is personally responsible for 250 million dollars in sales a year—certainly had bigger fish to fry, and easily could have assigned the problem to an underling. Instead, he chose to handle the problem himself. First, he reassured the employee that Olin didn't operate that way. Then he personally made some calls until he had tracked down the people who had typeset the directory. It turned out to be a simple typo—a typist had skipped a line while inputting the changes to the book. Then Cahill personally called the man and explained the error. Problem solved—and it was solved by a transformational leader who cared enough about his people to become personally involved in setting things right.[4]

Transformational Leadership
Listens and Demonstrates Teachability

People with this skill get their own egos out of the way so that they can continue to learn, grow, and adjust to change. They welcome feedback—including feedback from subordinates and frontline troops. The person who is not grateful for feedback is not interested in growth and change and is therefore *not* a transformational leader. In his book, *Transforming Leadership*, Leighton Ford writes,

> To lead is to struggle. In a world such as ours, in history as we know it, to choose the path of leadership is to be on a collision course with conflict. Why? The reason is quite clear. Leadership always involves change, moving people from one point to another, from the old way of doing things to the new, from the security in the past to the insecurity in the future. Within us there is a built-in resistance to change which seems to threaten our stability and challenge our power.[5]

Leadership is a process of continual improvement and growth, so leaders should intentionally create feedback loops in the organization to make sure that information is continually flowing their way. These loops should include close, trusted associates whose advice and counsel you respect and trust—people who will be candid with you about your errors and faults, people who will care enough about you to hold you accountable for change, people whose feedback will make you an even more effective leader.

Transformational leadership stands most of the old concepts of leadership on their head. A person who practices transformational leadership is not so much a boss as a guide, an encourager, a cheerleader, a mentor, a teacher. Transformational leadership looks beyond payoffs and tradeoffs. Instead of managing and controlling behavior, transformational leaders invest in people so that their personal growth, motivation, and enthusiasm will move the organization toward its goals.

The old corporate model of transactional leadership evolved during the Industrial Revolution, and it got the job done in manufacturing settings, where tasks were carried out on an assembly line and rarely changed. But transformational leadership is more appropriate in the new Information Age where most tasks are service-related and constantly changing. The kind of worker needed today is not a transactional worker ("I do my task for a paycheck"), but a transformational individual who is empowered to adjust to new situations and is motivated to find new and creative ways to get the job done. Transformational leadership unleashes the innovative and creative abilities of the members of the organization. Transactional leadership builds bureaucracy and stifles innovation, because it assumes that the world doesn't change and attempts to maintain the status quo. Once that happens, decline sets in. But transformational leadership assumes change, responds to change, and provokes change. It keeps organizations alive.

When we say that transformational leadership is the "new" leadership approach, we don't mean that it is a recent invention. Transformational leadership has been around since Jesus Christ, if not before. (Jesus was clearly a leader for his time—a time of great social upheaval and spiritual change.) So while transformational leadership may not be new, the rapid rate of change in our world makes transactional leadership obsolete, and makes transformational leadership the only viable model for the new millennium.

As we compare the old transactional model with the new transformational one, the contrast between old and new becomes clear:

OLD MODEL (TRANSACTIONAL)	NEW MODEL (TRANSFORMATIONAL)
Technical change	Adaptive change
Hierarchical pyramid	Relational web
Leader is perched atop the pyramid	Leader is at the center of a web of relationships
Leader dictates	Leader orchestrates
Leader directs	Leader supports
Leader controls people	Leader empowers people
Focus on position power	Focus on relationship power
Demands compliance	Inspires commitment
Confrontational and combative	Collaborative and unifying
Chain of command	Diffuse communication
Leader as decision maker	Leader as activator-stimulator
Employees viewed as subordinates	Employees viewed as associates and teammates
Power flows from the top down	Influence radiates from the center of a web
Rigid authoritarian structure	Flexible structure
Inflexible, complex rules	Elastic, simplified procedures
Desired place: top	Desired place: middle
Lead a meeting	Facilitate a meeting
Individual achievement	Group affiliation
Rigid job descriptions	Teams formed around specific tasks, disbanded, then new teams formed for new tasks
Will change only when forced to by crisis	Continuously learns and innovates

Clearly, this is not your father's leadership model. This is the emerging model for the emerging age, the emerging economy. It's not only the right, just, and humanizing way to lead in the new millennium—it *works*. Most important of all, it works at every level of the organization. This is not a model for the boss to employ from the ivory tower. It's a model that can be taught to *every member of the organization*, because no matter what position or arena he or she is in—from the boardroom to the mailroom—*every member is expected to exercise leadership*.

Here are some of the activities and abilities that can and should be learned by every member so that leadership can be fully implemented throughout the organization:

1. The ability to create a "holding environment." This means that a person has learned how to force a forum where change can happen. This is precisely why we use off-site retreats so often: to create a holding environment, one where people are brought into close contact with each other so that issues must be faced and can't be avoided. Change can't happen unless an environment is created where people expect change, and change is what a holding environment is all about.

2. The ability to command and direct attention. This means that a person has learned how to focus the attention of the group on the task or problem at hand. It is also the commitment to "hang tough" until a real and lasting solution is reached.

3. A willingness to grant access to information. Leadership involves providing as much information as possible. In former times, leaders hoarded information. Only a privileged few were allowed to be "in the loop." But the demands of authentic transformational leadership require that information be freely provided so that group members can make informed decisions.

4. The ability to control the flow of information. Authentic leadership doesn't overwhelm the group with information. Information overload produces frustration and cynicism. Leaders do not hoard information, but provide it when it is appropriate and relevant.

5. The ability to communicate persuasively. Leaders must be able to persuade, inspire, and motivate people. In a personal interview, Bert Decker of Decker Communications, Inc., told us,

> Anyone in leadership has to know how to move people to action with the spoken word. You can't afford to simply dump your information on the floor in front of people. You have to advocate your point of view effectively and believably. Whether you are addressing an audience of thousands or an audience of one, effective communicating is essential to effective leadership. You have to make an emotional connection with your listeners, communicate with energy, use

inflection, gestures, facial expression, and eye communication. These are the behavioral skills that make a great communicator—and every great leader is a great communicator.

(To improve your own communication skills, we recommend Bert Decker's excellent book, *You've Got to Be Believed to Be Heard,* St. Martin's Press, 1993.)

6. The ability to reframe issues. This is the ability to suggest that the Identified Problem is not the real problem. It's the ability to see beneath the surface of problems to the reality. Groups get stuck when they haven't properly framed the issues. Authentic leadership sees problems clearly, reframes them in solvable terms, and motivates the group to find the solution.

7. The ability to regulate stress. Authentic transformational leadership is willing to *push* the edge of the envelope—but not *break* it. Leaders know that people need to be motivated and challenged, but they never push people to the breaking point, never overwhelm. The right amount of stress and challenge keeps people moving toward change. Stress overload, on the other hand, produces paralysis and burnout, which in turn reduces productivity and increases unwanted employee turnover and employee downtime. Group stress is a tightrope, and stress regulation is a balancing act.

8. The ability to choose and clarify the decision-making process. Leaders establish the ground rules upfront. Is this going to be a unanimous decision or a general consensus? What happens if one person disagrees? The decision-making process should be clarified before every meeting. Typically, major issues such as strategic planning require a general consensus.

These are some of the key abilities that transformational leaders can and should acquire. And this is the beauty of the transformational leadership model: It can be *taught* and it can be *learned.* It can be practiced at any and all levels throughout the organization.

Unleash the Leadership Potential in Your Organization

We've heard it from employers around the country, in many different industries:

- ◼ "Our people aren't excited about their work."

- ◼ "The only thing that matters to them is the paycheck, the pension, and how much vacation time they get."

- ◼ "Their attitude is 'Don't do any more than you absolutely have to.'"

- ◼ "Nobody takes responsibility anymore. They all say, 'It's not my fault!'"

But employers aren't the only ones complaining. We've also heard comments like these from workers around the country, in many different industries:

- ◼ "I do a good job, I work hard, but around here, it doesn't matter what you do. It only matters who you play golf with."

- ◼ "My boss always takes credit for my ideas — so why bother thinking anymore?"

- ◼ "I haven't a clue why I do what I do. I just do what I'm told, then I go home."

- ◼ "Am I doing a good job? I dunno. I never get any feedback."

- ◼ "We have the craziest rules here—and none of them makes any sense."

- ◼ "No one ever listens to me."

If you want to have healthy members, you must start with the recruitment and hiring process. Recruit people with good attitude, good skills, and good motivation and inspiration. Once you have found them, trust them to lead, invest in their leadership, and empower them to lead.

Most companies can no longer afford to be vertical, rigid hierarchies in which leadership is isolated from the workers. The realities of the world today demand flat, flexible organizations made up of informal collaborative teams where leadership is exercised and power is shared at every level of the organization. The Thing in the Bushes often takes up residence in the corner offices of the executive suite, whispering messages of power, hierarchy, and control into the ears of the CEO and senior leaders.

Peter Coors of Coors Brewing Company observed,

> In the past, if we needed to fix up a machine shop, we simply went in and delegated: "Here are the bins, and these are the colors, and here's where the equipment will be, and there's where the tools will be kept. Now you go do it." This time we sat down with the employees to empower them and said, "Look, you have to work with this equipment, and so you design it the way you want it."

Empowering people in the workplace means:

■ People are given significant latitude and decision-making responsibility.

■ People know what's expected of them.

■ People have the resources and training to do their tasks correctly.

■ People believe their supervisors care about them as people.

■ People receive recognition and praise for good work regularly, and are accountable for mistakes.

■ People have the opportunity to do what they do best regularly.

■ People know that someone in the workplace encourages their development.

■ People know that they are expected to exercise leadership wherever they are, and they have been trained and empowered to feel confident in that role.

What happens to workers who don't feel empowered to exercise leadership? Well, all too often, they go out and start companies of their own—and they become your competitors! Workers who leave companies to start their own businesses usually have these complaints about the companies where they used to work:

- "I never had the opportunity to learn and grow."
- "No room for advancement."
- "I didn't feel like I was doing anything important."
- "I never got any encouragement or affirmation."
- "I was spinning my wheels."

To empower your people, let them know they matter. Let them know they are valued. Let them know how important their contribution is to the mission of the organization. Southwest Airlines built its phenomenal success story not on customer satisfaction but on a satisfied workforce. As company founder Herb Kelleher says of the culture at Southwest, "Customers come second. Our people come first." Customer satisfaction is an inevitable by-product of worker satisfaction.

When people feel valued, they can be trusted. Because they are valued and trusted, they are empowered. And when people are empowered, anything is possible. An empowered workforce tends to be a unified workforce. Unity means acceptance, not assimilation. In a healthy organization, people accept differences while working toward a common purpose and the accomplishment of a team mission. Many thriving organizations have near-cultic cultures that help build identity and unity. Employees take pride in identifying with the organization. Companies can promote that sense of identification with slogans and T-shirts that build an almost elitist pride in belonging.

All people long to be part of something larger than themselves. They want to feel connected; they want to belong. And a sense of community and belonging among workers creates profitable spin-offs for organizations. The combined creativity, energy, and IQ of a team is potentially much greater than that of an individual. As physicist Werner Heisenberg observed in his book *Physics and Beyond: Encounters and Conversations,* "Science is rooted in conversations. The cooperation of different people may culminate in scientific results of utmost importance." What is true of science is true in every other organizational endeavor. If your organization nurtures a culture of empowerment and shared leadership, your people will in turn empower the organization and lead it to undreamt-of heights.

The Greenlake Bank Story, Conclusion

"Am I holding up the show?"

That question from Don Larsen, president and CEO of Greenlake Savings Bank, hung in the air like a dark cloud. Sitting across the conference table from Don, we pondered that question — the same question he had asked us over the phone, days earlier: *Am I holding up the show?* Was it an unintended double entendre? Perhaps. You could take it two ways:

> *Am I the one who is solely responsible for the success of this organization, like Atlas holding the world on his shoulders?*

Or:

> *Am I the one who is obstructing the progress of this organization? Am I standing in the way of success?*

Paradoxically, the answer to both questions was yes. The very fact that Don saw himself as the *one and only person* responsible for the success or failure of Greenlake Savings Bank was in fact *hindering* the company's success. The Thing in the Bushes at Greenlake was Don's intrusive, micromanaging leadership style, which violated boundaries, destroyed communication, damaged trust, and knocked the entire relational network of the company off kilter.

"Am I holding up the show?" Don's anguished question continued to reverberate in the still air of the conference room for several seconds. Without exchanging a word, we knew: *This is it! The Thing in the Bushes!*

It was clear that Don was a fine human being, that he cared deeply and genuinely about all of his employees, and that he sincerely wanted each one to succeed. Though his employees resented his micromanaging ways, they actually liked Don as a person. He was, indeed, holding up the company in many ways. Like Atlas, he bore the weight of anxiety, responsibility, and worry for the company's future on his shoulders. But that also meant he was unable to empower his people to develop their own leadership ability. In his eagerness to make the company successful, he made himself the bottleneck, which held back the company's productivity, growth, and expansion.

Over the next two days, we led the entire staff of Greenlake through a weekend of leadership development. The first few round-table discussions with the staff were dominated (predictably) by Don. In those discussions, it was clear that he could clearly identify the problem at Greenlake — he had seen the enemy and it was him. Though he desperately wanted the staff to be empowered to carry out the company's mission, they couldn't do it because Don himself stood in their way. Even knowing this, Don couldn't help himself.

During the first day of the leadership development weekend, Don kept telling us how to do our job, how to facilitate the discussion, how to empower his staff. Even knowing he was the problem, he continued to perpetuate the problem. But over the course of the weekend, we gently eased Don out of a central position through some simple structuring exercises. Other members of the organization were brought forward and encouraged to speak and accept leadership roles. Managers were divided into three groups and each group was given an assignment. We intentionally gave Don's group the easiest assignment: identifying the organization's communication issues. The other two groups dealt with issues having to do with empowerment, leadership, and trust. In this way, we took Don out of the loop with regard to the most serious organizational challenges, and we put other people in charge of meeting and solving those challenges.

By the second day, other people had emerged as leaders. One young mid-level marketing director—not even a vice president—emerged as the real leader of the group. She skillfully elicited input from others, built consensus and clarified issues and decisions, and generally demonstrated a high level of leadership. As Don saw the high quality of leadership that emerged from the group, he began to see what he had been missing through all of his meddling and micromanagement.

And he began to relax his grip on the reins.

Oh, he still had a lot to learn and a distance to go before he would truly become the kind of empowerer he needed to be. But he had made a beginning. And so had Greenlake Savings Bank.

And it all began as the CEO started to see his company not as a pyramid but as a web of relationships, a network of leaders who could each be trusted to take the initiative and demonstrate executive ability without the boss's moment-to-moment, detail-by-detail intervention. When Don began to realize what real leadership means in the new era of organizations, The Thing knew it was beaten. It crept away, melted into the shadows, and disappeared.

And it hasn't been seen at Greenlake Savings Bank since.

4

PRACTICE RELATIONAL NETWORK THINKING

EXECUTIVE SUMMARY

Relational network thinking enables us to see and resolve *all* of the relational problems—both the Identified Problems and The Thing in the Bushes—at once. Real problems in an organization are rarely simple and isolated. They tend to involve complex issues of the entire relational network. So we must stop thinking simplistically. We must start approaching relational problems with *relational network thinking*. The principles of relational network thinking are:

1. Learn to focus on the whole, not just the parts. You cannot understand an organization merely by listing the characteristics of its individual members. In addition to those individual characteristics, there are complex dynamics at work, such as *synergy* (the interaction of two or more individuals so that their combined effect is greater than the sum of their individual abilities), *chemistry* (the way different personalities and capabilities interact and enhance each other), *rapport* (the ability of individuals to harmonize and get along), and *morale* (optimism, confidence, and esprit de corps).

2. Learn to focus on relationships, not just individuals. The old, ineffective way of assessing problems in organizations focused on individuals in isolation. In an organization, the web of relationships is everything. Being aware of the relationships in the organization means being continually aware of all the factors that affect those relationships, such as communication, boundaries, and trust.

3. Understand that organizations seek to maintain organizational status quo, which is often unhealthy. People tend to avoid change—even healthy change. Organizations, being made up of people, also avoid change. They seek to maintain a stable state—even if that stability is unhealthy and painful. Patterns of behavior and communication in relationships operate beneath the level of our awareness. Any attempt to change them is unconsciously but strongly resisted. Once we become aware of these patterns, we can make adjustments to produce good Relational Performance.

4. Learn to set appropriate boundaries. Healthy boundaries fence off the relational network of the organization from the outside world and also mark off the subnetworks within the organization. Healthy boundaries give form to healthy relationships. Those boundaries should be neither too rigid nor too lax.

Relational network thinking is a key to developing good Relational Performance.

"Jack, are you nuts! Or are you deliberately trying to destroy my work?"

Wade Martin's voice boomed throughout the office of *Metrolink* magazine. Everybody on the seventeenth floor of the Clayton Building dropped what they were doing. Throughout the office, editors, writers, layout artists, and advertising account people stepped out of their cubicles to see what the latest dustup was all about. Others ignored the shouting—this was, after all, the fourth time this week that Wade had blown a gasket.

The door to the private office of Jack Knight, the magazine's art director, was open. Inside the office, Jack leaned back in his swivel chair next to his Mac workstation, a sour expression on his face. "Look, Wade," said Jack, replying slowly as if explaining the concept of two plus two to a very dull child, "all I'm trying to do is make a halfway-decent magazine layout out of that wretched pile of Instamatic snapshots you turned in."

"You wouldn't know a great photo," Wade snapped, "if it bit you on the . . . "

"Wade," Jack interrupted, "if talent was dynamite, you wouldn't have enough to blow your nose!"

"My photos have won a shelf-full of awards!" Wade shot back. "And just look at what you're doing to them!" He pointed to the layout that glimmered on Jack's high-resolution monitor. "You completely destroyed the composition of that shot! You put display type across the top and knocked the caption out of that shadow area! That shadow is crucial to the whole esthetic balance of the shot!"

"Children, children!" admonished a strong alto voice at the door, a voice not unlike that of a very unhappy kindergarten teacher. Wade and Jack turned to see the stern face of Nanci Wallis, the managing editor, glowering at them both. "If you don't play nice, I'm going to have to pin notes to your sleeves and send you home to your mommies!" Neither her tone of voice nor her facial expression seemed as playful as her words.

"Nanci," drawled Jack, rising out of his chair, "will you tell this fathead that his job is to snap the pictures? Placing them in a layout is the art director's job."

"Is it wrong to care about excellence?" Wade lashed back. "Is it wrong to want my photographs displayed with taste and intelligence instead of seeing them trashed by some ham-handed a.d. who hasn't had a creative idea since 1975?"

Jack scowled. "Egotistical prima donna!"

Wade formed an L with his thumb and forefinger and stuck it against his forehead, leering at Jack.

"What does that mean?" Jack asked, offended—though he wasn't exactly sure why.

"If you weren't such a *loser,*" Wade sneered, "you'd know!"

"I don't have to take this from you!" snarled Jack.

"That's it!" shouted Nanci, cutting off whatever Wade was about to say. "I've had all I'm going to take!"

"Me, too!" Jack snapped. "I demand an apology."

"He's right, Wade," said Nanci. "Apologize."

"I'd sooner cut off my tongue," growled Wade.

Jack snatched a pair of red-handled cutting shears from his desk and proffered them in the photographer's direction. "Be my guest," Jack said tartly.

"That's it!" Wade turned on his heel and pushed past Nanci. "I quit!" he announced loudly, his voice and footsteps receding down the hallway.

Jack sat back in his chair, smirking. "At last," he said, "we can have some peace and quiet around here."

Seconds passed before the stunned managing editor regained the power of speech. "What . . . just . . . happened . . . here?" Nanci asked in wounded amazement.

What did just happen here?

It would be easy enough to blame this situation on Wade. After all, he is arrogant, demanding, rude, and insulting. He's clearly the problem, right?

Well, judging from this scene alone, you might be inclined to blame Wade. But if you knew a little more about the history of conflict in this office, you'd know that Wade is just the latest in a line of photographers at *Metrolink*. It seems that Jack, the art director, has a way of rubbing photographers the wrong way. He delights in cropping and recomposing their work in a way that drives them nuts. He exults in strategically placing type and other design elements right where it will do the most damage to the photographer's ego. Clashes between Jack and photographers are legendary at the magazine. So Jack is really the problem, right?

Well, Nanci, as managing editor, is directly responsible for both the art director and the staff photographers. This problem has been going on for years, yet Nanci has never solved it. Could there be something about her management and communication style that contributes to the problem? Are there problems of inadequate boundaries? Are there problems of trust? And what about the rest of the office? Could other people at the magazine be contributing to the problems that periodically rock the office?

Though we have changed the names and details in this story, we were called to this small magazine by the publisher precisely because ongoing patterns of conflict threatened to overwhelm and destroy the entire operation.

The relational dynamics in a family are much like the relational dynamics in an organization. A TAG senior partner, Joe Jurkowski, tells a story that clearly makes the point about how relational network thinking—viewing a situation as a multifaceted whole rather than as an isolated component—is crucial to solving relational problems and building good Relational Performance in organizations and in families.

During Joe's early training as a therapist, he studied under Jay Haley, the world-renowned family therapist. One day, a family brought their little boy to Haley to be treated for his fear of dogs. The boy and his phobia were the Identified Problem. But there was a deeper problem—The Thing in the Bushes—and this deeper problem was that the father and the boy had virtually no relationship. This is not to say that the boy's fear of dogs was inconsequential. The dog phobia was real and serious, but it wasn't the deepest problem.

Haley asked the father what he did for a living. "I'm a mailman," said the father.

"A mailman!" exclaimed Haley. "This is perfect!" He turned to the man's son and said, "Do you realize that your dad is an *expert* on dogs? He knows more about dogs than anyone else in the world! Well, that gives me an idea. Here's what I want you and your dad to do. I want the two of you to go together to the dog pound and the animal shelter and anyplace else that has dogs. I want you to keep visiting these places until you find a dog that is scared of *you.*"

The boy's eyes grew large. "But dogs aren't scared of me! I'm scared of dogs!"

"Well," said Haley, "somewhere out there is a dog who is scared of you, and I want you and your dad to find him."

It took the boy and his dad several weeks and many trips, but they finally found a puppy that ran at the sight of the boy. The results were (1) the puppy became the boy's pet; (2) the boy got over his fear of dogs; and (3) the boy and his father built a much closer relationship.

The dog phobia wasn't the real issue. The father-son relationship was. If Haley had seen the boy alone, without seeing the dysfunctional father-son dynamic, he could have helped the boy overcome his fear of dogs—but not only would the problem of the father-son relationship have gone unresolved, another Identified Problem would have probably emerged to take the place of the dog phobia (which, of course, was just a symptom of the deeper problem).

On the other hand, if Haley had simply told the father to spend more time with his son, the father might well have withdrawn in denial, creating an even greater wedge between father and son. By viewing the dog phobia not as an isolated problem but as one piece of the larger relational network puzzle, Haley was able to solve the entire puzzle—both the Identified Problem and The Thing in the Bushes—with a single therapeutic approach.

Whether we are dealing with the problems of a family or an organization, relational network thinking enables us to see and resolve *all* of the relational problems—both the Identified Problems and The Thing in the Bushes—at once. Relational problems in an organization are rarely simple and isolated. They tend to involve complex issues of the entire relational network. So we must stop thinking simplistically. We must start approaching relational problems with *relational network thinking.*

Whole-Brain Relationships

Each of us sees the world from a unique perspective, a singular vantage point. We easily forget that others see the same events and issues we see, but in a very different way. Some of the differences in our perceptions have to do with the way the human brain is constructed. The frontal lobes of our brain are actually made up of two sides, left and right, each dealing with the world in a different way.

Over the years, our culture has tended to place more emphasis on left-brain activity: information processing, the communication of verbal or textual content, mathematics, logical reasoning, science, engineering, technology, and so forth. Rational, symbolic ideas that can be expressed in words have been favored in our culture over the intuitive, the imaginative, the emotional, and the relational.

The left side of the brain, which is the dominant side for most people, is the brain hemisphere of which we are most aware. It operates out in the open, in ways that we consciously recognize. Books and e-mail messages are written, speeches are delivered, mathematical expressions are formulated, ships and airplanes are constructed, cities are built, and missiles and space shuttles are guided by the left side of the brain. The right side of the brain tends to work in the shadow of the left, gathering and processing its information underneath the level of human awareness.

The graph below compares the operations of the left and right hemispheres of the brain:

LEFT SIDE (AWARE)	RIGHT SIDE (UNAWARE)
Verbal I hear what you say.	Spatial I see what you're doing.
Intellectual That argument makes perfect sense.	Intuitive My hunch says this won't work.
Analysis Let's pull this problem apart.	Synthesis Let's fit the pieces together.
Directed Let's stick to the agenda.	Free Let's let our minds roam free.

Objective Let's base our judgment on the data.	Subjective I've just got a feeling about this.
Realistic Let's conduct ourselves in an orderly way.	Impulsive Throw caution to the wind.
Rational Give me the facts.	Metaphorical Tell me a story.
Individual It's all his fault.	Relational We should share the blame.

Let's look again at the troubled relationship between Wade and Jack at *Metrolink* magazine. We were called in to conduct interviews and assess the situation. In the process, we found that some people sided with Wade (the photographer) and blamed Jack. Others sided with Jack (the art director) and blamed Wade. Other people saw it as a problem between Jack and Wade, period—"a plague on both their houses," said one person. Still others blamed Nanci, the managing editor, for not taking assertive steps to solve the problem. But no one in the organization saw what we saw: there were distortions in the entire network of relationships at *Metrolink*.

As we worked with the management and staff, everyone began to understand that the problem was not just Wade, not just Jack, not just Nanci. The Thing in the Bushes lurked within the entire complex network of relationships. The blowup between Wade and Jack was just a visible symptom of a much larger but less visible problem.

In order to see that problem and solve it, the people at *Metrolink* would have to learn to move beyond looking at problems as simple isolated components. They would need to learn relational network thinking. The principles of relational network thinking are basic to the healthy functioning of any organization or group—from a family to a club to a church to a corporation to a government agency. The principles are:

1. LEARN TO FOCUS ON THE WHOLE
Relational network thinking looks at the forest, not just the individual trees. It looks at the organization as a complex whole, not a simple collection of parts. You cannot understand an organization merely by listing the characteristics of its individual members. In addition to those individual characteristics, there are complex dynamics at work, such as *synergy* (the interaction of two or more individuals so that their combined effect is greater than the sum of their individual abilities), *chemistry* (the

way different personalities and capabilities interact and enhance each other), *rapport* (the ability of individuals to harmonize and get along), and *morale* (optimism, confidence, and esprit de corps).

In his book *Ahead of the Game,* Pat Williams, the former general manager of the Philadelphia 76ers (and current executive vice president of the Orlando Magic), observes from his own experience that a basketball team is much more than just a collection of talented stars. In fact, during the 76ers' glory days, when the team was anchored by the legendary Julius "Dr. J" Erving, Pat discovered that a team can actually be *less* than the sum of its parts! He explains:

> We opened the '76-'77 season with a home game against the San Antonio Spurs. Dr. J led the charge, closely followed by a whole roster of marquee names: George McGinnis, Doug Collins, Darryl Dawkins, Lloyd Free, Caldwell Jones, Joe Bryant—a team that the sports reporters instantly dubbed "The Best Team Money Can Buy." Amazingly, however, the best team money could buy went out and lost its first two games.

> Coach Gene Shue and I sat down and talked about the disappointing start of the season. We decided that our win column was empty because our roster was too full. We didn't have a basketball team—we had a flying circus! We had too much talent—everybody wanted twenty shots a night. We had Lloyd Free proclaiming himself the Prince of Mid-Air. Darryl Dawkins, adopting a moniker that could not be topped, proclaimed himself All-Universe. Joe Bryant and Steve Mix continually elbowed each other for more court time—and the chemistry between Dr. J and George McGinnis was always touchy.

> We moved quickly to correct the situation, trading a couple players, putting a couple more on the injured reserve list, and waiving a few others. Once we had pared the team back, Gene Shue was able to get this expensive collection of talented egos under control—and the 76ers began winning games. After a 0-2 pratfall start, we went on to win 50 out of 82 games.[1]

That's the way it is in any organization. A successful team is more than a collection of individual talents. In fact, a team consisting of moderately talented individuals working in sync, with strong synergy, chemistry, rapport, and morale, will usually beat a highly talented "flying circus" of prima donnas and inflated egos. In a healthy organization, where relational network thinking is practiced, the whole truly is greater than the sum of the parts.

Take another example from everyday experience. The game of billiards is very simple if you only have two balls on the table: a cue ball and a billiard ball. Hit the cue ball at the billiard ball, and with a good aim, you can predict with great precision where the billiard ball will go. It's a matter of simple geometry. But if you break an entire rack full of billiard balls, the trajectories of the individual balls become much more complex and unpredictable. The path of any given ball—say, the seven ball—becomes less predictable because it is enmeshed in a network of relationships with all the other moving balls on the table. During a single shot, the seven ball's path will be jostled and deflected numerous times by contact with other balls. Where will the seven ball end up? Impossible to predict. The seven ball is one individual component in a complex network of dynamic relationships.

Those relationships become even more complex when you are dealing with thinking, feeling, living beings instead of unfeeling billiard balls. Newton's Third Law says that for every action there is an equal and opposite reaction. So, according to Newton, if you kick a ball, you will get an equal and opposite reaction from the ball. By transferring a certain amount of kinetic energy to the ball, you will send it flying in a fairly predictable way.

But when dealing with living beings, we need to know more than Newton's Third Law. If you kick a dog or a person, you cannot expect the same reaction you would get from kicking a ball. The dog might run and cower—or it might come after you and sink its teeth into you. If you kick a person, he or she might run away, kick you back, have you arrested, or sue you.

Living beings and living networks are much more complex and unpredictable than simple Newtonian systems. People are complex. The network of relationships within an organization is complex. Relationships among people in organizations are constantly changing, rearranging, and evolving. A change in any one member affects other members and the group as a whole. A change in the group as a whole affects each individual member. Every action is also a reaction. Individual members affect the organization; the organization affects individual members.

These ping-ponging, zig-zagging actions and reactions make it difficult to separate cause from effect. In situations like the crisis at *Metrolink* magazine, these actions and reactions make it difficult to assess blame when things go wrong. The question "Whose fault is it?" becomes extremely complex. More importantly, it is usually not even the right question to ask. It's not as simple a matter as "Wade yelled at Jack, so it's all Wade's fault." Often, as we begin to untangle all the various interwoven causes and all the many interrelated effects, we find that Wade yelled at Jack because Jack ignored Wade's request, because Nanci does not feel confident in exercising authority, because Hank, the editor-in-chief, has not set healthy boundaries within the organization, and because the board of directors has not established clear leadership parameters, all of which have generated a widespread mood of distrust throughout the organization, and on and on and on!

The point is not that we should excuse individuals and the poor choices individuals often make. There must be accountability. But at the same time, we need to broaden our thinking so that we can begin to grasp the complex relational dynamics that play out among people in organizations. When problems arise that threaten the overall effectiveness of an organization, the cause of those problems is usually found not in a specific individual, but in the relational network of that organization.

Relational network thinking is focused directly on such issues. Old-style simplistic thinking—the kind of thinking that is commonly employed in organizations—is incapable of even detecting such issues. The solution to most major organizational problems can only be found in the whole, not in the isolated parts.

2. LEARN TO FOCUS ON RELATIONSHIPS NOT JUST INDIVIDUALS

The old, ineffective way of assessing problems in organizations focused on individuals in isolation. The more accurate way of understanding problems in organizations requires us to look at relationships, at the way people relate to one another, not just at separate individuals.

We use an exercise we call "Relational Network Mapping." We begin the exercise by having people in the group identify the top six or seven specific problems affecting the organization. They frequently identify such problems as poor communication, conflict, lack of trust, and confusion over values. They may even identify a specific person as the problem. We write these different problems on a flip chart and circle each one, placing each in its own little bubble. That is how the group views the problems in the organization—each one in its isolated bubble.

But then we ask them to draw lines of cause and effect between the bubbles. "Well," someone says, "I can see that poor communication leads to lack of trust." So we draw a line between those two bubbles. "And lack of trust leads to conflict." "Oh, and confusion over values leads to conflict, too." Two more lines. And on and on, more and more lines connecting more and more bubbles. It quickly becomes apparent that what seemed to be a lot of isolated problems is actually connected by lines of cause and effect—lots and lots of lines, an uncounted number of lines.

And the group begins to realize that the bubbles aren't the problem and the people aren't the problem. The *lines* are the problem. And what are those lines? *Relationships!* And the entire group experiences an astounding breakthrough in understanding. They realize that you never find The Thing in the Bushes hiding in one of those bubbles, in the Identified Problems. It hides in the hidden space between the bubbles, in the relationships between the problems. This insight transforms our understanding of how to effectively solve relational problems in organizations.

In an organization, the web of relationships is everything. Being aware of those relationships means being continually aware of all the factors that affect them. (We'll explore these factors, including communication, boundaries, and trust, in detail in other chapters of this book.)

People in relationships are constantly communicating. Communication is the glue that holds relationships together. When we talk about communication, we mean *all* communication channels, both verbal and nonverbal. Relational network thinkers don't just focus on the verbal content, the "what" of communication. They also focus on the "how" of communication, the nonverbal, emotional, and relational elements of the communication process. With these elements in mind, the relational network thinker realizes that communication is never as simple as who said what to whom. Even the subtlest behavioral cues are recognized as important channels of communication.

For example, take another look at the conflict between Wade and Jack. During the time Wade had worked as a photographer for *Metrolink* magazine, he and Jack had continually been at each other's throats. They had developed a set, predictable pattern of communication. As a result, the patterns of communication and behavior among other coworkers were affected. People knew they had to avoid talking about Jack to Wade, just as they had to avoid the subject of Wade around Jack. Whenever Wade came into the office from one of his photo assignments, some people (especially those who were uncomfortable around conflict) found an excuse to leave the office. At the same time, others (those who tended to be placaters and peacemakers) would try to distract one or both of the combatants and prevent them from coming into contact with each other. The conflict between Jack and Wade impacted the entire office in a variety of negative ways, distorting the routine, the behavior, and the communication patterns of the *Metrolink* office.

The problem was much bigger than a struggle between two individuals. It was a dysfunctional dynamic that affected the entire relational network. The problem could only be solved by looking at *all* the affected relationships—not just at the individuals involved.

3. UNDERSTAND THAT ORGANIZATIONS SEEK TO MAINTAIN STATUS QUO (HOMEOSTASIS), WHICH IS OFTEN UNHEALTHY

People naturally tend to avoid change—even healthy change. Organizations, being made up of people, are no different. They avoid change. They seek to maintain a steady, stable state—even if that stability is unhealthy and painful.

Question: how is your golf swing? If you are at all like us, chances are you've got some bad golfing habits. Problem is, after performing a bad swing for a long enough time, doing it *wrong* begins to feel *right*. We easily become comfortable with an ineffective swing. Go take lessons with a pro, and you'll find that the pro is telling you to do some things with your golf swing that feel wrong and unnatural. You'd much rather stick to what feels comfortable, even though it causes you to slice like crazy. That's normal. That's human.

But it's also self-defeating.

The same is true of organizations. Because relational networks seek balance, predictable patterns tend to emerge, becoming repetitive, redundant, and counterproductive. We saw these patterns at *Metrolink*. In fact, it wasn't just a pattern. It was a *game*.

Wade would come into Jack's office, strut around and talk about his awards, and demand that Jack change his layouts to make his photos the focal point of the story. Jack, resentful of Wade's demands, would find ways to sabotage, camouflage, and obscure all the best elements of Wade's photos. He'd take one of Wade's favorite shots, with its subtle tones and highlights—and he'd posterize or solarize or dither it beyond recognition. When Wade saw his beautiful photos turned into something resembling Andy Warhol pop art from the 1960s, he would go ballistic—and Jack would sit back and grin.

At that point, Nanci would invariably rush in to find out what all the shouting was about. She would attempt to mediate the conflict by asking each person to recite his side of the problem, then she'd try to get both sides to "make nice." This little game—this *dance*—took place several times a week. It wasn't a disruption of the routine. It *was* the routine—but nobody seemed to realize it.

These patterns of interaction within organizations go largely undetected because people rarely step back and grok the big picture. Instead, people tend to focus on the details, the individuals, the issues of the moment, little realizing that the issues themselves are unimportant—mere minutiae. The *real* issue, the *bigger* issue, can only be found in the behavioral pattern.

Patterns of behavior and communication in relationships operate underground, beneath the level of our awareness. They are subtly constructed and elaborately maintained. Any attempt to change them is unconsciously but strongly resisted. Once we become consciously aware of the enormous influence of these patterns on the organization, we can make the changes and adjustments that produce good Relational Performance.

4. LEARN TO SET APPROPRIATE BOUNDARIES

Healthy boundaries fence off the relational network of the organization from the outside world, and they mark off the subnetworks within the organization. Healthy boundaries give form to healthy relationships. Those boundaries should neither be too rigid nor too lax.

As we assessed the problems at *Metrolink,* we found that a lack of healthy boundaries contributed to the destructive conflict in the office. Jack and Wade both allowed their personal, emotional agendas to invade the workplace. Instead of acting professionally for the good of the magazine, both became embroiled in personal, emotional turf battles. Professionalism went right out the window.

Nanci's attempts to jump in and mediate the disputes between Wade and Jack were yet another violation of boundaries. As a leader in the organization, she could certainly tell them that their bickering would not be tolerated, but she should not have gotten in the middle of their disputes. Instead of playing the mediator and peacemaker, she should firmly lay down the organization's rules and expectations for civil behavior. Then she should leave the two combatants to solve their own problem—and they should be held accountable for solving their own problem. The boundary should have remained intact around their conflict. Instead, there was no boundary; their disputes could be heard all over the seventeenth floor of the Clayton Building, and everyone in the office was affected.

When we were called in to assess this crisis, we began by interviewing everyone who was affected. A fascinating picture quickly emerged:

Nanci, the managing editor, and Hank, the editor-in-chief, were both nurturing and benevolent individuals who hated conflict within the office. Both showed a great deal of concern for their employees, allowing anyone to interrupt them to talk about office problems, personal struggles, and even issues having nothing to do with the magazine. Hank and Nanci had tried to make *Metrolink* a friendly place to work, with a breezy, informal, open-collar feel. In the process, however, a degree of professionalism had been lost. What seemed at first to be a plus—a laid-back, family-like atmosphere—also had its downside. "Family-like" is not always a compliment, especially when some members of the family are decidedly dysfunctional.

The family-like atmosphere at *Metrolink* also meant that there were a lot of family-like emotional issues in the office. People frequently took criticisms (which were meant constructively and professionally) in a personal way (perceiving them as destructive attacks). Some would bring their personal issues into the office. Leadership tended to act (and be perceived) as parents rather than business professionals. The entire relational network was unwittingly maintaining an atmosphere of sibling rivalries that were slowly sucking the life out of the organization.

We took the entire organization on a two-day retreat. During the first day, we nailed down the problem clearly: "*Metrolink* has become a family disguised as a business. Instead of acting professionally, the people in this organization behave like siblings in a dysfunctional family, bickering over personal issues and over who said what to whom and who got more than someone else." We showed the *Metrolink* staff how to think in terms of relational networks so that the hidden causes and contributing factors in these conflicts could become visible—and solvable. "Thinking in terms of the relational network constantly widens the lens," we told them. "In relational network thinking, we ask ourselves, 'How am I involved in this problem? Who else is involved? How do we interact with each other to create these problems?'"

The second day of the retreat, we worked on solutions. We talked about the need to behave professionally, about the need for conflicts to be contained within secure boundaries, and about the fact that issues should be examined not in isolation, but within the entire network of relationships. We showed the staff how to deal constructively with conflict and how to allow the combatants to solve their own differences without drawing others in.

Though Wade had resigned in the heat of the moment, Nanci had never accepted his resignation. She convinced him to take part in the off-site retreat, and by the close of the weekend he'd decided to stay with *Metrolink.* Within a few weeks, the office was functioning much more smoothly—and quietly. The friction between Jack and Wade didn't exactly disappear, but the open, explosive venting of their mutual hostility was no longer tolerated by the magazine's leadership. Jack and Wade still had their occasional fights, but they kept it between themselves. Nanci refused to mediate, and she refused to allow their bickering to disrupt the professional atmosphere at the magazine. (The principles they used to quell the conflict at *Metrolink* are explored in greater detail in chapter 6.)

We've checked back several times since the initial consultation, and the changes that were made at *Metrolink* are holding. Boundaries have been strengthened; leadership roles have been clarified (Hank and Nanci are carrying out their leadership responsibilities in a more professional and assertive manner); communication channels have become untangled and clear; and *Metrolink* is a much healthier, happier place to work. Linear thinking is out; relational network thinking is in.

Are Wade and Jack friends? Hardly. But for the purposes of getting out a magazine, they are something better than friends. They are colleagues.

5

CREATE HEALTHY BOUNDARIES

EXECUTIVE SUMMARY

You can't have Relational Performance without healthy boundaries. Boundaries are the fences that mark off our world, creating zones of safety, authority, and privacy. Boundaries are an essential component of Relational Performance because they define who is and who isn't part of the organization; what the roles and responsibilities are; who has authority for what; what is a priority and what is not; what is a professional issue versus a personal issue; and more.

Boundaries should be neither too rigid and inflexible nor too permeable and ambiguous. Healthy boundaries give structure to business relationships, but they should *de*fine, not *con*fine.

One of the most crucial boundaries that must be maintained in an organization is what we call "The Blue Zone" versus "The Red Zone." The Blue Zone is where people act within their professional roles. The Red Zone is where people move outside of their professional roles, reacting emotionally instead of professionally, taking issues and comments personally instead of professionally, and generally behaving like members of a dysfunctional family instead of members of a professional organization. This is a common hiding place for The Thing in the Bushes.

A wise, mature leader leads from the Blue Zone of the professional role, not the Red Zone of emotions and self. A relationally unhealthy leader operates from the Red Zone: he or she takes conflict and criticism personally, quickly becomes angry, and loses the ability to respond with logical detachment; he or she allows his or her attention to be diverted from issues to personalities.

When boundaries are out of whack in one area, they tend to be out of whack everywhere. Boundaries cannot be examined in isolation, but must be viewed in terms of the entire relational network.

Patrick Hughes (the name is fictitious), the CEO of a major land development company in northern Virginia, sat in our office. "The problem is my board of directors," he said. "Every time I try to—"

Deedle-deedle-deeeee! The electronic chirping came from somewhere on Pat's person.

"Excuse me," he said, whipping out his cell phone and flipping it open. "Hughes here," he said. "Oh, hi Tony. . . . That's what I told him. . . . Well, what did he say to that?"

We leaned back and waited.

"No way! That's totally unacceptable. . . . He really said that? Then it's no deal! . . . That's right. Tell him to forget it! . . . Yeah. Later." Pat snapped the phone shut and looked at us. "Sorry about that. Where were we?"

"You were saying that the problem is your board of directors," we replied.

"Oh, yeah, the board," said Hughes. "Every time I try to—"

Deedle-deedle-deeeee!

Out came the cell phone again. "Hughes," he said. "Yeah, Sherry. . . . Uh-huh. . . . Well, where are the specs? They were supposed to be here by ten o'clock. . . . You're kidding! They told you what? . . . Sherry, that's the stupidest excuse I ever heard! . . . No, I'm not waiting till next week! Tell 'em to FedEx 'em here by tomorrow morning, latest, and no more excuses! . . . Yeah, thanks, Sherry. Gotta go!"

Pat snapped the phone shut and grinned sheepishly. "This thing never stops ringing. I was telling you—" He paused and went blank.

"Your board of directors," we prompted.

"Right, you see, the problem I have is that every time I try to—"

Deedle-deedle-deeeee!

"Before you answer that," we said, "we see another problem we need to talk about. . . . "

Patrick Hughes didn't know it, but the biggest problem he had was a lack of boundaries. He didn't know the limits of his own role, and he had never articulated a well-defined role to the people in his company. As a result, they took every problem to him, rather than taking the initiative to solve their own problems. The Thing in the Bushes was present in every ring of the phone and in every problem he took upon himself to solve, every request that he fulfilled.

You can't have Relational Performance without healthy boundaries.

The Function of Boundaries

Boundaries are the fences, both physical and emotional, that mark off our world, creating zones of safety, authority, privacy, and territoriality. Boundaries are an essential component of Relational Performance because they

■ define who is and isn't a part of the organization;

■ define what belongs to each member of the organization;

■ fix roles and delineate what a member is and is not responsible for;

■ define lines of authority that are clear, yet flexible;

■ define the composition of teams within the organization;

■ restrict access and intrusions;

■ protect priorities; and

■ differentiate between personal and professional issues.

In some organizations, boundaries become too rigid, causing a bottleneck in the vital information flow that is the lifeblood of any healthy organization. This is especially true in transactional leadership organizations with their old-style pyramidal hierarchy, where boundaries are so rigid that policies and procedures are never to be questioned. When an organization cannot receive vital information from outside, it cannot respond to changing circumstances in the marketplace. When vital information is not passed along within the organization, gaps open up in the "assembly line," and important tasks "fall through the cracks."

In other organizations, boundaries become too permeable or ambiguous. In such cases, the integrity and cohesion of the organization is threatened by a lack of definition—a case of too many cooks spoiling the vichyssoise.

We are used to the visible boundary markers of our world: fences, hedges, traffic signs. Less obvious are the internal boundaries that mark off emotional territory: "These are my thoughts, my feelings," or "This is my responsibility, not yours." These internal boundaries are emotional barriers that protect and enhance the integrity of individuals and organizations.

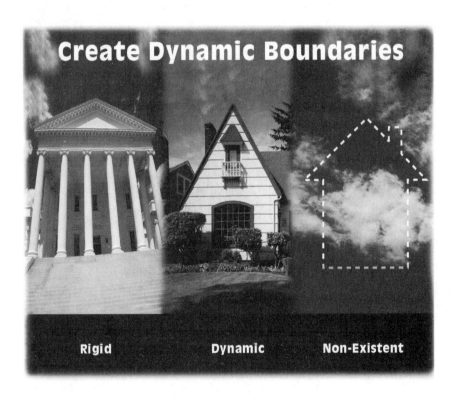

Here's a quick test to help you determine the strength and health of your own personal boundaries (based on ideas suggested by C. L. Whitfield in *Boundaries and Relationships*, Health Communications, 1993). See if you agree or disagree with the statements on the following page.

AGREE	DISAGREE	
		I have difficulty making up my mind.
		I have difficulty saying no to people.
		I feel my happiness depends on other people.
		I would rather attend to others than to myself.
		Others' opinions are more important than mine.
		People take and use my things without asking me.
		I have difficulty asking for what I want or need.
		I would rather go along with other people than express what I would really like to do.
		It's hard for me to know what I think and believe.
		I have a hard time determining what I really feel.
		I don't get to spend much time alone.
		I have a hard time keeping a confidence.
		I am very sensitive to criticism.
		I tend to stay in relationships that are harmful to me.
		I tend to take on or feel what others are feeling.
		I feel responsible for other people's feelings.

If you answered "Agree" to even two or three of these statements, you have at least some issues with unhealthy boundaries. The more statements you agree with, the greater your problem with maintaining clear boundaries.

Gaps and Overlaps

Boundary problems always arise at the extremes—where boundaries are either too vague and weak or too rigid and inflexible. Rigid boundaries produce gaps and weak boundaries produce overlaps. An organization with weak boundaries will have trouble discerning where one part of the organization stops and another begins ("What do you mean you processed the new hire today? I did that yesterday!"). These kinds of overlaps create organizational inefficiency with too many cooks in the kitchen.

Sexual harassment occurs more often in organizations where personal boundaries are not respected. In still other organizations, the boundary between personal life and work life is so vague that people are expected to put in long hours, to stay in contact at all times (even on vacation), and to generally surrender their lives to the good of the organization.

For over a dozen years, Rita Jones had been the comptroller in a small office of about twenty employees. Due to her expertise with computers, she also helped set up the company's computer network. It wasn't part of her job description, but she didn't mind—and her in-house expertise saved the company a lot of money. But as the office staff continued to grow, the company hired Jerome, an information systems professional, to manage the computer network. Problem was, Rita continued to take a proprietary interest in the computer network. After all, she helped set up the system. "I think of it as my baby," she said.

"But it's not in your job description," Jerome pointed out.

"I don't mind," Rita cheerfully replied, ignoring the note of aggravation in Jerome's voice. She continually interfered with his work, making changes in the network without informing him, and driving him crazy. Even though Jerome was hired as an IS specialist, everyone went to Rita for help when they had a computer problem—force of habit. Complaining of being treated like a fifth wheel, Jerome finally quit in disgust. The company lost a qualified professional because the comptroller didn't stick to comptrolling. She wouldn't acknowledge and respect Jerome's professional boundaries.

Bart and Susie have been married for over twenty years, and they manage a small restaurant together. Bart is the manager and chef, while Susie is the cashier and bookkeeper. There also is another chef, several waiters, and a bartender. Problem is, Bart and Susie can't seem to keep their marital problems out of the restaurant. Just the other day, Bart, as manager of the organization, directed Susie to perform a task. Susie, still fuming over an argument they had in the bedroom the night before, responds not as a business partner but as an angry spouse: "Just try and make me." Whenever Bart and Susie get into one of their on-the-job marital spats, the business suffers. Employees have quit, customers have been turned away, and occasionally the restaurant has even closed its doors, losing an evening's receipts, because of childish behavior that knew no boundaries.

Healthy boundaries give structure to business relationships, but they should *define*, not *confine*. Boundaries that are too rigid and confining usually create gaps in organizations. New tasks or roles tend to fall through the cracks ("That's not my job—that's marketing's job!"). Rigid boundaries also indicate a lack of trust within the organization. Sondra, an executive in a well-known telecommunications company, recently told us that her company had such paternalistic and rigid boundaries that even top executives were made to punch a time clock and account for every hour of every day. Information was rigidly controlled between departments. Rigid policies and procedures stifled creativity and innovation. The result: morale was low. So Sondra, a talented and energetic executive, was seeking employment elsewhere because, as she put it, "I'm tired of coming to work in a straightjacket every morning. There are plenty of companies out there who respect and trust you, and where your talent is encouraged, not stifled."

Healthy organizations respect the boundaries of each individual ("I am respected for who I am. I'm seen as a person, not just a function."). Healthy organizations also respect the boundaries between the organization and the private life of each individual member ("When I'm home, I'm home. I don't have to worry about what's going on back at work.").

Healthy organizations maintain clear boundaries in terms of responsibilities and authority. Members of a healthy organization have a clear sense of who does what, but they are also flexible enough to cover for each other, make allowances for each other, and occasionally stretch the limits of their job descriptions for the good of the organization.

Roles Are Boundaries

Churches are relational organizations, too.

Like any organization, a church needs to have good Relational Performance—and that means that churches need healthy boundaries. We were once called to a church to help solve a problem between the ruling board and the senior pastor. After assessing the situation, we found that the pastor had been at the church for nearly ten years, was dedicated and hard working, and wanted to do the right thing by his board. The board was made up of members of the congregation who had been elected to it for three-year terms. Each member had joined with a strong sense of commitment and desire to do a conscientious job. There were no "bad guys" in this organization. Unfortunately, considerable conflict had arisen between the "good guys" on both sides.

The problem, it turned out, was confusion over roles and boundaries. As often happens with boards in organizations ranging from multinational corporations to corner churches, these board members had only a vague idea of what their roles entailed. When some of the newer board members began receiving calls from parishioners regarding this or that thing the pastor had done, they began to doubt the pastor's ability to lead. They didn't realize that, in a church of over five thousand parishioners, complaints were inevitable: "His sermons are too long," or "He doesn't do enough visitation of the sick and shut-ins." The most serious complaint involved the way he had dealt with a personnel issue involving the music minister, who was very popular with many of the congregants.

"Our music minister's marriage was in serious trouble," the senior pastor explained to us in confidence. "His wife had found out he had a problem with Internet pornography, and she wanted to leave him. As senior pastor, I worked closely with the personnel committee to keep this matter confined to a few people with a need to know. We got our music minister and his wife into counseling and kept him on the payroll for a full year to give him a chance to get his life together. I felt we had bent over backward to help this couple toward restoration. But stories circulated that I had simply railroaded him out of the church because of some personality clashes we'd had in the past. It wasn't true, but I couldn't defend myself without causing damage to our music minister and his wife."

During a board meeting, several of the newer board members strongly criticized the pastor over his "poor job performance." They proposed reversing his decision regarding the music minister, and they started suggesting topics that should be addressed in his sermons. It was a clear-cut case of treating the Identified Problem and ignoring The Thing in the Bushes.

This is a familiar story, not only with church boards, but also with corporate boards. Regardless of the organization, we always suggest that a board spend 60 percent of its time discussing policy, 25 percent making decisions, and only 15 percent in monitoring and oversight. Unfortunately, boards usually find their time spent in the reverse order—and that's what was taking place at this church.

A board is not the pastor of a church, not the CEO of a corporation.

Boards and executive officers have very different functions and roles. If the boundaries that circumscribe those roles are not understood or not observed, the result is confusion and conflict. Where there is healthy Relational Performance, there is a clear understanding of what the roles and responsibilities of the board are versus the roles and responsibilities of the chief executive officer. In a broad sense, it is the difference between *strategic* matters and *tactical* matters.

The *strategic* realm is the role of the board. Strategic matters have to do with code, long-range planning, policy-making, overall governance, and the mission and direction of the organization. In its policy-making role, the board should be proactive, anticipating future needs, not reacting to each little problem and formulating a policy to remedy it (which is micromanagement by committee, a fatal mistake). Proactive policy-making covers broad issues, not a multitude of details. In a church setting, this often involves the statement of faith, theological orientation, polity, and such matters. That is the strategic realm, the sphere of the board's operations and influence.

The *tactical* realm is the role of the CEO or pastor. As the top executive in the organization, he or she is responsible for executive decision making and the day-to-day functioning of the organization, the daily details. While a good CEO or pastor is proactive and visionary, this individual must also be reactive, dealing with problems and crises that arise. That is the tactical sphere. That is what it means to be an *executive* officer — what the board determines in broad outline, the CEO *executes* in concrete detail.

To put the strategic-tactical duality into military terms, the board determines the overall strategy: on what fronts the war should be waged and how resources should be allocated to fight it. The general decides how to deploy his troops most effectively to get the job done.

In a real sense, the board of an organization has only one employee: the CEO. The board should determine the overall direction of the organization, and then turn the operation of things over to the CEO, trusting that individual to carry out the wishes of the board, but also demanding a regular accounting from that individual (the old principle of "trust but verify"). The CEO must have the character traits and leadership skills to perform the day-to-day operations in an effective and trustworthy manner. If the CEO is able to do this, then the board will be less likely to worry about that individual's performance and less tempted to interfere.

When we conducted our assessment of this church, we found an organization where the board had usurped the role of the pastor. It had gone beyond the boundaries of its role and had invaded the boundaries of the pastor's role. What few people on that board understood was that by trampling these boundaries, reversing the pastor's decisions, and telling him how to handle a staff problem, they had effectively undermined their own ability to hold this pastor accountable. He no longer held executive authority, because they had wrested that authority from his hands.

After studying the situation carefully, we confronted the board members with the result of their action. "You are telling your pastor, 'We no longer have faith that you can run this organization, so we are going to run it for you,'" we explained. "So now you have to ask yourselves, 'Why do we even have a pastor? We've taken over those functions.'"

Once the board members saw their action in terms of a violation of roles and boundaries, they willingly reversed themselves, voted confidence in the pastor, and formulated policies to formalize healthy boundaries in their own role and the pastor's role. Today, that church has healthy Relational Performance.

Strong boards need strong leaders; strong leaders need strong boards. That's a balance that must always be held in tension, each side understanding its own role and function. Just as good fences make good neighbors, healthy boundaries make healthy companies.

Here's a true story: Robert was the head of an organization that had completely turned itself around from a failing proposition to a going concern. He enjoyed an excellent relationship with his board, which trusted him completely. They turned the day-to-day operations and tactical concerns over to him without interference.

Robert's main competitor was a man named George, the head of another, much larger organization in the same field as Robert's. George was attempting to negotiate a hostile takeover of Robert's firm. Unfortunately for George, there was considerable mistrust and cynicism between George and his board. The board tended to second-guess George's decisions and micromanage his tactics. Understandably, George resented and resisted the board's meddling by withdrawing and sharing little of his organization's day-to-day operations with the board. When the time came to initiate the takeover, George sensed the lack of board support, made a number of tactical errors, and ended up blowing the whole deal.

The Robert of this story was Robert E. Lee, head of the Confederate Army. His board consisted of the Confederate president, Jefferson Davis, and the Confederate high command. George was General George McClellan, Union commander of the Army of the Potomac. McClellan's lack of trust in President Lincoln and the high command was legendary. The hostile takeover was the bloody battle of Antietam, one of the most famous battles of the American Civil War. Though McClellan's forces and

CREATE HEALTHY BOUNDARIES

resources far outweighed those of Lee, the battle was fought to a draw in the summer of 1862.

It was a battle that McClellan should have won, and his failure to achieve victory is almost certainly a result of the fact that his organization was hamstrung by unhealthy boundaries. McClellan's forces staggered on through the war for well over a year after Antietam. Finally, President Lincoln and the Union high command had had enough of McClellan. They replaced him with a general in whom they could place their trust: Ulysses S. Grant. Once Grant was in command, the Union high command stopped micromanaging the war. Lincoln and the high command went about their function of broad strategic oversight while trusting Grant to successfully prosecute the war—which he did.

It was a classic case of a strong CEO and a strong board achieving success through good communication, healthy boundaries, and clearly defined roles.

The Red Zone and the Blue Zone

Another important boundary division in organizations is the division between *first-order boundaries* and *second-order boundaries*. First-order boundaries include such technical matters as deadline dates, responsibilities, duties, departments, divisions, and measurements. These technical kinds of boundaries are relatively simple to define, understand, and maintain. This is the realm of itemization and specification. They are easily reduced to rules and categories.

But second-order boundaries are another thing altogether. They are personal rather than technical boundaries. They often involve such "fuzzy" issues as relationships and emotion. Second-order boundaries involve the realm of "where I stop and you begin," the balance between personal and professional, the balance between home and office, the balance between *my* roles and responsibilities and *your* roles and responsibilities. Most importantly, second-order boundaries involve the precarious balance between "who I am in my professional role" versus "who I am in my emotions, my inner security and insecurities, my hurts and sensitivities, and my humanness." The most crucial and sensitive second-order boundary of all is the balance between what we call "The Blue Zone" and "The Red Zone."

We recently consulted at a small (forty employees) high-tech company that was going through a severe crisis, threatening the very existence of the company. A number of high-level managers within the organization, which we will call ZIP, were at odds with each other. This pitched battle had drawn in people from all over the organization and was seriously affecting the quality of products and services the company delivered. Arguments broke out in view of customers. Deadlines were missed. Several prime clients had defected. The future of the company was in doubt.

We were brought in to analyze the problem and find solutions to end the civil war at ZIP. After making an on-site inspection of the situation, we set up an off-site meeting for the ZIP management. We reviewed the nine principles of Relational Performance. We asked the participants about their expectations. We asked each one to define the problem in the organization. We listened to complaints. What emerged was a clear picture of an organization that was at war with itself over the issue of boundaries.

As they probed the boundary issues at ZIP, we heard these complaints:

Time boundaries among coworkers were ambiguous. "I'm in my thirties and single," said one young woman, "so everyone here assumes I don't have a life. It's like everyone thinks I don't have anyone to go home to like married people do, so they just take advantage of me. 'Ginny, can you stay late tonight? Ginny, would you cover for me? Ginny, do this, Ginny, do that.' So I've been working late night after night so other people can go home to their families. Look, I'm willing to work hard, but I'm tired of sacrificing my life so that other people can have more quality time with the remote control or whatever. I have a life, too!"

Emotional boundaries among coworkers were ambiguous. "I care about the people I work with," said another member of the organization, "but when my coworkers are constantly coming to me with their problems and complaints, I just can't absorb it all! It's too emotionally draining. People tell me things I shouldn't hear, and I say, 'I don't want to know that!' but they tell me anyway!"

Emotional boundaries involving clients and suppliers were ambiguous. "I feel like Dear Abby and Dr. Laura all rolled into one," said another member. "One of our clients is going through a messy divorce right now. When he walks in, I say, 'Hi, Chuck, how ya doin'?' And he says, 'Not so good,' and proceeds to tell me his whole life story. Am I getting paid to fix this guy's problems? I've got problems of my own, and one of them is that I can't get my work done because of people like Chuck who take up all my time."

Boundaries between workers' private and professional lives were ambiguous. Ian, a salesman with a chaotic personal life, brought his chaos into the workplace. He always had a number of past and present girlfriends who were either calling him at the office, stopping by the office to entice him into taking a "long lunch," or storming into the office to tell him what a two-timing lowlife he was. He had also made inappropriate advances toward some of the female members of the organization. The sexual tension and animosity that swirled around Ian were a highly combustible mixture, like gasoline and an open flame.

There was not enough margin in the employees' lives. Deadlines were tight; hours were long; praise was rare. Pressure and long hours depleted employee energy. The leadership at ZIP was squeezing all the margin out of the lives of the workforce by driving people hard without replenishing their lives with praise and celebration. Workers would seek out the approval of their leaders, but the leaders would respond, "So you closed a deal, so you completed a project. That's what you get paid to do. Don't expect a medal for it."

There were no boundaries around personality clashes and internecine conflict. Conflict in the office was frequent and never seemed to stay between the two original combatants. Other people in the organization were constantly drawn into the conflicts, either to side with one party or the other, or to act as reluctant referees. The more people got drawn into the conflicts, the more those conflicts seemed to swirl out of control.

As the weekend seminar progressed, a new way of understanding these problems began to emerge. We helped the members of the organization reframe their understanding of the company. ZIP had become a dysfunctional family disguised as a business. The various members of the organization actually filled familial roles. The leaders and owners were like emotionally remote parents: demanding, authoritarian, and loath to give out praise and affirmation. The rest of the members of the organization filled other roles in a dysfunctional family setting: the ne'er-do-well playboy brother, the bossy sister, the battling siblings, the peacemaking child, the molesting uncle, and on and on and on.

Most of the problems in this organization took on the qualities of family conflicts rather than professional difficulties. It was as if the coworkers had two selves: a professional business self in which they went about doing their jobs in a competent manner and a personal self in which they acted more like highly sensitive, emotionally charged family members. People kept stepping back and forth between the two worlds: the personal and the professional. They could not establish a boundary between what they felt personally and what they did as professionals within the company.

To illustrate the concept of these two worlds, we used two Magic Markers, a blue one and a red one, to draw the two zones on a large white board. The Blue Zone was where people acted in their professional roles. The Red Zone was where people acted emotionally, taking issues, problems, and comments personally, and behaving like a dysfunctional family. The graphic looked like this:

THE BLUE ZONE = PROFESSIONAL MODE
THE EMOTIONAL COOL ZONE
Focus on efficiency and effectiveness.
Structures of the business are closely monitored and respected.
Job descriptions and performance evaluations.
Business issues are highest priority.
THE RED ZONE = EMOTIONAL MODE
THE EMOTIONAL HOT ZONE
Focus more on feelings than results.
No set standards of acceptable behavior.
No mechanism for monitoring standards of behavior, because no consistent standards exist.
People act like family members.
Family roles are assumed at work.
People expect organization to be a family.
Common family roles appear: *Mom and Dad:* Workers craved approval from the owners, but never received it. *Caretakers:* "Here, let me help you (even though you didn't ask)." *Isolators:* "I can do it myself, so leave me alone." *Warring siblings:* "She got more than I did!" *Peacemakers:* "Can't we all just get along?" *Distracters:* "How 'bout a joke?"

One of the most important boundaries in any organization is the boundary between the Blue Zone and the Red Zone. In fact, this is often where The Thing in the Bushes is found. When that boundary becomes blurred, miscommunication, distrust, irrational behavior, and destructive conflict become inevitable. Whereas Relational Performance assumes a certain level of healthy Blue Zone conflict, in which different viewpoints and ideas collide to produce stronger ideas and solutions, Red Zone conflict is almost impossible to resolve because the real emotional reasons for the conflict are usually buried beneath superficial issues, rationalizations, denial, and unreasoning hostility.

When an organization operates in the Red Zone, its boundaries are unhealthy by definition. People in the Red Zone allow their professional behavior to be driven by personal, emotional, and unprofessional motives. But when an organization operates in the Blue Zone, the members work together on a healthy, professional level. When there is good Relational Performance, business relationships and behavior always remain in the Blue Zone.

In the final day of the seminar, we asked the members of ZIP what they wanted for their organization. The number-one answer on everyone's list: "A *fun* place to work!" They wanted a place where professionalism reigned and where personal issues were left outside the door. So then the discussion turned to what they would need in order to achieve the kind of organization they desired and envisioned:

■ They would need to monitor their communication and make sure that all communication remained in the Blue Zone (professional mode). They needed to monitor not only the "what" of their communication but the "way" of their communication—not only the content of their words, but also the tone of voice, eye communication, body language, and other nonverbal cues that affected the message. The way we communicate says much more to others about how we feel about them and the relationship than the what of our words.

■ They needed to recognize and take responsibility for their own Red Zone (or personal) issues. Until they honestly acknowledged their Red Zone issues, they would remain stuck there. Honest acceptance of the reality of those issues was the first step toward moving into the Blue Zone.

■ Every member needed to monitor his or her own boundaries. They needed to ask themselves: "Am I allowing personal business to intrude into the workplace? Am I inappropriately absorbing the emotional debris of my customers, suppliers, and coworkers? Do I take personally statements and actions that are not meant in a personal way? Is it appropriate to discuss this matter in the workplace? Am I operating from the Blue Zone or the Red Zone?"

■ They needed to minimize the arenas of conflict. If there was a conflict between two people in the organization, it should stay between those two. No one else should be drawn into the fight.

■ All members—including Ian the Casanova—were put on notice that there would be no tolerance for private issues disrupting the efficiency of the workplace.

We checked back periodically after our consultation to make sure that the positive changes were still in place. After six months, the leaders at ZIP told us that the whole atmosphere of the company had been transformed. It had become a *fun* place to work.

Leading from the Blue Zone

Good Relational Performance requires a leader who understands the difference between the Blue Zone and the Red Zone:

THE BLUE ZONE = ONE'S ROLE	THE RED ZONE = ONE'S SELF
THE EMOTIONAL COOL ZONE	THE EMOTIONAL HOT ZONE

A relationally healthy leader understands that when people respond to his or her actions in the organization, they are responding to that leader's role, not to the person. A wise, mature person leads from the Blue Zone of that role, not the Red Zone of self. This is one of the key boundary areas for Relational Performance.

A relationally unhealthy leader operates from the Red Zone. He or she takes conflict and criticism personally and responds in kind, usually with harshly personal, biting, even insulting attacks. Emotions run high as people in the emotionally hot Red Zone become angry and lose the ability to grapple with a problem coolly, rationally, and with logical detachment. Operating from the Red Zone easily leads to misunderstandings and misdiagnoses of issues. Every problem becomes a highly personal, emotionally charged problem. Colleagues become combatants as attention is shifted from issues to personalities.

A relationally healthy leader operates from the Blue Zone, where conflicts and criticisms are seen as part of the role of being a leader. A Blue Zone leader maintains a zone of safety around his or her soul. Conflict is kept external. The leader is able to hear criticism without feeling personally attacked or destroyed. This enables everyone involved to think and communicate more logically, clearly, and constructively. Attention remains focused on the issue, not on personalities.

By understanding the forces and dynamics of the Red Zone whenever they arise, we can make a conscious, deliberate, logical choice to remain in the Blue Zone in all our interactions. The Red Zone is like the force of gravity, always pulling on us, always trying to snatch us into its orbit. It gnaws at us from within, filling us with fear, resentment, and self-doubt: "Am I competent? Do people really accept me? Are people trying to control me? Have I done my job well enough?"

Externally, the Red Zone tugs at us through people and circumstances. When our opinions are challenged, we may become defensive and angry—or we may retreat. When we are under pressure, we may become indecisive and uncertain. Continual criticism or a series of setbacks may make us overly sensitive to what others think or say about us. Worries and uncertain circumstances may make us edgy and irritable. We may become unreasonably angry when others disagree with our opinions or suggest a better way to do something.

Our challenge as leaders is to recognize the existence of the emotionally charged Red Zone, to be wary of its influence on our emotions and behavior, and to continually work to keep our reason in control of our emotions. With this awareness, we can lead from the relationally healthy region of the Blue Zone.

Relational Performance means that there must be healthy boundaries of many kinds—boundaries between the professional Blue Zone and the emotional Red Zone; boundaries between the organization and the outside world; boundaries between my role and your role; boundaries between family life and work life. In our experience, we have found that when boundaries are out of whack in one area (such as the boundaries between members' roles or between the Blue and Red Zones), then boundaries tend to be out of whack everywhere. So, again, the issue of boundaries cannot be examined in isolation, but must be viewed in terms of the entire relational network.

"Be All That You Can Be"

Healthy boundaries are critical to the health of every organization—even military ones. In 1999, Bruce Garwood, a professional facilitator with the U.S. Army Corps of Engineers Trans-Atlantic Center, called to ask for our help. The corps needed someone to facilitate strategic planning, but Bruce felt he couldn't do it because he was too close to the situation. He asked us to facilitate.

We know very little about engineering, and even less about military culture. But strategic planning is a process that works regardless of our knowledge of the inner workings of a given industry. Just prior to beginning our consultation in earnest, we received a call from the commanding officer, Tim Wynne. "We've brought consultants in before," he told us, "and the results have hardly been spectacular." It quickly became clear from Wynne's remarks that these consultants had done little to address the relational climate in the corps, and particularly in this division. As commanding officer, Wynne was under a lot of pressure to improve his division's productivity.

The U.S. Army Corps of Engineers has a long and proud history of service to the nation, building the infrastructure of the U.S. military and its allies during wartime, and also serving the national and international communities with construction projects in peacetime. It has undergone many changes in organizational structure over the years, reflecting the rapid rate of change in the world and in the army itself.

In recent years, the corps has been heavily impacted by a number of factors, including government downsizing, military cutbacks, and increased global competition in construction. The result: Rivalries had flared up among divisions within the corps, producing conflict and distrust. Individuals were becoming increasingly concerned about the shrinking job picture. Morale was slumping. Energy and motivation were sagging. The corps' Trans-Atlantic Center was losing the battle to maintain its esprit, its confidence, and its focus. "Be all that you can be" is an army recruiting slogan. Well, in order to be all that it could be, this army organization was going to have to develop its Relational Performance.

We began our consultation with a Relationally Healthy Organization (RHO) Factor Survey and a two-day strategic planning retreat with the leadership. Approximately fifteen leaders were present, both men and women, both military and civilian. The first day of the retreat was productive and energetic, with a lot of good discussion of the characteristics of Relational Performance. The group quickly built a consensus around the need for improved morale and teamwork, and was able to build clarity about the corps' code and mission.

Everything seemed to be going smoothly, until we got to the principle of healthy boundaries. Suddenly, it was as if an emotional grenade had gone off in the room. We could feel the charge crackling in the air. Something was wrong, something that had to do with boundaries. We had stumbled onto The Thing in the Bushes at the Army Corps of Engineers. Without interrupting the presentation on the Relational Performance principles, we moved on through the rest of the principles, knowing we would get back to boundaries. That was where the pay dirt was.

After the session on Relational Performance principles, the group discussed strategic initiatives — the big-picture initiatives an organization decides to address over the next two to three years in order to achieve its desired future — but consensus was nowhere to be found. This was curious, because these initiatives normally flow smoothly right out of the desired future that the group has agreed upon. Something was stopping the flow — but what? We began pressing, looking for The Thing in the Bushes.

At about that time, Wynne's skepticism suddenly resurfaced in a vocal way. He pointed out that the organization had already done strategic planning with another consultant. In fact, that strategic planning session had produced a five-hundred-page document that was still sitting on the shelf in his office.

"Why wasn't that plan implemented?" we asked.

No one had an answer, not even Wynne.

At that point we let the discussion grind to a standstill. No one spoke. No one even moved. Everyone sat there in apparent defeat. We let the group stay at that point of "stuckness" for some time. People tend to be afraid of stuckness. The silence makes them feel impatient and uncomfortable. People want to fill up the silence with talk. They change the subject, move in a different direction. But in our experience with group dynamics, we know that stuckness is golden. It tells us

THE THING IN THE BUSHES

where the problem lies. If we just ride out the stuckness, it will lead us straight to The Thing in the Bushes.

After allowing the group to simmer in its stuckness for a while, we allowed them to proceed to other matters. But we knew we'd be back. The core issue that was keeping the group stuck would resurface later, and the group would have to confront it—or admit failure.

Sure enough, late in the second day, the core issue resurfaced. We were challenging individuals to make commitments to implement the group's strategic initiatives when we began to realize that military cultures thrive on competition against an opponent. During wartime, it's clear enough who the opponent is—it is "the enemy." But during peacetime, the clarity disappears. A military unit's sharpness, focus, and motivation will decline unless there is a new opponent or "enemy" to compete against. And that is precisely what had happened in this organization.

As the corps' motivation and energy waned, new enemies appeared within the corps itself—among the divisions, departments, and units. The members of one part of the corps began to see other parts as the enemy. Even individual members began to square off against each other. Instead of team members, they became antagonists, and this distrust forced internal boundaries in the organization to become rigid and fixed, like trenches in a battlefield. No one would take responsibility for the lack of implementation of the strategic plan. Because of distrust and antagonism, everyone said, "It's not my fault, it's not my problem; it's his fault, it's her problem." Members blamed everyone but themselves.

So The Thing in the Bushes was now in plain sight. The people in the corps needed a common enemy, an external opponent, in order to regain a sense of shared responsibility and shared focus. What did a common enemy provide? A firm boundary around the organization, creating organizational identity while separating the organization from the outside world. If we could create a firm *external* boundary around the organization, then there would be less need for such rigid *internal* boundaries. That would enable people in the organization to become more flexible, more trusting of their coworkers, and more responsible and accountable for the strategic objectives of the organization.

So there we were, late in the final day, and we decided it was time to challenge the group once more and confront The Thing in the Bushes. It was time to get the group to confront the boundary issues that were keeping this organization stuck in the same place.

We began by reminding the group of the previous day's stuckness over poor implementation of the strategic plan. "Everyone in this room," we said, "is aware of a hidden dynamic that has been tearing down the morale and productivity of this organization. Yet no one was willing to confront it yesterday. Are you willing to confront it today?"

It was amazing, the difference a day made. The group was arranged in a circle, and there was a spontaneous reaction to our question. One by one, going all the way around the circle, every person in the group responded, taking full personal responsibility for his or her own contribution to the failed implementation of the strategic plan.

"In my own mind," said one, "I blamed the C.O. for not implementing the plan. Fact is, I was the bottleneck. I wasn't carrying out my responsibilities. It was easier to lay the blame on leadership than to do what needed to be done."

"I should have shown more leadership and initiative," admitted another. "Instead, I deferred to the commander. I see now that leadership isn't supposed to be invested in one person; it's to be exercised throughout the organization. In one way or another, we're all expected to demonstrate leadership. From now on, I will."

The crowning touch was when the commander—the ranking officer in that meeting—was able to let a subordinate officer take responsibility for driving this initiative so that he could focus on other tasks. As a result, one month after the consultation, the group came up with a new code, a new culture, and a new definition of what it meant to be a "good citizen" of the U.S. Army Corps of Engineers. Boundary confusion had created many hiding places for The Thing in the Bushes. The clarification and shoring up of healthy boundaries tamed The Thing.

Three months later, the commander reported high praise for the results, noting that his staff was showing tremendous initiative and leadership. Morale and teamwork had soared. He was personally confident that his unit was going to achieve divisional goals that, just a few months earlier, had seemed impossible.

When everyone in the organization understands his and her role and responsibilities, keeps family and work life separate, knows to keep what's inside the organization in and what's outside out, and operates in the Blue Zone instead of the Red, you have the makings of a healthy organization. Every organization, even an army, should have Relational Performance—and you can't have Relational Performance without healthy boundaries.

6

NURTURE EFFECTIVE COMMUNICATION

EXECUTIVE SUMMARY

Today, conversations can often be the most important form of work. Communication is the glue that holds an organization together, and when communication breaks down, organizations fragment and fall apart. Why does communication seem so difficult at times? Because the process of *communication,* which is the act of transmitting and receiving meaning, is much more complex than we assume. The Thing in the Bushes often lurks in the dark recesses of our fumbling attempts to communicate with each other. Factors that commonly distort communication include:

Metaphors. Not only words but also behaviors are often used as symbolic stand-ins for other issues within the organization. People often use metaphors without consciously realizing it, conveying through metaphoric symbols what they find too threatening or uncomfortable to say directly.

Obliqueness. Indirect communication can produce major problems in an organization. Indirect communication involves both sides: the speaker and the hearer. It is incumbent upon speakers to speak plainly and directly, and it is incumbent upon listeners to listen closely for nuances, emotions, and subtleties in the speaker's message.

Cultural, generational, and gender differences. Words, concepts, body language, and other verbal and visual cues mean different things to different people, often according to where they were raised and which side of the gender divide they come from. We can never assume that the other person means what we would mean by those same words, that same inflection, or that same body language.

The "what" of communicating versus the "way" of communicating. Communication is more than just the words we say. Sometimes a look, a gesture, a facial expression, or an action says more than ten thousand words. The way we speak—our tone, inflection, and body language—often carries more weight than the verbal content of our message. Communication is a multichannel process involving most of the senses. The verbal component is the "what" of communication; the nonverbal component is the "way" of communication. Unfortunately, most people concentrate on the "what" dimension and forget the "way" dimension (nonverbal cues such as tone of voice, body language, eye communication, gestures, and so forth). The "way" of the message communicates our view of the relationship between speaker and hearer. To communicate clearly, the "way" must match the "what." If not, our message will be blocked.

To keep the communication lines open, follow these principles:

■ *Set a good example of open communication, expressing yourself with clarity and confidence.*

■ *Shorten the lines of communication by building relationships with people in your organization.*

■ *Invite opinions, ideas, and dissent.*

■ *Create a warm, friendly, relaxed environment.*

■ *Build a horizontal relational network rather than a vertical hierarchy.*

■ *Be a good listener.*

■ *Keep everyone in the loop.*

■ *If you are in a subordinate position, put yourself and your ideas forward.*

■ *Face conflict squarely and honestly. Build trust by demonstrating integrity.*

■ *Use the Five Dialects of Appreciation (verbal affirmation, quality time, rewards, acts of service, and physical touch).*

■ *Practice the 7-11 Principle (the average message must be repeated between seven and eleven times before it sinks in).*

The Snoozewell Mattress Company and the Sleepytime Spring Company were preparing to merge (both names are fictitious). Snoozewell, a conservative "blue suit" company, had planned such a merger two years earlier, and the fresh, innovative climate of Sleepytime made the perfect complement. The CEO of Snoozewell, Ken Watson, and the CEO of Sleepytime, Paul Flores, had been meeting for months, hammering out the details of the merger with their attorneys. Unfortunately, both Ken and Paul had completely misunderstood each other as to who would be in charge. Though they talked about the merger as a joint venture, each had a very different idea of what the term "joint venture" meant. And The Thing was lurking in the shadows of that disparity, waiting to pounce.

Ken's organization, Snoozewell, was in a stronger financial position due to the meticulous implementation of their long-range scenario-based business plan. The merger scenario was right on target, so he assumed Snoozewell's carefully crafted plan would drive the newly formed organization's overall direction and vision. Paul's role? Well, Ken figured he would help decide the implementation tactics. After all, Ken and his team had already developed a complete business plan based on the merger scenario.

Paul assumed that both sides of the newly merged company would have an equal say from the get-go. It never occurred to him that his decision-making role might be subordinate to Ken's.

Only when the day came to consummate the merger did these differences in perception come out. As they were about to sign the final agreements, Paul began to talk about his vision of the future for the newly merged company. Ken laughed, thinking his partner-to-be was joking.

Surely, Ken thought, *Paul knows I'm the one who'll be calling the shots—and Paul had seen the business plan.* But Paul wasn't joking. Tempers flared, and an argument broke out. Paul folded his arms, spun about in his chair, and muttered an obscene (and anatomically impractical) suggestion. Ken snarled, "I heard that!" then jumped up and stormed out.

The merger never took place. Both CEOs had a powerful tool at their disposal: clear, healthy communication. But The Thing in the Bushes deceived them into making false assumptions rather than communicating effectively to understand each other. The moral to this true story is that Relational Performance doesn't just happen. It is the product of clear, healthy communication.

Communication: The Act of Transmitting and Receiving Meaning

Communication is the glue that holds an organization together. When communication breaks down, organizations fragment and fall apart. Why does communication seem so difficult at times? We all speak the same language, don't we? "I know what I said, I know what I meant." So why do other people mistake our meaning or find something sinister in what we say? Why don't we understand each other?

Fact is, the process of communication is not nearly as simple as we assume. Communication—the act of transmitting and receiving meaning—is a much more complicated process than most of us suspect. It is complicated by many factors, and The Thing in the Bushes often hides in the tangled underbrush of poor communication. Factors that commonly distort communication include:

METAPHORS

A metaphor, as everyone knows, is a figure of speech. You take a word or phrase that normally has a literal meaning, and you use it in a poetic, figurative, or ironic way to designate something else: "all the world's a stage," or "she was a deer in the headlights," or "you're dead meat," or "I'm toast."

But in the sense we are using the term *metaphor* here, we are talking not about words, but about *behaviors* that become symbolic stand-ins for other issues within the organization. What you see is not always what you get. To illustrate the concept, here is an example from an actual TAG consultation:

The people down in the Human Resources department of a government contractor complained that their offices were too cold. They began to wear heavy sweaters and bring portable heaters to work. Management heard their complaints and spent a great deal of money rearranging the heating ducts to channel more heat to HR. No sooner was the ductwork completed then the HR people began complaining about something new: too much dust coming from the vents.

If you take the complaints literally (as the management of this company did), then you will only be able to think of one particular kind of solution—and you will go looking in the ductwork for The Thing in the Bushes. Fortunately, we happened to be in the building, conducting an organizational assessment, when this problem came to light. We wondered if the lack of warmth down in HR was a literal problem involving thermostats and ductwork and a furnace—or if it was a metaphor describing a very different kind of problem—*a relational* problem.

What were the people in HR really trying to say? People often use metaphors without consciously realizing it. Sometimes they convey through metaphoric language what they find too threatening or uncomfortable to say directly. "What if the people in HR are talking about the cold treatment they get from other parts of the organization?" we wondered.

We went down to HR, posed this possibility to the people there—and they immediately seized upon the idea as totally valid. The company quit trying to change the ductwork in HR. Instead, they changed the lines of communication, the lines of caring and interaction between HR and the rest of the company. From then on, there were no more complaints from HR about a lack of warmth.

OBLIQUENESS
Another form of communication problem is the tendency many people have to be oblique and indirect in their communication. Sometimes, indirect communication can produce major problems in an organization. It can even get people killed.

On January 13, 1982, a Boeing 737 prepared to take off from National Airport in Washington, D.C. The plane—Air Florida Flight 90 to Fort Lauderdale—was running two hours late because of the icy midwinter conditions. Though the copilot had logged many hours in snowy conditions, the pilot had not. As the plane idled, waiting for the go-ahead from the tower, the copilot seemed to be chatting casually with the pilot—but in reality, he was trying to *warn* the pilot, obliquely and indirectly, about the danger of ice buildup on an airplane.

"Look how the ice is just hanging on the tail of that plane—see that?" the copilot said. "See all those icicles on the back there?"

"Yeah," the pilot replied. If he realized the copilot was trying to warn him, he gave no indication of it.

"It's been a long wait since the last de-icing," the copilot said a few minutes later. "A lot of time for new ice buildup in this storm. You know, this is a losing battle, trying to de-ice these things. It just gives you a false sense of security."

The pilot ignored the copilot's concerns and continued preparing the plane for takeoff. Minutes later, Flight 90 was cleared to go. The pilot throttled up the engines. The plane rolled down the runway. The copilot anxiously monitored the instruments as the plane lumbered up into the sky. "Look at that indicator! That doesn't seem right, does it?" he asked. "Uh, that's not right."

"Yes it is," the pilot responded. "There's eighty."

"No, I don't think that's right," the copilot responded worriedly. "Well, maybe it is. . . . I don't know."

That's when the stall warning began to sound. The plane had stopped climbing and was now wallowing back toward the ground.

"Come on! Forward! Climb! Climb!" the pilot pleaded, trying to urge his plane back into the air by human will alone. Ten seconds of anxious silence passed.

"Larry, we're going down!" moaned the copilot. "Larry—!"

"I know it—" answered the pilot.

Those were the last words on the cockpit voice recorder.

An instant later, the plane's belly cut like a scythe through a half-dozen vehicles on the 14th Street Bridge over the Potomac, killing four people in their cars. The plane continued on, plunging nose-down into the ice-coated river. Most of the plane simply vanished beneath the surface of the river. Only the blue Air Florida tail section was still visible. Five people survived that crash; the pilot and copilot and most of the passengers were killed. A total of seventy-eight people lost their lives that day—because of indirect, oblique communication.

Flight 90 didn't have to go down, and seventy-eight people didn't have to die. The copilot knew that the conditions for taking off were dangerous, and in his roundabout way he tried to warn the pilot. But he didn't state his case plainly and clearly, and the pilot didn't listen to what his cold-weather-wise copilot was trying to tell him.

The problem of indirect communication involves both sides: the speaker and the hearer. It is incumbent upon speakers to speak plainly and directly, and it is incumbent upon listeners to crane their ears for nuances, emotions, concerns, meaning, and subtleties in the speaker's message. There are two sides in every dialogue; both sides are responsible for the success and clarity of the communication process.

The Thing in the Bushes often lurks in oblique, indirect communication styles—and The Thing can be deadly. Flight 90 was brought down by a failure to communicate—and your organization can be brought down in much the same way. So avoid disaster. Communicate clearly. Listen carefully.

CULTURAL, GENERATIONAL, AND GENDER DIFFERENCES

Problems in communication arise between people of different cultures, between people of different generations, and between men and women. Words, concepts, body language, and other verbal and visual cues mean different things to different people, often according to where they were raised, whether they are baby boomers or members of Generation X, Y, or Z, and what side of the gender divide they come from. We can never assume that the other person means what we would mean by those same words, that same inflection, with that same body language and set of gestures.

It is a commonly held stereotype that women tend to be less confident than men. But is that true, or is it a stereotype rooted in a misunderstanding of another gender's communication style? To find out, a team of researchers led by psychologist Laurie Heatherington conducted an experiment among incoming college freshmen. In the experiment, the researchers asked hundreds of incoming college freshmen to predict what grades they would achieve in the coming year. The students were divided into two groups: One group was asked to make sealed, written predictions. The other group was asked to offer predictions verbally in a group setting. According to Heatherington,

> More women than men predicted lower grades for themselves if they made their predictions publicly. If they made their predictions privately, the predictions were the same as those of the men—and the same as their actual grades. This study provides evidence that what comes across as lack of confidence [among women]—predicting lower grades for oneself—may reflect not one's actual level of confidence but the desire not to seem boastful.

Researchers have traced the origin of gender-based differences in communication styles back to childhood. Deborah Tannen observes,

Although both girls and boys find ways of creating rapport and negotiating status, girls tend to learn conversational rituals that focus on the rapport dimension of relationships whereas boys tend to learn rituals that focus on the status dimension. . . . The result is that women and men tend to have different habitual ways of saying what they mean, and conversations between them can be like cross-cultural communication.[1]

These linguistic patterns can also affect who gets promoted and even who gets hired. Organizations may be squandering, underrecognizing, and underrewarding the talent and abilities of bright, creative, capable people—particularly women. At the same time, those organizations may be promoting people who are more outspoken but less qualified.

Every person is an individual, and communication styles vary from one person to the next, from man to man and woman to woman. Not all generalizations apply to every individual. However, it can certainly be said that, in general, men and women have different styles of communicating. These two styles can be broadly categorized as follows:

MEN	WOMEN
Find it difficult to subordinate themselves to another person	Find it less difficult to subordinate themselves to another person
Tend to downplay doubt	Tend to downplay certainty
Tend not to account for the feelings of others	Modify talk to account for the feelings of others
As leaders, give orders	As leaders, offer suggestions
Focus on rank and status	Focus on relationships
Enjoy center stage	Enjoy the center of the relational web
See apologizing as accepting blame	See apologizing as restoring the balance to the conversation and to relationships

The more conscious we are of different communicating styles, the more clear and effective our communication will be.

THE "WHAT" VERSUS THE "WAY"

In the new economy, conversations are the most important form of work. The job of a leader in an organization is to create an environment where members can have meaningful, effective conversations, and where the risk of miscommunication is minimized. To do this, everyone in the organization needs to understand the true nature of communication.

Communication is more than just the words we say—much more. Communication is really about *all* the many ways we transmit and receive meaning. Sometimes a look, a gesture, a facial expression, a posture, or an action says more—and says it more powerfully and eloquently—than ten thousand words. The way we speak—our tone, body language, and inflection—often carries more weight than the verbal content of our message. Communication is a multichannel process involving most of the senses. Even a touch on the arm can convey a lot. In a real way, *all* behavior has communication value: we cannot *not* communicate.

Katherine's boss enters the room and asks her what she thinks about the new marketing plan. Katherine has been in the company for two months. Although she disagrees with many aspects of the plan, she knows her boss is proud of the program and expects some positive strokes. Being new and insecure, and having seen this boss react badly to criticism, Katherine doesn't want to do anything that might jeopardize her job. How can she say what she really thinks? Katherine communicates verbally, "I think the plan is terrific, Mr. Jones." But Mr. Jones frowns as he subliminally detects the hesitancy in her voice and the look of disapproval that flashes in her eyes. Her nonverbal communication has canceled out her verbal communication.

Even tiny, involuntary nonverbal cues can affect how a message is received. For example, when we see something that gives us pleasure, our pupils dilate; when we see something we don't like, our pupils contract. This is an involuntary reaction, but it is visible to another person. Some studies have shown that people are able to subconsciously register such tiny nonverbal cues, and when the nonverbal cues don't match the verbal cues, trust is diminished and the communication process is jeopardized.

We refer to the verbal components of communication as the "what" of communication; we refer to the nonverbal components as the "way" of communication. When people communicate, they tend to concentrate on the "what" dimension. Yet the "way" of communication often says even more than the "what." Through our nonverbal cues—our tone of voice, body language, eye communication, gestures, and so forth—we communicate our view of the relationship between us. Our words may say, "Have a nice day," but our tone of voice and body language may convey something entirely different: "I'm superior to you," perhaps, or "You are of no value to me."

To communicate clearly, the "way" must match the "what." Our tone of voice and other nonverbal cues must match our words. If not, the content of our message will be blocked.

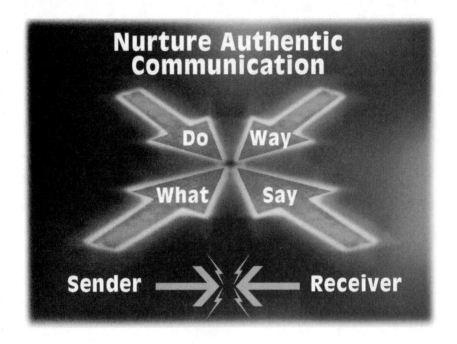

There are sound business reasons for being aware of the various communication channels and for making sure that the "way" and the "what" of our message are congruent. Clear, congruent communication enhances efficiency. Garbled communication causes relationships to break down and processes to disintegrate. When we use multiple communication channels to get our message across—and we use them all in a congruent way—those channels reinforce each other and help ensure that our message is received with clarity and impact.

Healthy organizations make use of as many communication channels as possible: verbal, written, visual, and electronic. And they realize that individuals relate differently through these various media. We once consulted with a company in which management was extremely frustrated with the customer service staff for not paying attention to messages. "We send out memos," said one manager, "but they ignore every one." After conducting a couple of focus groups, we realized that these customer service reps were *verbal* people—they didn't read *anything*. So we encouraged management to communicate new information to the customer service reps verbally in weekly meetings. It worked.

Communication channels are tools, and just as you would not use a hammer to do the work of a saw, you should not use one channel to do the work of another. There are some messages that can be effectively communicated by e-mail; when the stakes are higher and the possibility for misunderstanding greater, the message should not be entrusted to a single-channel medium like e-mail. It should only be conveyed by voice — by phone if necessary, but face-to-face if possible. Yes, you can put little smiley faces and similar emoticons in an e-mail message to add some semblance of a visual channel, but it doesn't compare to the feelings dimension that is added to a message by eye communication, inflection, facial expressions, and gestures.

As Max De Pree, author of *Leadership Is an Art* (DTP, 1990), told us in an interview,

> E-mail is not the appropriate way to communicate in certain situations. For example, using e-mail to solve relational problems and misunderstandings doesn't work. That requires face-to-face interaction. The problem with e-mail is that no one rereads it and reflects on it before they send it out. So often when you write something, you ought to take a look at it the next day and see if it really ought to go out or not. But once you press "send," it's sent, it's out there. It's instantaneous.
>
> I often tell people you are not going to solve the problem until you call the guy and tell him you are coming over to have a cup of coffee in his office, and then you can talk about it. But you see, people think e-mail is so wonderful because it's so quick. And I say, "Well, could it be *too* quick?" In many cases, e-mail *is* too quick, and it complicates communication problems instead of solving them.

In our own organization, we feel so strongly about effective communication that we have instituted a series of communication guidelines:

■ We never communicate emotional issues over e-mail.

■ Voice mail gets an answer within twenty-four hours.

■ E-mail gets an answer within eight hours.

■ Memos get an answer within one week.

■ Person-to-person communication gets an immediate response.

These simple guidelines help all of us to operate more effectively, maintain healthy relationships, and serve our clients in a responsive way. We believe these guidelines would serve any organization well, particularly those businesses where the goal is to get as close to the customer as possible and where effective use of time and efficient response and turnaround become the benchmarks of success.

How to Keep Communication Lines Open

Here are some ideas and suggestions for maintaining Relational Performance through healthy communication:

1. Set a good example of open communication. Always make a point of expressing yourself with clarity and confidence.

2. Shorten the lines of communication. It is said that the best way to have *open* lines of communication is to have *short* lines of communication. As a leader, be available and accessible at all times. It's not enough for people to know your door is always open; you have to walk out the door and mix and mingle with the members of your organization. Walk the floors and hallways of the building. Greet people by name. Eat in the employee lunchroom and really get to *know* people. You build better communication when you build relationships.

3. Invite opinions, ideas, and dissent. Some people are shy and self-effacing; draw them out. Make sure everyone in the organization knows that his or her ideas and opinions are valued. Make full use of the creativity, experience, and unique perspective of every individual in your organization. Great ideas often come from unexpected sources, including the mailroom or filing clerks. It is often the lower-echelon people who are closest to the customers, to the problems, and to the opportunities in the marketplace.

4. Create a warm, friendly, relaxed environment. Nothing shuts down communication like emotions of anxiety, distrust, and unease. As people tense up, they clam up. So keep it loose; keep it friendly; keep it relaxed.

5. Build a horizontal relational network rather than a vertical hierarchy. Good communication flows from feelings of shared commitment and a shared relationship. When everyone feels committed to a common goal, vital information naturally flows more freely. People become less protective of their own interests and more focused on organizational results. Sharing information is then seen as an opportunity to advance the organization's goals rather than a threat to one's own hegemony or personal advancement up the hierarchical ladder.

6. Be a good listener. Give verbal and nonverbal feedback to let people know you are truly hearing them: "Uh-huh, right, exactly." A nod of the head. Steady eye communication. A smile. After the speaker has spoken, reflect his or her words back: "What I'm hearing you say is . . . " Be careful not to start answering while the other person is talking. Make sure you fully *hear* what the other person says before you respond. Listen carefully to nuances and subtleties, especially when you are around people who tend to be shy or express themselves indirectly. Find ways to draw such people out — their input is valuable, too.

7. Keep everyone in the loop. When all the members are well informed, they will be sure to keep *you* informed. Don't hide information from employees. Never display an attitude that says, "You don't need to know." Solutions to problems often come from the people you'd least expect, so give them the information that makes creativity and ideas possible.

8. If you are in a subordinate position, put yourself and your ideas forward. Make yourself heard in a respectful way. Make yourself known as a person of ability and creativity. In social situations, after work, sharpen your small-talk skills. What's that? You're shy, you say? Then work on your assertiveness! Remember, advancement and rewards come to those who display competence — and confidence.

9. Face conflict squarely and honestly. It is a common mistake for groups and individuals to avoid conflict. The truth is that a certain amount of visible conflict in an organization is healthy. And note that word *visible.* All organizations have conflicts, but many keep their conflicts hidden and invisible. Hidden conflict simmers below the surface. It eats away at morale and productivity. It destroys.

In unhealthy organizations, members suppress communication and conflicting ideas in order to maintain the surface illusion of cohesion. When organizations or teams become polarized and views become entrenched, factions form and communication shuts down. Defensiveness and wariness set in. Forward momentum and progress stop.

Visible conflict, handled in a healthy, honest way, can be a great catalyst for growth and positive change. It is not the absence of conflict, but the *healthy management* of conflict through open, candid communication that denotes healthy Relational Performance. The free flow of ideas—including *conflicting* ideas—is crucial to creative thinking.

10. Build trust by demonstrating integrity. Become known and trusted as a person who always tells the truth, who has no hidden motives or hidden agenda. Good communication is built on trust, and trust is built on a good reputation, and a good reputation is built on integrity.

11. Use the Five Dialects of Appreciation. Dr. Gary Chapman has identified the "five languages of love" within a family relationship (verbal affirmation, quality time, gifts or rewards, acts of service, and physical touch) in his book *The Five Love Languages* (Northfield, 1992). In much the same way, we have identified five corresponding dialects of appreciation that leaders and managers can practice with members of their organization:

- Verbal affirmation ("Great job!" or public recognition)

- Quality time ("Let me take you to lunch.")

- Rewards (a plaque, flowers, a week in Cancun)

- Acts of service (washing your employee's car or doing his or her job for a half-day)

- Physical touch (a handshake, a pat on the back)

The Relational Performance model makes the best and most appropriate use of each of the five ways of showing appreciation to members, according to the relational needs of each individual member. One employee may respond best to words while another responds best to a tangible gift or "face time" with the boss.

It is important to remember that we all tend to *show* appreciation the same way we like to *receive* appreciation. If we love to receive verbal compliments, we tend to assume that verbal compliments motivate everyone. That assumption is a trap that leaders should assiduously avoid. Time and again, we have interviewed employees who say, "Sure, raises are nice and I can use the money, but once, just once, it would be great if the boss would give me a little recognition in front of my peers." When healthy relationships are built on a foundation of healthy communication, leaders are able to assess the most appropriate form of appreciation for each individual member.

12. Practice the 7-11 Principle. Communication experts have found that the average message must be heard between seven and eleven times before it sinks in. That's the 7-11 Principle. Never assume that simply because you have said it, it has been heard. Don't be afraid of appearing redundant. Make sure your message gets across—again and again and again. If you only say it once, you haven't really said it at all.

"Should We Kill Him?"

In the 1990 Oscar-winning movie *Dances with Wolves,* there is a scene in which a tribe of Sioux Indians discovers a mysterious white soldier (Kevin Costner) near their camp. In this early pivotal scene, about two dozen tribe members gather to determine what they should do about this enigmatic white man. Should they kill him to send a message to other white soldiers who might follow him? Or should they let him live, and thus display a willingness to get along with newcomers?

This scene is a great example of Relational Performance in action. As the tribe members meet, they model a healthy communication process. They speak openly and place all the options on the table. The members listen carefully to each other before responding. All input is heard and valued. There is disagreement as various ideas come into conflict, but the disagreement is handled in a healthy, honest fashion. All sides of the issue are allowed to speak. Some of the speakers incorporate the ideas of others in their own arguments.

In the discussion, every member works to find a solution that is congruent with the belief structure of the tribe, the code of this Sioux organization. When a member of the group makes a proposal that is incongruent with that code, others in the council either attempt to find harmony or reject the suggestion.

In the process of openly communicating about this situation, the tribe fulfills a number of other functions of Relational Performance. These wise leaders successfully navigate a transition in their environment and respond appropriately to change—that change being the introduction of the white man to their region. They successfully hold onto their code—their core principles—even while addressing this radical change in their environment. They realize their need to think about the greater community and about how the decision they make regarding this man will affect not only the future of their village but also the future of dozens of other Indian villages in the region. Good relational health—as exemplified in the movie's tribal meeting—is the foundation of organizations that are financially successful, productive, innovative, energetic, and enduring. And healthy communication is one of the keys to Relational Performance.

7

BALANCE TRUST AND CYNICISM

EXECUTIVE SUMMARY

Good Relational Performance strikes a healthy balance between trust and cynicism. Trust is a key ingredient to growth and success. It is the basis of all relationships—and honesty is the basis of trust. You cannot trust someone unless you believe that person will keep a promise, be candid with you, and never betray you.

Trust is the glue that holds an organization together. And it is a two-way street. Employees will invest more trust in an organization that invests trust in them.

It takes time to build trust in an organization, but cynicism grows like a weed. Runaway cynicism (distrust) is corrosive to the well-being of an organization. While cynicism cannot be completely eliminated, it can have a positive role to play in an organization. Trust and cynicism need to be balanced in order to maintain Relational Performance. There is a place for healthy cynicism in Relational Performance.

For example, it is appropriate to be a little cynical when hiring a new employee. New hires are rarely as competent in the job as experienced veterans. Leaders must supervise and monitor the new employee, controlling quality and demanding accountability. This is organizational cynicism; that is, the organization puts institutional controls, account-ability, and monitoring mechanisms in place until trust has been earned. However, if controls are too rigid, bureaucratic, and stifling, the result will be low morale and high turnover. Trust and cynicism must be balanced so that there is healthy accountability within an overall atmosphere of healthy trust.

Organizations earn trust by giving trust. Trust can be built over time and cynicism can be managed all the time. A balance of trust and cynicism is essential to good Relational Performance. The Thing in the Bushes arises whenever an imbalance exists.

In 1989, filmmaker-comedian Michael Moore produced a satiric docu-mentary called *Roger and Me.* In that film, Moore is seen trying to get an interview with the chairman of General Motors, Roger Smith, so that he can ask Smith why GM is allowing thousands of jobs to leave Flint, Michigan. The film comes off as equal parts *60 Minutes* and *Saturday Night Live* sketch comedy. In June 1998, nine years after *Roger and Me,* Moore returned to Flint—his hometown—to encourage some 9,200 GM workers who had walked off the job.

"The strike was not about wages or more benefits or pension plans," Moore said. "The strike was precipitated by GM taking the machinery out of the plant in the middle of the night on a holiday weekend, so they could build [GM parts] someplace else."[1]

The GM strikers were convinced that their employer had misled them and betrayed them. They claimed that GM had promised to make three hundred million dollars in new investments in their factory, but instead of stepping up production, it had made clandestine moves to scale back production—and scale back jobs. As Moore noted, GM had taken advantage of a holiday weekend to quietly remove major assembly machinery from the plant and ship that machinery elsewhere. With that machinery went a lot of jobs. GM had already eliminated fifty thousand jobs in Flint; by 1998, only twenty-eight thousand GM jobs remained in Flint—and now even those remaining jobs were in jeopardy.

The walkout closed not only the Flint plant, but also every other GM plant in North America, because the parts made in Flint were used in nearly every GM vehicle. Almost 150,000 workers at over one hundred parts and assembly plants in the United States, Mexico, and Canada were idled by the strike in Flint—and the final price tag of the strike, due to lost production, totaled over one billion dollars.

That's a high price to pay for a lack of trust. For that, in fact, was the real crux of the matter. "There's no trust between the United Auto Workers union and GM—none whatsoever," said UAW President Stephen P. Yokich as the walkout began. "We have tried everything we can do to work with them. I don't know . . . they don't want to work with us."[2]

It is hard to imagine a more unproductive organization than a company that is paralyzed by strikes, with workers and plants idled in three countries, losing a billion dollars in a matter of weeks. Healthy organizations build trust by acting in harmony with their words. Unhealthy organizations build cynicism and distrust, resulting in a loss of productivity, public confidence, and profitability. What an organization says must match what it does, or the entire organization—from the leaders to the workers to the shareholders—will pay the price. In an organization with good Relational Performance, people trust each other. Without trust, a relationship is not possible.

At the same time, it might surprise you to know that while the opposite of trust is cynicism, a little dose of cynicism can be a healthy thing in an organization. Fact is, you can never completely eliminate cynicism, so you might as well learn to live with it and manage it in a healthy way. In many organizations, The Thing in the Bushes is a lurking mood of cynicism—but The Thing can be tamed. It doesn't have to destroy you. Relational Performance strikes a healthy balance between trust and cynicism. If that sounds contradictory, stay tuned. In the next few pages, you'll see how it all makes sense.

Trust Is the Key

Most organizations start with lofty ideals. Mission statements are carefully crafted, printed, and posted behind the counters of all the organization's offices and outlets. At meetings, pronouncements are made concerning the nature of the organization, its values, its vision, its goals, its sense of responsibility toward employees and the community.

But as time passes, practical considerations outweigh cherished principles. Something crucial gets lost between the dreams that created the company and the realities of daily business life. A dissonance arises between stated principles and actual practice.

. . . And trust is the victim.

How do an organization's values and principles get lost in the shuffle? Sometimes they slip through the cracks between layers of an organization.

The values and principles do not get properly communicated from upper management to middle management. Or those principles are not consistently applied between one division and another. Or circumstances and market conditions change, and someone in leadership decides that the principles that held true in the good times no longer apply in tough times.

As incongruity drives a widening wedge between what we say as an organization and what we do, trust is shattered, cynicism and resentment grow, morale declines, and commitment and motivation diminish. As the quality of products and services falls off, consumer confidence and market share drop. As employees stop innovating and stop helping each other, initiative and teamwork suffer. As superior employees leave and marginal employees do not improve, increased turnover and lower productivity eat into profits—big time. The cost of replacing and retraining just one employee is estimated to be in excess of twenty-five thousand dollars, so it is easy to see that "intangibles" like distrust and cynicism can quickly convert into a very tangible impact on the bottom line.

Trust is a key ingredient to the growth and success of an organization. Runaway cynicism is corrosive to the well-being of an organization.

As we write these words, we have just completed a consultation with an association that represents a large group of professionals on the East Coast. This association offers an array of services to its members, including legal services. But the director and staff have a dirty little secret: "We are actually incapable of protecting our members from ninety-five percent of the legal difficulties they are exposed to," one association attorney explained to us. "We just don't have the power and the legal clout that our members think we do."

"But," we asked, "the members of your association think that they have excellent legal coverage. They trust you to defend them if they encounter a legal problem in their professional lives. What happens if they get sued and they turn to you for help?" Our question was met with worried shrugs.

"But don't you see," we asked again, "that this association is living a lie? You are promising something you can't deliver."

"But we have to promise them legal coverage," said the director of the organization. "We couldn't hold onto our membership if they knew the truth. Legal coverage is one of our main drawing cards."

"But it's a lie!" we said.

"Well, we prefer to think of it as a secret."

"No matter what you prefer to call it," we insisted, "it's a lie. And sooner or later, when one of your members gets slapped with a summons, the lie will be exposed. What then?"

"We can't help that," the director said. "Our existence depends on our ability to attract and keep members. If we told the truth, we'd lose members for sure — and we would cease to exist."

We walked away from that organization with a sick feeling inside. We couldn't help them. They were lying to their members — and they were lying to themselves, deluding themselves into believing that somehow they could keep their dirty little secret under wraps. That organization was a house of cards, and sooner or later, it would collapse.

It is a dangerous thing to keep information from people who need it. Secrets have a nasty way of shaping who we are as people and what our organization is. People make plans, alter their lives, and make decisions based on the information they receive. If we withhold vital information from them, we can potentially cause great harm in their lives. Why do we keep these dirty little secrets? Usually, it is because we are afraid of the consequences that the truth will bring.

But what about the consequences of a lie?

A great deal of energy is expended in keeping secrets. Cover-ups and lies are deadly to trust and relationships. People form coalitions and factions and cliques: those who are "in the know" versus those who are "out of the loop." Coalitions and factions and cliques divide organizations.

And what happens when the truth comes out (as it usually does)? The greatest casualty is trust.

Trust Is the Glue

The Duke University Blue Devils is one of college basketball's greatest teams. The reason: Duke's legendary "Coach K," Mike Krzyzewski (pronounced Shuh-SHEV-ski), who has guided the fortunes of the Blue Devils for nearly two decades. Coach K's philosophy is simple: "Our kids have really believed in us. . . . We trust one another."[3]

Where does that trust come from? Only one source, says Coach K: *honesty*. His greatest accomplishment, he says, is not getting his team to the Final Four or coaching them to a national championship. Rather, his greatest sense of satisfaction comes when "that kid who plays here knows that I've been honest with him."[4]

Coach K's fans see it, too. "One trait seems to wind its way through Duke basketball coach Mike Krzyzewski's success — honesty," wrote one Blue Devils fan in the Letters section of *Sports Illustrated*. "He is honest with his players, their parents, the student body, his athletic director, the press and, most important, himself. Krzyzewski's philosophy is a breath of fresh air."[5]

Trust is the basis of all relationships—and honesty is the basis of trust. You cannot trust someone unless you believe that person will keep a promise, be candid with you, and never betray you. The first time you discover you have been lied to, all faith is gone. It takes a long time to rebuild broken trust, if it can ever be rebuilt at all.

Trust within organizations is built on a foundation of promises. When the organization makes a promise to its members—*and demonstrates that it can be trusted to keep those promises*—it becomes a safe place for its members. A promise is a declaration assuring the listener that a person or group will do something—or not do something. Promises look to the future. In fact, a promise is the only way to overcome the unpredictability of the future. It is designed to produce certainty and trust by assuring someone, "I am reliable. If I say it, you can depend on it."

Organizations are only possible because of our human ability to make, keep, and trust promises. The U.S. Constitution is a promise that makes our government and society possible. Churches, clubs, and corporations also have documents, handbooks, policies, and procedures that embody promises that enable people to work together in an atmosphere of trust. Imagine living in a nation, working in a company, and worshiping in a church or synagogue where no one can trust any other person to keep promises.

Promises bind people together, setting boundaries and outlining expectations and obligations. As promises become more formal, they move from unspoken to spoken to written form. Your faith in an organization is commensurate with its ability to keep promises. So if you want to engender trust and loyalty in your organization, you must make promises—and *keep* them.

Other key concepts for building trust include:

Consistency. When a person or organization behaves in a consistent manner, others can know in advance what that person or organization will or will not do. The future becomes predictable, because it is based on a consistent track record. Of course, to be successful, you must build a track record that is consistently *good,* not consistently poor or consistently mediocre. If you are consistently good, consistently reliable, consistently trustworthy, then you are practicing . . .

Dependability. A person or organization is dependable if he, she, or it can be relied upon to act in certain ways. If I do what I promise, over and over, I'm considered to be trustworthy and dependable. Dependable organizations say what they mean and mean what they say. They can be relied upon when the chips are down. In situations where other people or organizations might break their word and destroy trust, dependable organizations keep faith and maintain trust. People like working for, and doing business with, organizations that are dependable, because they are practicing . . .

Predictability. Consistency and dependability look to past experience, to an organization's track record. Predictability looks to the future. When we have confidence that we can predict the behavior of a person or organization, then we have trust in that person or organization. We know we can place our faith in that organization, and we know that our faith will not be disappointed.

Trust is built by people and organizations through behavior that is consistent, dependable, and predictable. When those qualities are absent from an organization, the result is distrust, resentment, hostility, and a sense of betrayal. Motivation and morale suffer. Organizational cohesion and esprit de corps collapse. Instead of moving toward a common goal, members of the organization think, *Every man for himself!* Success is rarely achieved in a dog-eat-dog environment. Success thrives on unity, and unity feeds on trust.

It is important to understand, however, that trust is a two-way street. Employees will tend to invest more trust in an organization if the organization invests trust in them. Jan Carlzon, president of Scandinavian Airlines, explains in his book *Moments of Truth* (Ballinger, 1987) that trusting employees was one of the keys to saving the airline when it was facing bankruptcy. Carlzon decided to trust his employees with the power to make decisions at the point of interaction with customers. If someone came to the customer service desk with a problem—even if it was the customer's own mistake or carelessness that caused the problem—the employee had the authority to fix the problem as he or she saw fit. That was a lot of power to entrust to the rank and file, but the fast, simple solutions to problems that resulted from that trust helped to build customer loyalty for the airline—and put Scandinavian back in the black.

Less obvious but equally important, trusting and empowering employees also helps to build pride and loyalty. When a member of an organization sees that he or she is trusted, it is much easier for that member to give trust in return. The result: higher morale, increased productivity, lower turnover.

Trust is the glue that holds an organization together.

Is There a Place for Cynicism?

Have you noticed that it takes time to build trust in an organization, but cynicism seems to spread like crabgrass? Have you seen how quickly cynicism can change the environment of your organization? It can be a corrosive, destructive force—The Thing that stalks your office corridors and lurks around your water cooler and growls menacingly in the interoffice e-mails that flash from desk to desk. And let's face it: cynicism cannot be completely eliminated. When tamed, cynicism can play a positive role in the life of your organization. Indeed, trust and cynicism need to be balanced to maintain Relational Performance.

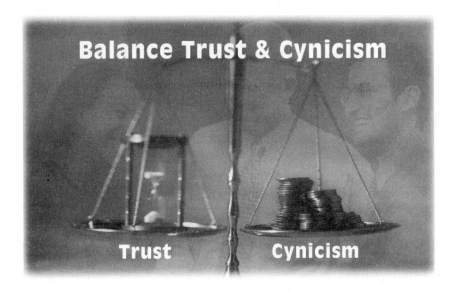

Dan McAllister, Ph.D., assistant professor in the McDonough School of Business at Georgetown University and a research affiliate of TAG, talks about balancing trust and cynicism:

> When you're driving down the road and see a car coming toward you in the other lane, you have to trust that it's going to stay in its lane, and that it's not going to swerve into your lane and hit you. In everyday life, we operate a great deal on that kind of trust. We have to be confident in people's behavior, or we wouldn't be able to get out of bed. Trust is the positive expectation that the things you hope for will actually happen. When there is trust, it becomes easier

to make decisions and get things done because you have confidence in the probability of the outcomes that you desire.

So we need trust in order to live our lives. But cynicism also has its benefits. Cynicism reduces complexity in decision making. Let's return to my driving example: If it is late at night and the car driving toward me swerves toward my lane, I might suspect that the driver is intoxicated and I might elect to stop at the side of the road until the car passes. In this situation, I cynically assume that, apart from intervention on my part, the other car is likely to hit me. My distrust of the approaching driver reduces the complexity of the situation and allows me to act in a prudent manner. In this case, cynicism creates an expectation that what I fear might take place.

Just as trust has survival value for an individual or an organization, so does cynicism. Trust is healthy, but there is also such a thing as a healthy dose of cynicism. You can't do the things that build trust unless you've done the things that manage cynicism.

For example, it is appropriate to be a little cynical when hiring a new employee. New hires are rarely as competent in the job as an experienced veteran. Leaders must supervise and monitor the new employee, controlling quality and demanding accountability. This is *organizational cynicism* (or, as McAllister puts it, "institutional distrust"). It's nothing personal. It's not a matter of saying to the person, "I don't trust you." Rather, the organization puts institutional controls and accountability and monitoring mechanisms in place, which take the place of personal distrust.

People have strengths and weaknesses, and these strengths and weaknesses must be managed. Healthy cynicism prompts us to use controls that enable us to diminish the possibility of harm from an employee's weaknesses and flaws while still allowing the organization to utilize that employee's strengths and capabilities. Can an organization put in too many controls? Yes. And this is why we talk about the need for organizations to *balance trust and cynicism.*

It's important to recognize that there are two kinds of cynicism: healthy and unhealthy. Unhealthy cynicism never allows trust to grow. Healthy cynicism fosters a safe, controlled environment in which trust is the ultimate goal. For example, when you are teaching a child to ride a two-wheel bike, you don't just sit him or her on the seat and give him or her a push down the driveway. Being cynical (in a healthy way) about your child's beginning ability on two wheels, you employ several safety precautions: The bike may have training wheels at first, and you keep him or her away from the street. When the training wheels come off, you go with the child, keeping one hand on the bike to steady it until you know he or she can be trusted on two wheels. That's healthy cynicism.

Now, if you never took off the training wheels, if you never let go of the bike, if you never allowed the child to experience a gradual increase in freedom and trust (saying to yourself that the child will ride his or her bike into the street and get killed), that would be unhealthy cynicism. The goal of healthy cynicism is always to increase trust and to unleash and empower people to operate at full capacity. Organizations that keep members on a short leash are practicing unhealthy cynicism. Healthy cynicism is characterized by flexible controls and growing trust. Unhealthy cynicism is characterized by rigid, bureaucratic, confining controls and a stifling atmosphere of distrust.

Employees understand the need for a certain amount of control and structure and accountability, but most employees will react badly if they see management supervising their behavior too rigidly. People don't like working in organizations that are overly paternalistic and controlling, and our experience in consulting with many organizations has shown us that paternalistic, rigidly controlling organizations tend to have a much higher turnover than those that balance trust and healthy cynicism.

The presence of too many bureaucratic procedures and controls sends a message loud and clear. The employee says to himself or herself, "You've put all these measures in place because you don't trust me." Feeling watched and distrusted, the employee does not feel any sense of loyalty or trust in return, and those negative feelings are invariably hurtful to the organization's goals and its bottom line.

Many organizations are learning the value of balancing trust with healthy cynicism. The monitoring processes are in place, but those processes are fair and flexible, not rigid and controlling. The challenge for managers is to put as much control as possible in the hands of employees, preferably through a team approach. When employees are able to police themselves and take responsibility for the quality of their own output, they feel a sense of ownership and pride: "This is *my* organization." They feel empowered, and this sense of empowerment helps them to buy into the organization's code, values, mission, vision, culture, rituals, and so forth. All of these shared assumptions create an *intrinsic* control within the employee so that you don't need to impose rigid, external, extrinsic controls. As people buy into the code of the organization, less control is needed.

Organizations earn trust by giving trust. They also earn trust by demonstrating trustworthiness over the long term. When a company says, "We care about our employees," and backs it up by offering a good working environment, benefits that demonstrate caring, and worker-friendly policies, people respond by giving that company their trust, their allegiance, and their best efforts. A company that has been in business ten, twenty, or thirty years without ever laying off an employee is a company that workers are likely to trust and feel good about.

But if a day ever comes when, out of a sheer need to survive, a company must lay off a percentage of its workforce, the entire atmosphere can shift in a heartbeat. Instantly, employees will begin to feel that trust has been breached. Cynicism can run rampant, along with wild rumors that are readily believed and spread. People who once loved their organization and were proud to identify with it begin to say such things as "You did this intentionally! You don't care about us! All you care about is making more money!"

Cynicism can quickly become epidemic as people begin to attribute the worst imaginable motives to the organization they once trusted. And it seems as if the more loudly an organization proclaims its caring for its people, the more extreme the cynicism becomes if the company is later forced to do something as "uncaring" as salary freezes or layoffs. People are extremely sensitive to a perception of incongruence, to the appearance that the words of a person or organization do not match the behavior. How can leaders help to avert a cycle of runaway cynicism during a difficult passage in the life of an organization?

"Every organization experiences problems and mishaps that can lead to employee cynicism and distrust," says McAllister. "The solution is to build such a strong atmosphere of trust that the organization can weather these periodic storms and remain firmly on course."

Prevailing over Cynicism

A pair of stories from *Harvard Business Review* will demonstrate how two managers found ways to restore trust and relational health to an organization that was crumbling under the weight of financial problems, labor troubles, and skyrocketing cynicism.

In the early 1970s, Gene Cattabiani became general manager of the Westinghouse Steam Turbine Division in Philadelphia. It was a troubled era for Westinghouse. Falling profits, layoffs, and strikes had produced an ugly stalemate of distrust and cynicism on both sides. Management viewed the workforce as fat and lazy; workers saw management as isolated and unfeeling about the needs of the working person.

Cattabiani saw the problem in different terms. He didn't view either side as the bad guy. He knew that the real bad guy in this situation was something intangible—the dreaded Thing in the Bushes. Though labor and management were locked in a struggle, Cattabiani knew he had to bring the two sides together or *everyone* on *both* sides would be out of a job when the division collapsed. The common enemy was distrust on both sides. Spiraling cynicism was The Thing in the Bushes at Westinghouse, and Cattabiani was determined to hunt it down and kill it.

Cattabiani made a courageous decision to go directly to the workers, explain the company's financial situation, and ask for labor's support for the painful austerity measures he needed to implement. It was going to be a tough sell—no doubt about it—but he believed it was the right thing to do. Ignoring the advice of advisers, he held a series of face-to-face meetings with the workers, closing each meeting with an extended question-and-answer session so that workers could voice opinions and ask questions.

The first few meetings were disastrous. Cattabiani was greeted with jeers, catcalls, and threats. Other Westinghouse managers begged him to call off the rest of the meetings, but he persevered. "I have to get them to listen," he said, "and I have to show them that we are willing to listen. We can't stay in business without trust between labor and management."

Cattabiani went out on the factory floor and into the shops—something no previous manager had ever done. He talked individually with workers on the floor, responding calmly and levelly to those who were angry and accusing. After a few days, he noticed a change: many of those who had once attacked him now gave him grudging respect. Some would even shake his hand. Gradually, the workers in the Westinghouse plant began to see Gene Cattabiani not as the enemy, but as a man who was trying to do his job. He gained their trust and respect—but even more, he learned from them.

Over the next few weeks, labor-management relations began to improve. Responding to the workers' criticisms, Cattabiani instituted changes. He introduced ideas for greater flexibility in schedules and procedures, and he made changes resulting in higher quality and productivity standards. Sometimes, with deep regret, he laid off workers. There was still anger and bitterness in the Westinghouse plant, but the distrust and cynicism had begun to melt. Workers had learned to trust that Cattabiani was doing his best for both Westinghouse and the workers, even if they didn't always agree with his decisions. More importantly, there were no more strikes, and the mood of violence that had hung in the air subsided. Soon, the profitability of the division improved—and hundreds of jobs were saved.

The Thing in the Bushes had been dealt with effectively.

A witness of the turnaround at Westinghouse was William Peace, one of Cattabiani's young assistant managers. Less than a decade after Cattabiani confronted the problem at the Steam Turbine Division, Peace was promoted to general manager of the Synthetic Fuels Division at Westinghouse. He never forgot the lessons he learned from Gene Cattabiani. In the early 1980s, Peace found himself faced with a problem similar to the one Cattabiani had solved: declining oil prices meant declining profits, and the division faced liquidation. The only solution Peace saw was a layoff, but he knew that the unionized workforce at Westinghouse would not accept it without a fight.

Peace checked the personnel records of his workforce and found that every person in his division was a good worker with an excellent performance history. There wasn't one person who deserved to be let go. The thought of writing even *one* pink slip made him sick at heart—and he was going to have to write *fifteen*. Remembering how his mentor had courageously handled the tough chores personally, Peace decided to talk to each person who was being laid off. He not only owed the workers a personal explanation, but he believed that by handling the job face to face, he could head off any rumors about wholesale firings.

In those one-on-one meetings, some workers became angry, others wept openly, and some just stared numbly in disbelief. A few argued or accused him of ingratitude. Peace calmly absorbed their anger and explained that the layoffs were based on fiscal realities, not on any dissatisfaction with the workers' performance.

Several months passed after the layoffs. Eventually the Synthetic Fuels Division was back in the black. Because of its sound financial condition, the division became attractive to prospective corporate buyers, and Westinghouse decided to sell. The new corporate owners kept Peace on as general manager and expanded the division. To his delight, he found that he was now in a position to rehire many of the people he had laid off. When he offered them their old jobs back, every one accepted, even those who had already gotten jobs elsewhere. Instead of having to train new hires, Peace was able to reassemble his experienced workforce.

Gene Cattabiani and William Peace are two managers who had learned the value of balancing trust and cynicism. They learned how to tame The Thing in the Bushes—the thing called cynicism. Authentic caring, honesty, and the courage to relate to people face to face, one on one, even in tough circumstances—these are qualities that pay off in trust, loyalty, and respect. Learning to control cynicism is crucial to building organizational trust—and it can be the key to organizational survival and success.[6]

Here again, we see the crucial importance of relationships in organizational life. Trust cannot develop *except* within a relationship. When there is no relationship, no personal connection, no sharing of information, we give cynicism a place to grow like bacteria in a Petri dish. Leaders who make themselves accessible and available and organizations that demonstrate genuine caring even in tough situations are the ones who earn trust and loyalty. Leaders and organizations that prove themselves trustworthy will prevail over the beast of cynicism when the chips are down.

Trust and Cynicism—Side by Side

Frank Washburn was the original manager of a small Canadian farming cooperative in the mid-1970s (names and locations are changed; the story is true). His wife, Emily, volunteered countless hours as his administrative assistant. When Frank died a few years later, Emily continued to run the organization quite successfully, turning the little mom-and-pop operation into British Columbia's leading service provider and political advocate for Okanagan farmers. This little lady from Kelowna had earned a large reputation from Victoria to Prince George.

After a quarter-century at the helm, Emily was thinking about retirement. At around this time, she asked us to facilitate their strategic planning and help develop a fair compensation system for her position as CEO. Although everyone acknowledged that Emily had been the driving force behind the co-op's success and growth, the board didn't know how to objectively quantify and reward her effectiveness.

Emily knew everything there was to know about the business—more, in fact, than anyone on the board. The entire organization trusted her completely, viewing her as a wise and benevolent matriarch. In fact, everyone's trust in Emily was so complete that no one could imagine trying to run the business without her in charge. She was the "mom" who took care of everything, so whenever she mentioned retirement, people tended to panic. After all, there was no plan for replacing her, no orderly line of succession. The board's solution to the problem was to simply move it off into the future. They offered her a "golden handcuffs" package—a $100,000 "signing bonus"—if she would agree to stay on for at least three years instead of retiring.

We worked closely with Emily and the board, and together they crafted an evaluation and compensation process for the CEO position. We built a system that was objective and that enabled us to remove subjective, emotional, personal issues from the equation. Problem was, there was still a mom-and-pop-store mentality in the organization. As Emily's role changed within the organization, she didn't like it. She called us and e-mailed us, and a typical comment was "Things have worked just fine all these years! Why can't you just leave it alone!"

It was around this time that Emily and the board brought in a new executive vice president from a co-op in Calgary, who would be groomed to eventually succeed Emily. His name was Chad, and he came with good credentials and references. But what the credentials and references didn't show was that Chad was a playboy. He charmed the ladies and alienated the men. His presence drove a relational wedge right down the middle of the co-op.

Chad had been aboard for about two months when Beth, vice president of operations, announced her decision to leave in order to care for her ailing father. At 5 P.M. of Beth's last day on the job, Chad walked into her office and said, "Well, you're no longer employed around here, right?"

"That's right," Beth said.

"That means there's no company policy against what I'm about to say to you," he said, and then proceeded to make a sexual proposition. Shocked and shaken, Beth—who was a married woman—rejected his advances and left the building.

That night, at a going-away party for Beth, Chad showed up with his wife on his arm. Beth tried to avoid him, but he wouldn't be denied. He got away from his wife and cornered Beth behind a potted plant. Once again, he made a sexual proposition—this time even more boldly and crudely. And once again, Beth excused herself and got away from him. A few drinks later, Chad began talking loudly about the sexual attributes of a young member service rep who had just been hired—in front of his wife and everyone else in the room. He even described how he would often leave his office and stroll behind the counter to admire the pretty young woman. Everyone within earshot was too stunned to speak.

The day after Beth's going-away party, Emily called and told us all about it. Then she called an emergency meeting of the board. The board voted to fire Chad on the spot. It was a wise decision. An atmosphere of cynicism and distrust had been created by one person's toxic behavior, but Emily and the board acted quickly to control the situation. The board's next move was to conduct an executive search for Chad's replacement—the person who would ultimately replace Emily.

One moral we can learn from this story is that trust and cynicism are not mutually exclusive. Sometimes they exist side by side in the same organization. Emily was the embodiment of trust—a leader so trusted she was looked upon as Mom. If anything, her long tenure had created an excess of trust so that no one in the organization could imagine trusting any other person as CEO. At the same time, Chad had sewn seeds of distrust and cynicism. Clearly, this organization needed some sort of structure that would enable trust to flourish while keeping cynicism from spinning out of control.

We helped them locate a successor: a person who not only had a good track record, but who also had superior character references. We knew that there would be no repeat of Chad's behavior with this person. But the people in the organization had been burned once, and now they were gun-shy. "How do we know we can trust the new executive?" they asked. We explained that trust is only built with time and experience; you shouldn't expect to have instant trust when a new person comes aboard. Yet even though you can't manufacture instant trust, you can manage cynicism.

We did that by building four main safeguards into the search process:

1. *No manager could be fired within the first twelve months without board consent.* This allayed many of the fears that long-timers had about being pushed aside by a "new guard."

2. *The management team, board, and potential CEO would engage in a full day of reviewing the existing business plan,* making sure that everyone had bought in to the organization's vision.

3. *The managers, board, and potential CEO would spend a day outlining how their relationship would work:* who is involved in strategic planning, who attends board meetings, how often managers and board members interact, and so forth.

4. *The executive candidate would meet the managers before being hired.*

These four policies helped this organization to manage cynicism. It reframed the problem from building instant trust (an impossible task) to managing cynicism (a doable task).

Trust can be built over time, and cynicism can be managed all the time. The organization that learns to balance trust and cynicism is well on its way to developing good Relational Performance.

8

PROACTIVELY

MANAGE CHANGE

EXECUTIVE SUMMARY

There is hardly any organization in the world that has not been impacted by the enormous changes of the past few years—changes brought about by the global economy, by the changing culture, by changing tastes in the marketplace, by technological change, by computers and the Internet. Those that adapt will thrive; organizations that resist change will die. Healthy organizations tend to be more flexible and responsive to new situations and more likely to thrive in changing times.

Here are the top ten changes caused by the rise of e-business:

1. The change from mass markets to markets of one. The world has moved from an economy of mass production to mass customization. Instead of marketing to the masses, organizations must learn to cater to markets of one.

2. The rise of the experience economy. In the twenty-first century, successful organizations offer more than products and services; they offer an experience.

3. Hiring for competencies instead of skills. The old assembly-line economy rewarded specific skills and tenure on the job. But in the new economy, where people flow in and out of organizations as conditions change, hiring and compensation must reflect a person's ability to adapt, think, communicate, lead, and innovate.

4. The elimination of geographical boundaries. Technology is creating a world without geographical boundaries. Replacing the old geographical boundaries are new "virtual boundaries" such as mission, values, common focus, and vision.

5. The rise of automation. Successful organizations focus on the intangibles that can't be automated, such as emotional experiences, intellectual creativity, and Relational Performance.

6. Employee mobility replaces employee loyalty. With unemployment at its lowest level in three decades, employees can pick and choose jobs. Compensation factors being equal, they tend to choose the better Relational Performance environment.

7. Management authority gives way to employee leverage. Today's pool of available talent is scarce, and employees know they have leverage. Managers must treat employees like volunteers who can quit at will and find another job down the street.

8. The spread of short-term thinking. Today's younger generation does not think long term, but organizations must think long term to respond to changing situations.

9. The information explosion. Information overload creates a niche for companies that can help people locate, sort, sift, organize, and analyze pertinent information.

10. Face time is shifting to virtual time. The transition from personal contact to virtual contact makes it more difficult to establish trust. Even in a virtual organization, time must be set aside for face-to-face relationship building.

Change is rarely pleasant and never easy, but the ability to safely navigate change is one of the vital signs of Relational Performance.

In recent years, the headlines have blared with stories of Medicare reform, physician dissatisfaction trends, and new practice-management technologies. Large multispecialty medical groups are declining. Hospitals are no longer purchasing medical practices. What drives these profound changes in the medical profession? To a large degree, it is the rise of health maintenance organizations (or HMOs; also called "managed care").

These changes have been confusing and frustrating for patients and physicians alike. Patients used to a long-term relationship with the family doctor now find themselves cared for by an array of different doctors. Third-party payments by insurance companies have become a thing of the past for many patients. Some doctors now find themselves forced to join an HMO—or find themselves without patients and income. These doctors, once used to setting their own fees and making their own rules, now find their income and treatment options tightly regulated by the corporation. Many doctors have reluctantly acceded to the strictures of medicine's Brave New World.

But some physicians have chosen an alternative.

"I'm a Doctor, Not an Accountant!"

Rejecting the rigid constraints of the managed care environment, some physicians have made the decision to band together, forming single specialty practices of twenty or thirty doctors. These practices have many of the advantages of an HMO, but without the corporate mandates that restrict a doctor's treatment decisions—and a doctor's earning potential. But while such practices have many advantages over HMOs, many physicians in these large practices have discovered problems they had not expected. Often, these problems are, at base, *business* problems. In order to survive and thrive, these practices must do more than offer good medical care. They must learn good business habits. They must develop Relational Performance.

The Cardiovascular Group of Northern Virginia (TCG), the largest group of cardiologists in northern Virginia, is an organization that discovered how to increase Relational Performance in its practice. TCG consists of twenty-four physicians and almost a hundred support staff members. It is a prototypical example of a newly formed practice responding to the rapidly changing environment in the health-care profession. Though the physicians of TCG have experienced all the problems one would expect from a transition to a new way of delivering health care, this organization is an excellent example of how to overcome those problems and successfully navigate the stormy seas of transition and change.

Our association with TCG began when the executive director, Lauri Rustand, called us and requested our help in resolving some problems. Lauri told us that the organization lacked coherent direction. The doctors, who had all been in smaller practices before, were having trouble getting in step with the new system. There were twenty-four physician-shareholders, six of whom were on the board; they had hired a team of four nonphysician managers to oversee the staff of nurses, receptionists, clerks, and other support personnel. The problem: decisions made by the four managers were not being implemented.

We agreed to do an organizational assessment and to facilitate three days of strategic planning at an off-site location. We met individually with a number of physicians to perform the initial assessment and determine the problems and needs that existed at TCG. Upon completion of the assessment, several issues emerged:

1. The organization lacked a comprehensive business plan.

2. The decision-making process was ineffective; when decisions were made by management, they were frequently undermined at the implementation level.

3. The six members of the board, all doctors, were so involved in the daily operation of the practice that they were unable to effectively focus on strategic issues.

4. The doctors had unresolved differences over code, values, and clinical procedures that needed to be addressed.

In the course of a three-day strategic planning retreat, we began the process of helping this organization restructure itself. During the strategic planning session (which all doctors and managers attended) the lack of effective leadership throughout the organization, from the board through the staff, emerged as the single issue preventing TCG from realizing its mission. Leadership was continually reacting to the crisis of the day rather than setting long-range strategy. This reactive cycle began to unravel relationships, causing people to feel frustrated, angry, and hurt. Several people in the organization took these frustrations and hurts personally.

In the course of the retreat, however, they were able to see that these frustrations and hurts were actually the result of an organization trying to feel its way around during a time of change, uncertainty, and transition. The Identified Problem was conflict. But the real problem, The Thing in the Bushes, was the organization's inability to navigate change. The very things that made the physicians competent in the operating room—command, control, and individuality—kept them from moving forward as a business. Everyone in the organization was moving through *terra incognita,* and there were no road maps or guidebooks to tell anyone at TCG how to do things that had never been done before.

There was plenty of cynicism during the first day of the retreat: Would people arrive on time and actively participate? Would anything meaningful come of these meetings? Or would it all be a waste of time? We set firm ground rules, such as starting on time, and no late arrivals. By setting firm ground rules, we raised expectations for this meeting. We showed that this was a process that would be taken seriously. The first night, everyone arrived on time—and with a businesslike attitude. Everyone in the organization was ready for change.

The key issue we faced was in defining organizational values. Prior to becoming part of a larger medical group, these physicians had all run successful practices. For years, they had known only one way of running their practices, and they did not readily let go of the autonomy they had enjoyed in the old environment. They considered themselves doctors first, not business people, so they hired competent people to run the business side of TCG. When the nonphysician managers made decisions, the doctors would often take a position like Dr. McCoy on *Star Trek:* "I'm a doctor, not an accountant!" Management decisions were often undermined by the physicians themselves.

This would set in motion a cycle of reaction: Management would give orders. Physicians would resist those orders. Management would have to put out fires and solve problems when the system didn't work the way it was supposed to. This took time away from training and staff building—and ultimately from patient care. It also created resentment as managers and staff members began to feel excluded from making a real difference. The result was increased complaining and decreased efficiency in the office. It was a reactive cycle that slowly ate away at the organization.

The desire these physicians had to maintain control and autonomy was not a bad thing in and of itself. In the operating room, a surgeon needs to be in charge and call the shots. You can't perform a critical open-heart procedure by committee. Quite properly, these doctors were used to giving orders and getting their own way.

But this was a new day. These doctors needed to recognize that the practice of medicine could not be done the way it used to be—at least outside the operating room. They needed to be willing to give up a degree of control and autonomy (particularly in nonmedical issues, such as office management) for the good of the entire group. We spent several hours wrestling along with the doctors and managers of TCG. To the credit of these physicians, they all realized that the only way for them to succeed as individuals was for the entire organization to synergize and succeed.

Once this hurdle was crossed, once the collective decision was made to sacrifice a certain amount of individual autonomy for the greater good, the group began to move forward in productive ways. That day, decisions were made that produced lasting results. Some people predicted that we would never get twenty-four physicians to move together as a cohesive group—yet we did. But we certainly can't take the credit for this. These doctors were open to change and to new ways of doing things. Their receptivity to the changes we proposed made our job much easier.

TCG was on its way to outstanding Relational Performance. It was not there yet. The process would take time. But as these doctors, managers, and staff members learned the principles of Relational Performance, the group began to change—and it was definitely a change for the better.

The Quickening Pace of Change

The health-care industry is just one of many undergoing radical transformations. There is hardly any business, any organization in the world that has not been impacted in one way or another by the enormous changes of the past few years—changes brought about by the global economy, by the changing culture, by changing tastes in the marketplace, by technological change, by computers and the Internet. Some organizations live on the razor edge of change, constantly adapting, upgrading, retooling, retrenching, reinvesting, reinventing. These are the organizations that become the leaders in their corner of the marketplace.

And then there are those organizations that resist change. When the next wave comes, they drown, they disappear. When the speed of external change outpaces the speed of internal change, companies begin to die. The organizations that are the most likely to make a healthy transition through times of external or internal change are those with good Relational Performance. A healthy organization tends to be more flexible and responsive to new situations, less set in its ways. An organization's ability to adapt and respond to change can spell the difference between success and extinction.

Charlie Chaplin was a comic film star during the era of silent movies. His world abruptly changed with the 1927 release of *The Jazz Singer,* the first "talking picture." Chaplin was slow to grasp the meaning of adding sound to motion pictures. In 1931, he predicted that the "fad" of talking pictures would soon pass away. "I give the talkies six months more," he said.

When was the last time you saw a silent movie? Change is inevitable, but keeping up with change is not. That takes work and awareness. If you do not adjust to change, your company is doomed to become the organizational equivalent of silent movies.

In the prologue of this book, we listed the top ten changes caused by the rise of e-business. It's a dot-com world out there, as the proliferation of e-business commercials on TV (especially during the Super Bowl) attests. And if you are a frequent flyer, you know you can't fly to places like Seattle, San Francisco, L.A., or D.C. without seeing a lot of tattooed and pierced twenty-something passengers in first class—they are the new dot-com executive class. Quick: name one business of any consequence that can't be found at doubleyou-doubleyou-doubleyou-dot-whatever. No question, the arrival of e-trading, e-retailing, and e-everything-else has totally transformed the way business is done. The world is changing at a rate of millions of mouse clicks per second. Just look at these trends:

1. THE CHANGE FROM MASS MARKETS TO MARKETS OF ONE

The world economy has evolved from an economy of mass production (Henry Ford's assembly line) to continuous improvement (process reengineering as evidenced by the Japanese electronics industry in the 1970s) to mass customization in the twenty-first century. Instead of marketing to the masses, or even improving the speed of delivering products to the masses, organizations must learn how to cater to markets of one.

For the majority of the twentieth century, industries tended toward standardization. A product that is one-size-fits-all is obviously cheaper to make than a large array of varieties. Standardization makes assembly lines possible, and assembly lines reduce the cost of products for the masses. Employing this mass-standardization mindset, the United States became the industrial leader of the world.

But mass standardization was based on tangible assets, or physical assets. In the new economy, the value of tangible assets is being replaced by intangible assets: knowledge, information, name recognition (brand), market share, and innovative business practices. In the old economy, for example, if Ford Motor Company built an automobile, only one consumer could purchase that automobile at one point in time. In the new economy, a virtually unlimited number of consumers can purchase the same knowledge on an Internet website at any one point in time. The new economy has de-emphasized the cost-effectiveness of mass standardization.

Concurrently, the rise of the new generations, all of whom resist conformity, has created an increasing demand for products and services that are custom-tailored to individual needs. This demand has led to a customized economy in which choices among options, sizes, shapes, and colors abound. New leaps in technology are making it possible for unique products to be produced in response to individual tastes—at lower costs. For example, Ford Motor Company's eConsumer Group is leading the way in "build to order" automobiles, following the same strategy that propelled Dell to the top of the computer industry.

New, more flexible computer software is transforming the delivery of products and services, enabling smaller, leaner companies to outpace larger institutions. Nearly 50 percent of the pioneers in PC banking, for example, were credit unions ranging in asset size from fifty to five hundred million dollars or small start-up Internet banks such as Security First Network Bank. The larger, multibillion-dollar megabanks were the last ones to come to the dance.

To move from a mass-market mindset to catering to markets of one, organizations must retool their thinking. Custom-tailoring products and services requires organizations to integrate three components:

Focus on Customer Needs
What do your customers care about? What do they worry about? How can your product or service improve their lives and reduce their wor-

ries? How important is price to your customer? How does your price structure compare with that of the competition? How convenient is your product or service to use? How reliable is your product or service? Does your organization give customers a sense of empathy, touch, personal interaction, and genuine concern?

In order to market to individuals and tailor your product or service to a market of one, you must be aware that your customers are not a faceless, homogeneous mass. They are individuals. The answers to all of the above questions should not be totaled and averaged; they should be placed on a "needs matrix" or grid. Some individuals will place the highest premium on price. Others will place a high premium on choice of options or colors, or on ease of access and operation, or on personal empathy and touch with your organization. By offering customized varieties of your product or service that are individually tailored to appeal to the needs and tastes of your highly individual customers, your organization becomes responsive, flexible, and successful in the new economy.

Reengineer Processes

The second step in mass customization is to reengineer your product or service around discrete units of work. This means that you focus on the smallest activity or cost unit that can be measured, and then you reassemble those units into a product or service and deliver it in a way that is flexible enough to meet the individual needs and wants of your customers. Whereas the ability to *mass produce* is based on the ability to make as many look-alike products as possible, the ability to *mass customize* is based on the ability to quickly, economically assemble discrete units of work into a variety of patterns to meet highly individualized consumer demands.

For example, when you buy a Lego set for your children, it doesn't come preassembled as a car or an airplane or a bridge. It comes as a box full of varicolored building blocks in different sizes and shapes—each a discrete unit of plastic. You can build virtually anything you like out of Legos.

The key to reengineering your product or service is to break it down into those Lego-like units that can be reassembled in a variety of ways to please and serve a variety of customers. If you can accomplish this, you have taken the next step in assuring your organization's success in the new economy.

The food industry has understood this better than others. Beau Jo's Pizza in Colorado, for example, allows consumers to choose between four types of crust, four levels of thickness, six sauces, a dozen varieties of cheese, and dozens of ingredients.

Develop New Systems

The third and final step in mass customization is to create the systems that will enable your organization to match reengineered processes to individual customer needs. These systems can be divided into two categories: people and technology. The people component involves training the members of your organization to think and act in terms of customer needs and wants. It involves teaching them and equipping them to assemble and deliver the discrete units of work, the "Legos" that combine to satisfy the individualized demands of your individual customers.

The technology component involves supplying your employees and customers with the equipment and tools to manage a large number of variables and to assemble the discrete units, the "Legos," into products and services that meet your customers' needs and demands. Care must be taken to make sure your technological components work effectively and interact seamlessly. That means hardware, software, operating systems, and peripherals must be compatible, integrated, and completely user-friendly.

Successful organizations in the new millennium will be those that are able to move from mass marketing to markets of one. Your ultimate goal may be to reach a thousand clients, a million clients, or even a billion clients—but never forget that you have to reach them one by one.

2. The Rise of the Experience Economy

The world has evolved from an agrarian economy (preindustrial) to a production economy (the Industrial Revolution) to a service economy (post-World War II) to the experience economy of today. In the twenty-first century, customers look for the experience rather than the service. That is why organizations such as Starbucks and Nordstrom offer not just products and services, but also a sensory experience.

Take a cup of coffee, for example. In the production economy of the industrial age, coffee beans were a raw commodity ground and packed in tin cans and sold on the grocery shelf for the equivalent of a few cents for a cup of coffee. In the service economy, that same cup of coffee could be sold as a service in a coffee shop for fifty cents. But today, in the experience economy, that cup of coffee is now premium roasted, exotically flavored, converted into latte or espresso, and sold in fine dining establishments and java hangouts for three dollars a cup. Raw commodities that are mass-produced (goods) are coupled with services, which are ultimately transformed into experiences. At each level of transformation, the value to the customer increases—and so does the price.

The bottom line is that today's consumers don't buy a product. They buy an experience. Young consumers will scrimp on the staples of life in order to have more money to spend on a weekend snowboarding at Vail or mountain-biking in the Andes. They crave the *experience.* Volkswagen has a well-established reputation for delivering a quality product. But they realized that a quality product is not the only way to strengthen relationships with customers. Their customers want experience. In June 2000, VW opened Autostadt, a Disney-esque theme park. The five-hundred-million-dollar complex in Wolfsburg offers intense driving simulations that rival other theme park experiences. "In the past, Volkswagen sold four wheels and an engine," says Jack Rouse, an American theme-park designer who has played a leadership role in the German project. "With Autostadt, the company wants us to bring emotion to the customer."[1]

Companies like Barnes & Noble and Borders have successfully reshaped the bookselling business—not just by discounting prices, but also by offering an enjoyable ambiance with cafe latte and elegant lounges. In short, they have turned book browsing into an *experience.* Nordstrom department stores feature live music, exquisite décor, and a sales staff that is fanatically dedicated to customer satisfaction. Shopping at Nordstrom is different from shopping at any other department store. It's not a chore; it's an *experience.* Successful organizations today are those that offer more than products and services; they offer an experience.

3. Hiring for Competencies Instead of Skills

The old economy rewarded specific skills and tenure on the job. Mass standardization required proficiency in doing a few tasks well—the assembly line approach. The people who performed these tasks efficiently and loyally were typically the most experienced, or tenured, employees. Compensating for tenure made sense in the old economy. In the new economy, where people flow in and out of organizations according to changing conditions, hiring and pay are based on the ability to adapt, think, change, communicate, lead, flex, and innovate. Companies can no longer afford to reward skills and tenure alone; human resources decisions must increasingly be made on the basis of other competencies such as traits, values, and motives (see chapter 2).

4. THE ELIMINATION OF GEOGRAPHICAL BOUNDARIES

Technology is creating a world without geographical boundaries. Corporations (and the people in those corporations) no longer see themselves as "American" or "Brazilian" or "Swiss." Their allegiance to the company has nothing to do with geographical boundaries or national identities. Replacing the old geographical boundaries are new "virtual boundaries" such as mission, values, common focus, and vision.

5. THE RISE OF AUTOMATION

Technology is automating everything that can possibly be automated. Successful organizations will be those that distinguish themselves by focusing on the intangibles that can't be automated, such as emotional experiences, intellectual creativity, and relational health.

6. EMPLOYEE MOBILITY REPLACES EMPLOYEE LOYALTY

With unemployment at its lowest level in three decades, employees can pick and choose jobs. If compensation and interest are basically the same, they will choose the better environment. Even if compensation and job interest are slightly lacking, they will choose the relationally healthy atmosphere.

The old model of the paternalistic corporation offering lifelong jobs, guaranteed advances, and a testimonial dinner and gold watch at age sixty-five is a thing of the past. In the new model, companies are flexible, offering employees an opportunity for personal and professional growth in an environment that, in a best-case scenario, is open and honest and treats them fairly. Today's employees no longer build loyalty, they build résumés — and this fact is understood and accepted on both sides. After channel surfing and web surfing, the next logical step was job surfing. Loyalty and lifetime job security are out; the contract between employer and employee (like everything else in our society) has *changed*.

7. MANAGEMENT AUTHORITY
GIVES WAY TO EMPLOYEE LEVERAGE

Managers used to have authority over employees. They could threaten to fire an employee or dock the employee's pay. But today's pool of available talent is scarce, and employees know they have leverage. In the twenty-first century, managers must treat employees like volunteers who can quit at will and find a job that's as good or better right down the street. Managers have a lot to learn from nonprofit leaders (ministers, social service workers, and so forth) who know the value of motivating volunteers through vision, servant-leadership, self-sacrifice, and encouragement.

8. The Spread of Short-Term Thinking

Every day another tech start-up has an IPO that jumps an average of 80 percent the first day. This creates an elite class of young entrepreneurs whose penny-a-share stock has split four times and is valued at fifty dollars a share. Implication: this generation is not thinking long term—a problem that could spell disaster for an economy focused on short-term rewards for the few rather than long-term gains for the good of all. Today's younger generation grew up on pizza in thirty minutes or less, microwaves, ATMs, and other instant-gratification innovations. These people think short term. Time has become the newest measuring stick of success. Companies must be responsive and adaptive. But Relational Performance also focuses on the long term as part of a healthy code.

9. The Information Explosion

The amount of information in the world doubles every eighteen months. This is a problem—and an opportunity. Information overload creates a niche for companies that can help people locate, sort, sift, organize, and analyze pertinent information for customers. But information overload also creates a cynical society. The average American receives 4,200 advertising messages per week. The extension of choice tends to lead to the evasion of choice. Remember when your parent's television had three channels? You chose a channel and stuck with it for a full half-hour or sometimes even an hour. We don't believe the message because we are bombarded with so many. We become skeptical and cynical of anyone who has a message. Is it any surprise that new employees in today's society begin work with a standoffish attitude? It takes more time than ever to overcome that cynicism and to establish trust. But we have less time than ever to accomplish that task. And we are forced to do with less face time than ever.

10. Face Time Is Shifting to Virtual Time

Traditionally, face time established trust. The transition away from personal contact to virtual contact makes it more difficult to establish trust at the very time when trust and relationships are becoming all the more crucial in conducting business. Companies used to take for granted that employees are aware that they are helping each other simply by being in proximity. Now, even that can't be taken for granted. From telecommuters to virtual offices, employees and employers must pay special attention to going the extra mile in communicating expectations, achievements, affirmation, and other relational information. Even in a virtual organization, time must be set aside for face-to-face relationship-building events, such as retreats, no-agenda meetings, and so forth.

In today's environment, organizations must stay on top of changing conditions. They must be fluid and constantly changing, because conditions are fluid and constantly changing. People come and go, moving out of old roles and into new ones. Conditions change. New technologies emerge. New laws and regulations are promulgated. Economic and market conditions fluctuate. In a rapidly evolving world, healthy organizations navigate change with alacrity and agility, while clinging firmly to their core principles. Those organizations that do not manage change are doomed to be managed by it—if not flattened by it. Those that manage change well are the innovators and leaders in society.

External Change Versus Internal Change

Coping with change was the primary challenge at TCG. The medical group was formed, as you'll recall, in response to changing conditions in the health-care profession—an external change. Yet equally problematic for TCG were internal changes and the relational issues that normally arise from transitions and changing conditions within an organization. During our initial consultation, as we were attempting to move on to strategic planning, we quickly ran into The Thing in the Bushes once more—and this time, to our surprise, it was a Thing of a different color. The color purple, to be exact.

Now, a color might not seem to be a major issue at first glance. But a controversy came about because TCG management had been trying for months to create a consistent corporate image, including a corporate dress code. Everyone at TCG was expected to wear a uniform shade of purple—a decision made by management. This color scheme extended from front desk attire to operating room scrubs. Some of the staff liked the dress code; others hated it. TCG had nine office locations, and at one location there was so much controversy over the dress code that some of the doctors had told staff members they could ignore it. Management complained that the doctors had undermined their decision. Having one renegade office in the group created resentment among the managers, and lowered staff morale in *all* the offices ("How come *we* have to follow the dress code and *they* don't?").

During an all-day session with the entire staff, we observed that the dress code kept emerging as an issue. Staff members kept raising it, and managers kept changing the subject. We became convinced that the dress code itself was not the issue, but it was symbolic of The Thing in the Bushes, the hidden problem or distortion in the relationships at TCG. Finally, near the end of the day's session, executive director Lauri Rustand said, "We need to deal with this issue and get beyond it."

"Are you willing to hear what the staff has to say?" we asked. "Would you be willing to respond to their concerns and make changes?"

"Yes," said Lauri. "I'm willing to do anything that will move us forward." It was a courageous stance.

We facilitated a discussion with the staff regarding dress code. It lasted forty-five minutes, and we were amazed how positive the atmosphere became during that discussion. Though no consensus was reached by the end of that time, it was clear that staff members felt included, respected, and listened to. But they were still stuck. During the talks, the dress code issue was boiled down to three options, and the group was pretty evenly split between those three options.

"Would everyone be willing for management to make the final decision based on what has been said here today?" we asked the entire group.

Heads nodded. Smiles broke out. A major breakthrough: the staff had reached a consensus to allow management to lead!

As the meeting was about to break up, one employee commented, "It's too bad we had to spend so much time on one little issue."

"Oh, we don't think it was a little issue at all," we replied. "The dress code may seem like small potatoes, but it symbolizes a major obstacle that has been keeping TCG from moving forward. Staff had felt excluded from decision making, and managers felt they were continually under fire. Now staff feels included, and management feels empowered to lead. That's a significant shift!"

The purple people-eating dragon had been slain. The Thing was dead. TCG was ready to go forward and tackle the real task, the task of planning its future.

Leading Through Change

Change is inevitable in life and in business. The rate of change is undeniably accelerating. Whereas previous generations only had to deal with gradual change in life and in business, today's must deal with bewildering, quantum-leap change—what Intel CEO Andrew Grove calls

"10X Change." This refers to the difference between change that progresses arithmetically (1, 2, 3, 4, and so on) and change that progresses geometrically, by factors of 10 (10^2, 10^3, 10^4, 10^5, and so on). In his book *Only the Paranoid Survive* (Bantam, 1999), Grove says that 10X Change is instigated by what he calls "Strategic Inflection Points," or SIPs. When a Wal-Mart store first opens in a city, that is an SIP for all the smaller, locally owned retailers in town: the level of competition undergoes an overnight 10X Change.

Here's another example of gradual change versus 10X Change: For thousands of years, books were copied by hand. In the fifteenth century, Gutenberg made the printing press possible by inventing movable type. In 1885 (480 years after Gutenberg), Ottmar Mergenthaler introduced the Linotype "hot lead" typesetter, which mechanized typesetting by setting "slugs" of type from a typewriter-like keyboard. Phototypesetting was born in the 1940s with a primitive machine called the Intertype Fotosetter, but it wasn't until the photo imaging "back end" was married to the computer display "front end" that computerized phototypesetting became widespread in the 1970s. Even so, the job of a Linotype operator was very secure from the 1880s to the 1970s, when widespread sales of computerized phototypesetters (cold type) edged the Linotype (hot type) aside.

The job security of cold-type operators was extremely short-lived by comparison: By the late 1980s, when desktop publishing made almost every computer owner a typesetter and graphic designer, the specialized career of typesetter was gone forever. All previous changes had been gradual, but computers and desktop publishing represented a 10X Change in the publishing and typesetting arena.

Leaders in organizations must learn to lead through times of rapid change. They must pay attention to Strategic Inflection Points and learn to discern which SIPs are mere passing fads and which are likely to force 10X Change upon the organization. The rise of new competitors, the rise of new technologies, the obsolescence of old technologies, changes in global conditions and foreign economies, changes in government regulations (including deregulation), changes in customer demographics and tastes—all of these factors have the potential of imposing 10X Change on your organization.

How, then, does a leader lead through times of enormous external and internal change? Here are some suggestions:

1. Be aware and be proactive. Make sure you stay up on trends, changes, and influences on your organization's environment. Read, study, talk to experts, consult with consultants, find out what people are saying, thinking, and doing in your industry. Beware of becoming isolated or insulated within the ivory tower of your corner office. Be informed about opportunities before they become *missed* opportunities. A reporter once asked Wayne Gretzki why he was such a great hockey player, to which he replied, "I skate where the puck is going to be." Identify where your "puck" is going to be, and proactively lead your organization there.

2. Listen to your intuition. There is nothing mystical about intuition. It is the ability of our brains to sift through mountains of input, experience, memories, and events at a subconscious level and, out of all of that input, produce a decision or an idea. Sometimes we can perform all the studies, examine all the graphs and charts, analyze all the data, and listen to all the consultants and focus groups, yet still come up with a sense that "I've got to go with my gut on this one." That's intuition. Visionary leaders are those who have learned to tune in to their intuition, even when it saws across the grain of logic, in order to take advantage of opportunities before they would normally present themselves to the logical, "sensible" mind. The ability to intuit is a priceless ability. Cultivate it.

3. Listen to organizational dissonance. In times of 10X Change, there is often a difference, a dissonance, between what an organization says and what it does. Executives, CEOs, managers, and board members may be charting one course while the people on the frontlines are moving in a different direction. Who is right? Who is out of step with reality? Who is responding to change? Who is resisting change? Never assume automatically that the senior leadership has all the answers. Sometimes the people "at the top" are isolated and out of touch, while the people in the trenches have a better feel for what's going on. But not always. Sometimes the leadership is on the cutting edge while the frontline troops just don't want to deal with change. As a leader, when you encounter dissonance in your organization, it is up to you to sift through the dissonance and find out where the truth lies.

4. Pay attention to your number-one competitor. Why is your competitor doing so well? What is your competitor doing that you are not—and vice versa? How is your competitor responding to changing conditions both outside and inside the organization? What does your competitor see that you might be missing?

5. Listen to your staff. The people on the frontlines of your organization are closest to potential Strategic Inflection Points. Encourage them to be observant and ask them about the changes in the environment of your organization. Wander around and ask your employees what they observe. Suggestion boxes or reports rarely work because they are anonymous and not relational. Include as many employees as possible in your strategic planning process. Employees want to be heard, and they want immediate feedback.

Good things come to those who listen. The most successful and innovative companies in America know that the majority of corporate innovations come from frontline workers, not managers. In fact, at least three-fourths of all product-improving and money-saving ideas come from the workers who deal with the products every day. The best companies worldwide find they receive at least fifty ideas per employee per year.

Listening is really a form of idea management. When an organization effectively manages small ideas, big ideas are sure to follow. So encourage a free flow of ideas. Listen. Affirm creativity. Encourage innovation. When you receive an idea from an employee, follow through immediately (within days, not months). Employees will eagerly offer great ideas if they know that their ideas will receive a fair, timely hearing and that valuable concepts will be implemented quickly.

6. As you work through changes in your organization, never lose sight of what must not *change.* Your organization's code—its mission, values, and vision—should not shift with every wind of change. When your organization responds to external change, or when it initiates internal change, *all* of those changes must be evaluated within a framework of fulfilling the organization's permanent mission and realizing its enduring vision.

7. When you, as a leader, come into an existing situation to make changes, be careful not to condemn the past. Always frame your vision in a positive, upbeat way. You have not come to erase the past, but to encourage an even brighter future. The people you have come to lead did not fail in the past; rather, you have come to spur them on to even greater success. These people were a part of that past—they lived it, they identify with it—and if you condemn it, they will feel condemned. As you focus on the future changes, be sure to always build on the past, not tear it down.

We saw the importance of these principles of leadership through change during our consultation with TCG. Over the next few months, we continued working with the medical group's management to develop a comprehensive business plan. The plan was designed to overhaul the way business was conducted and move the organization onward toward a shared vision. Our goal was to help the TCG board focus on long-range strategic issues while empowering the managers to deal with the day-to-day tactical issues with a free hand. We also worked with the entire staff to build consensus, map out processes and procedures, and clarify the lines of accountability within the organization.

But our most important job was leadership development with the board and management. We suggested that the board elect a chief medical officer (CMO) to serve as the go-to person when crucial executive decisions were needed. The CMO would also be responsible to articulate the mission, enforce the policies, and direct the focus of the organization. He or she would also interact directly and regularly with the executive director, Lauri Rustand, to both empower her to make key decisions and to hold her accountable for outcomes and results—but all, of course, without micromanaging!

Clearly, the CMO position required certain character traits and competencies that went well beyond surgical skill. It soon became apparent that one person had emerged as everyone's choice for that position: Dr. Warren Levy. A wise man who knew just when to be hands-on in a situation and when to be hands-off, Dr. Levy defined the role and made it his own.

Meanwhile, changing circumstances within TCG were forcing Lauri to confront her biggest challenge as executive director. She knew that TCG needed a comprehensive information-systems overhaul. After careful research, she selected Gateway Electronic Medical Management Systems (GEMMS)—a platform designed especially for cardiology practices. The price tag? Close to one million! The purchase of this system would require each doctor to take a significant salary hit over the next couple of years. So we constructed two financial scenarios: (1) a baseline built upon no change at all, and (2) a scenario based on the purchase of GEMMS. This task was difficult because there was so little useful historical data due to the various mergers, but Lauri's careful financial analysis began to establish her leadership credibility.

Both scenarios looked grim for the next couple of years, but the *real* problem was not money; it was boundaries. Would the doctors give Lauri the authority to implement their strategy? Would Dr. Levy be able to keep the doctors focused on strategic issues? Would Lauri exercise her leadership role firmly and decisively?

We arrived at the Country Club of Fairfax to observe the evening presentation to the physicians. Lauri and her management team were the presenters. The management team was not exactly looking forward to asking the doctors to take a salary hit. Dr. Levy opened the meeting, setting the tone for the evening, reminding his fellow physicians of their shared vision, their shared goals, and their shared values. Lauri followed up with a masterful presentation of the changes that had taken place in the organization's external and internal environments. Things were going well as the discussion turned to strategic initiatives and goal statements.

Then came the financial presentation. The room grew silent as Lauri presented the plan to implement the GEMMS medical management platform. At first we didn't know what to make of the silence. We could feel a lot of energy in the room, and at first it was hard to identify what kind of energy it was. Were these doctors all excited about the potential and possibilities of the new system, or were they incensed over the price tag? But then a moment came when the tension broke—like a bubble popping. There were smiles and nods all around, and it was clear that everyone in the room was on board.

It was awesome to see. For the first time since these docs had undergone the enormous transition of merging all their practices into a single group, they were all moving together as one unit, totally in sync with each other. Dr. Levy led the strategic sessions and Lauri handled the tactical matters. One doctor admitted after the session that it was the first time he had ever seen smiles in this group!

A motion to accept the business plan was promptly moved and seconded, but then came a hitch in the agenda. "Just a moment," said one of the doctors, an august and imposing figure of a man with steel-gray hair and piercing, skeptical eyes. Just as it seemed the group was about to move forward, this doctor—one of the leading cardiologists in the nation—appeared to be applying the brakes. "Before we approve this motion," he said in a deep, commanding voice, "I want to hear from everyone in this room."

When Dr. Herron interjected, our hearts sank—until we realized what he was doing: He was building consensus! He wasn't stopping the process; he was building on it.

So every doctor in the room offered his comment on the plan. Immediately afterward, the plan was approved. As we write these words, TCG is still moving forward, still navigating new internal and external changes—and still developing better and better Relational Performance. Old issues that had held the group back are being resolved, and there is a renewed sense of mission and excitement at TCG.

Change is rarely pleasant and never easy, but the ability to safely navigate change is one of the crucial vital signs of Relational Performance. A static organization is headed for extinction, but the ability to adapt and respond to change is the key to success and a bright future.

9

FOCUS BEYOND YOURSELF

EXECUTIVE SUMMARY

Although The Thing in the Bushes would have us believe otherwise, a healthy organization understands its responsibility as part of a greater community: the neighborhood, the city, the state, the nation, and the world. This doesn't mean that organizations should simply engage in charitable giving. Many companies find they can improve their service, products, and bottom line by involvement in the social sector.

By tackling chronic social problems, organizations often find they solve their own problems, including problems with product quality or profitability. For example, Bell Atlantic installed a prototype computer network in a public school system. This win-win solution gave the school system a state-of-the-art computer network while enabling Bell Atlantic to beta test its latest technology under real-world conditions.

There are many kinds of return on investment. The organization that invests in its own community will get back an incalculable ROI, both in intangibles such as good will and good public relations *and* in hard, bankable, bottom-line returns. A healthy organization is an organization that *matters* to the community and to the world.

W e sat in the elegantly appointed waiting room outside the office of Kevin T. Kennelly, president and CEO of Park Meridian Bank in Charlotte, North Carolina. A photo album sat open on the beveled-glass coffee table in front of us. There were photos of people in work clothes at a construction site. They were operating Skil saws, carrying two-by-fours on their shoulders, installing plumbing and electrical fixtures, nailing shingles, sanding, painting, and more. Looking closer, we realized we had seen many of those same people in the lobby when we entered the building. They were loan officers, assistant managers, tellers — and there was even a photo of Kennelly wearing a hard hat.

"Sorry to keep you waiting," said Kennelly, emerging from his office.

"That's all right. We were just noticing this photo album — "

"Oh, that!" Kennelly beamed with pride. "That was a Habitat for Humanity house we built for a working poor family." He went on to explain how *all* of the employees pitched in — and so did a number of customers. From pouring the foundation to the final coat of paint, they got the house built in just one week. "That experience knit our people together like nothing we've ever done, before or since," he said. "The goodwill that project built in the community is something money just can't buy. And so is that good feeling" — he thumped his chest — "right here."

Kennelly knows. There's more to being in business than making money. A lot more. An organization with good Relational Performance is one with a conscience, a soul, a worthwhile purpose. A healthy organization focuses beyond itself.

Another bank that demonstrates that kind of outward, community-conscious focus is Vermont National Bank. This bank offers the Socially Responsible Banking Fund® (SRB Fund), which allows depositors to earmark money for worthy social enterprises such as financing affordable housing for low-income families, environmental and conservation projects, agriculture, education, and community businesses. The bank's corporate conscience has won many new friends — and nearly one hundred million dollars in new deposits to the fund.

The bank's website explains how the SRB Fund works:

> When you choose the SRB Fund, your FDIC-insured deposits are loaned to local individuals and companies

which make positive contributions to the environment,
their communities and their employees. We will not support
companies with negative records in energy, employee relations or the environment. Nor will we support alcohol,
tobacco, gambling or weapons production.

In addition, deposits, loans and cash balances in the
Socially Responsible Banking Fund® are managed separately
from other bank funds to ensure that your deposits are
used exclusively for socially responsible lending. Our SRB
Community Advisory Board, comprised of community leaders committed to socially responsible business practices,
provides us with insight on the lending issues facing local
communities.

One of many worthy organizations that has received a helping hand
from Vermont National Bank's SRB Fund is Spectrum Youth and Family
Services in Burlington, Vermont, a nonprofit group with a thirty-year
track record of creating life-changing programs for troubled youth:
substance abuse counseling, job development, health care, family counseling, emergency services, and more. Spectrum's thirteen-bed youth
shelter was largely funded by a loan from the SRB Fund. As Spectrum's
executive director Will Rowe recalls,

Some time ago we started doing basic banking with
Vermont National, and one thing was clear immediately:
the people were very friendly and very helpful. There was a
personal touch and an interest that was very different from
other banks we've worked with, and it meant a lot to us.
. . . The relationship has gone beyond banking. We've had
volunteers from VNB do community service. Our loan officer, Brian Meyer, calls us when there is furniture available
for donation. . . . They always keep us in mind.

Could the big heart and caring social conscience of Vermont National
Bank have anything to do with the fact that, in the past few years, it
has grown to become the largest bank in the state? We think so—and
the bank's 19-percent market share speaks for itself. We have seen it
again and again, in one organization after another: Being a good corporate citizen is good for business. When you give, you get back—in
ways you never would have imagined.

Healthy Organizations Are Dedicated to the Public Good

In an organization with good Relational Performance, everyone understands that it does not stand alone. It is part of a greater community. In fact, it draws its life and support from the community, and so it has a moral obligation to give something back.

What is the community? It may be the neighborhood, the city, the state, the nation, or the world. As David Packard, cofounder of Hewlett-Packard, once observed, "The company should be managed first and foremost to make a contribution to society." And management guru Peter F. Drucker agrees: "Moral vision and commitment to social values are the foundation of enduring business success."

Here are a few examples:

Millions of people in the African tropics lost their sight to onchocerciasis, more commonly known as "river blindness," caused by parasitic worms that invade the body tissues, ultimately attacking and destroying the eyes. Today, river blindness has been virtually eliminated by a program coordinated by the World Health Authority (WHA), using medicine developed and donated by the pharmaceutical firm Merck & Company. The WHA estimates that the sight of as many as thirty million people has been saved, thanks to the generosity of Merck, which not only donated the medicine but also invested heavily in its development without any prospect of a dollar of financial return.

Before the development of this new medicine, outbreaks of river blindness often resulted in as many as 15 percent of a village becoming blind, and it frequently caused entire river communities to migrate from their villages to hostile desert locations, producing hardship and famine. The medicine, called ivermectin (it is trademarked by Merck as Mectizan), only needs to be taken twice a year to provide complete protection.

While Mectizan was in development, Merck knew that it was a drug with a huge market. But the company also knew that there was a big drawback to that market: the people who needed the drug could not afford to pay for it. Merck chose to continue production and distribution of the drug at its own expense. Why? Because Merck's researchers viewed themselves as people on a mission to preserve and improve human life. How would they have felt about that mission if Merck had turned its back on a crying human need? How would the members of the organization have felt about themselves and their company? It would have been demoralizing—and it would have been wrong. Merck did what it had to do to remain true to its code, its vision, and its values: the company provided more than one hundred million Mectizan tablets free of charge.

In 1995, a seven-foot sculpture entitled "The Gift of Sight" was unveiled at Merck's headquarters in Whitehouse Station, New Jersey. The statue depicts a young African boy leading a blind man by the hand. Thanks to Merck's social conscience, such scenes are finally becoming a thing of the past in African village life.[1]

Another company that has recently rediscovered its social conscience is Dutch Shell, the world's largest publicly traded oil company. It has been the target of withering international criticism in recent years over such issues as its collusion with the corrupt and repressive government of Nigeria and its environmentally unfriendly disposal of the Brent Spar oil platform in the North Sea. Now headed by Mark Moody-Stuart of London, Shell is undergoing a transformation into a paragon of social and environmental responsibility.

In 1998, Shell issued a report called *Profits and Principles: Does There Have to Be a Choice?,* an amazingly candid corporate self-examination. The document disclosed that Shell had caught and fired twenty-three staff members for soliciting or accepting bribes and had canceled ninety-five contracts because contractors had violated Shell's standards of ethics. Moreover, Shell sought the opinions of thousands of people, both within and outside the company, and learned that it had a profound image problem with regard to the environment and human rights. "We had looked in the mirror," admitted the report, "and neither recognized nor liked some of what we saw."

The key to Shell's transformation is the company's decision to adhere to what it calls a "triple bottom line," in which the company reports not only on its financial bottom line, but on its environmental and social performance as well. "The old Shell was pretty smug," says Moody-Stuart, "and didn't bother dealing with the outside world." He attributes his own growing social conscience to the influence of a Quaker wife and two Quaker sisters. Under his leadership, Shell now embraces the United Nations' Universal Declaration of Human Rights. Moody-Stuart says that he realizes that the corporation must behave as a stakeholder in society, not the other way around. When the society as a whole suffers, so does business; but when society is sound, it creates a better environment for corporate success.[2]

David Bollier, author of *Aiming Higher: 25 Stories of How Companies Prosper by Combining Sound Management and Social Vision,* observes:

It is customary to think of a business in terms of its capital assets—the building and technology and material resources. But increasingly, the depth and integrity of a company's human relationships are becoming critical factors in business success. . . . The "soft" factors in business—moral integrity, a sense of fairness and cooperation, social vision—critically affect the "hard" bottom line more than is commonly realized. . . . A company can deal with some issues through skillful PR while ignoring the underlying concerns. But this is a short-term expedient that can easily backfire; the most effective long-term business strategy is to walk the talk.[3]

Bollier goes on to cite a number of companies, some large, some small, that "walk the talk":

There is Fel-Pro, an Illinois company that manufactures gaskets for the automobile industry. Fel-Pro, says Bollier, is a family-friendly company that gives employees enormous flexibility through on-site childcare, college counseling, tuition scholarships, and more.

The McKay Nursery Company of Waterloo, Wisconsin, offers its migrant workers an employee stock-ownership plan—a radical innovation given the seasonal nature of its workforce. Most companies look at part-time and seasonal workers as a place to trim the cost of benefits. But McKay has found that by offering the stock-ownership plan to its migrant workers, it has been able to reduce costly turnover and maintain stability in its workforce.

Starbucks Corporation provides a comprehensive benefits plan (including stock options) for all workers, including part-timers. The result: low turnover, employee loyalty, and great service. These factors have put the perk in the coffee retailer's growth and staying power.

Starbucks' social conscience also extends south of the border. The company has recently begun using its coffee-buying muscle to persuade Guatemalan plantation owners to improve wages, working conditions, housing standards, and safety standards for coffee workers in that country. Starbucks also donates heavily to CARE, which provides water-quality improvement projects in that country. The coffee company was awarded the 1996 Corporate Conscience Award for International Human Rights from the Council on Economic Priorities.

The Thing whispers to us that profit, ROI, and ROE are everything—the business of business is business, period. But that is a lie. No individual is an island—and no organization is an island either. Relational

Performance understands that organizations do not exist solely for themselves, solely for the stockholders, solely for the sake of profit. As healthy organizations reach out to strengthen and nurture the surrounding community, they strengthen and nurture themselves. A healthy organization focuses beyond itself and is dedicated to the public good. Maintaining a healthy outward focus is a good way for an organization to keep its bushes trimmed, leaving no place for The Thing in the Bushes to hide. Here again, the key is *relationships*—in this case, the organization's relationship with the surrounding community and with the world at large.

Making a Better World

Many companies are finding out that they can improve their own service, products, and bottom line by becoming involved in the social sector; that is, in inner-city neighborhoods, in welfare-to-work programs, and in public schools. By tackling some of the chronic problems that plague our society, organizations often find that they are able to solve many of their own internal difficulties, including issues with product quality or profitability.

For example, when companies create jobs in the inner city, they often find that the result is higher consumerism and greater sales in the inner city. Also, many companies have learned that needy communities can be ideal proving grounds for new ideas and new technologies. Such companies don't look at their social involvement as charity or do-gooderism, but as research and development.

Here's a prime example: In 1991, Bell Atlantic installed one of its prototype computer networks in the Union City, New Jersey, public schools. The company not only installed the school network, but also donated 135 new computers. This innovative system enabled students and teachers to connect with each other, conduct research, and improve skills. At the same time, Bell Atlantic was able to "test drive" in the schools a working prototype of a system it planned to market. The company continually monitored and upgraded the system, finding new ways to manage data transmission over the network. The schools gave the computer system the real-world shakedown it needed in order to work out all the bugs — and the school system got a state-of-the-art computer network, plus continuous tech support, all free of charge.

The school system's need for a computer network and Bell Atlantic's need to develop and field test new networking technologies under real-world conditions came together as a perfect hand-and-glove solution. The Union City schools helped Bell Atlantic refine and perfect some of its most important technologies of the 1990s, including video and high-capacity data transmission.

Though this project (dubbed Project Explore) gave a big educational boost to thousands of inner-city children, Bell Atlantic didn't view Union City schools as a charity case. The project was funded out of operating and R&D budgets, not philanthropic funds. The company got at least as much back as it gave — a huge return in know-how, technological improvement, and profits on sales of the network to businesses and educational institutions over the next decade. The lessons learned from Project Explore in Union City led directly to the highly successful introduction of Bell Atlantic's Infospeed DSL product line in 1999.[4]

Project Explore was the perfect yes-yes solution.

Another company that discovered higher profits through social action is the hotel chain Marriott International. This company offers its 130,000-plus employees a toll-free, twenty-four-hour hotline that offers help with personal problems, from finding affordable housing to locating childcare to responding to domestic violence and abuse. Marriott estimates that it saves nine dollars for every dollar it invests in the hotline; the savings come primarily from reduced absenteeism and employee turnover.

Marriott also offers Pathways to Independence, an innovative training program to help its people develop both job skills and life skills. It is aimed primarily at the low-skilled people who tend to comprise Marriott's housekeeping, maintenance, food service, and security staff, many of whom are making a transition from welfare to work. Though many companies shy away from the challenge of developing the skills and work habits of the chronically unemployed, Marriott has gained a lot of valuable insights about how to train, place, and manage people who traditionally do not do well in the workforce—and these insights have proven useful in better training and managing of Marriott's *entire* workforce. The result: while creating thousands of new opportunities for people coming off welfare, Marriott enjoys the benefit of a stable and reliable workforce, while offering customers the highest degree of service in the hotel industry.

Marriott's Pathways to Independence program works in concert with nonprofit organizations such as Goodwill Industries, the Jewish Vocational Service, and the Private Industry Council to find the participants for their training programs. The benefits are easy to measure. About 70 percent of Pathways to Independence grads are still employed at Marriott after a year versus 45 to 50 percent of new hires who do not go through the Pathways program. If the program graduate is still working at Marriott after eighteen months or so, Marriott figures it has recouped the cost of the program. In fact, Marriott does not consider Pathways to Independence a charitable program at all; it is treated as a trade secret, with the details of the program not to be divulged outside the company. Why? Because the program gives Marriott a *competitive advantage* over rival hotel chains.

Pathways to Independence may look like a do-gooder program from the outside, but for all the thousands of people this program helps, it does more than enable Marriott to *do good* in society. It enables Marriott to *do well* in the business.[5]

There is clearly a role for traditional charitable activity in business. However, many organizations are discovering that the social sector offers opportunities for developing the organization, training employees, and field-testing products. Society as a whole benefits, but so does the organization. These are not just the intangible benefits of warm-fuzzy feelings and a better corporate image. These benefits are reflected in the bottom line, benefits you can take to the bank. As Rosabeth Moss Kanter observes in *Harvard Business Review*,

> High-impact business contributions to the social sector use
> the core competencies of a business—the things it does

best. . . . The community gets new approaches that build capabilities and point the way to permanent improvements. The business gets bottom-line benefits: new products, new solutions to critical problems, and new market opportunities. . . . Today these examples are still works in progress. But tomorrow they could be the way business is done everywhere.[6]

Whatever your organization does, wherever it is located, you can be sure of one thing: There are plenty of social problems all around you — problems your organization can help solve. Donating to charity is the easy, short-term way to alleviate a problem and make you feel better. But your organization can and should do more than write a check. Relational Performance understands the need to do *more* than write a check and treat a symptom.

Organizations with good Relational Performance choose to get involved and solve root problems — problems that can be at least partially solved by aiding education, by strengthening families, by helping troubled youth, by promoting neighborhood revitalization, by moving people from welfare to work, by providing housing and opportunities for the poor, and much more. These are areas where your organization can have a powerful impact.

As Max De Pree, author of *Leading Without Power,* told us in an interview,

To me it is a great mystery that relatively few people in this world can have accomplished so much technologically, but we have been unable to share it effectively with the rest of the world. I just can't understand that. I can't understand why there aren't really good schools in Africa. And I can't understand why African villages don't know how to deal with their waste materials, they don't know how to find fresh water, and they don't know how to pump fresh water to every family. That is so elementary and yet we haven't been able to transmit that knowledge to people.

That was the original mission of the Peace Corps, but it never got off the ground, other than being a training ground for a few people. And there are other organizations in the world — missionary organizations such as World Vision — that are doing a good job improving conditions.

But you don't see these initiatives coming from the institutions and corporations that really have the wherewithal to make an impact. You don't see the business world looking at the suffering people in the world and saying, "Their problems are our problems." The greatest social force in the world has been business—yet business has done next to nothing about the social problems in the world.

I was talking with a CEO of a billion-dollar company recently, and he asked me, "Do you think we ought to be interested in India?" And I said, "Well, you know, I think you should be, but I don't think we are talking about the same subject. You are asking if your company should be selling its products in India, am I right?" And he said, "Yes, exactly." And I said, "When you ask me that question, I wonder what does India need from you?" And he looked puzzled and asked, "Like what?" And I said, "Well, do you ever wish you could be on the cover of *Forbes?*" And he said, "Sure, all the time!" And I said, "One of the ways you could get there would be to adopt an Indian village. It wouldn't cost you much at all. Just pick a village in India and give them a water system and a sewer system and build them a school. And then you could call up *Forbes* and say, 'How would you like to see a success story in India?' If you could do that, I guarantee you'd get the cover of *Forbes*. And think what would happen if a hundred other companies said, 'Gee, we can do that, too!'" And he said, "Oh, I don't know, I don't think we could do that."

Well, it was disappointing that he couldn't catch that vision, but we had a wonderful conversation anyway. And finally he said, "Do you think there is anything good we can do in *this* country?" I said, "Sure, I've talked to a number of people and I have a standard suggestion for business leaders like you: Why don't you open an innovative operation in South Chicago? You know, you've got all of these young men in South Chicago and . . . they have no hope. When you have no hope, anything is rational. If you don't think you are going to live beyond age twenty-one or so, it doesn't matter what you do; the most dangerous and irrational choices seem rational." He hadn't thought about that. I said, "A real innovation in South Chicago would be for you to establish a manufacturing unit that is also a school. And you hire only . . . teenagers and you make them go to school in the morning and you give them a job in the afternoon, and you'll turn the place around because what you'd be offering is hope." And he said, "Well, I don't think we could do that either!"

Now, why is his thinking so narrow in this area? One reason is because businesspeople have to be taught a new way to think. The business schools are teaching them to always think "return on investment," and ROI is always measured in dollars. But the kind of investment I'm talking about would also yield a rich ROI. Ultimately, it would return in dollars, because when you improve the lives of people, they become consumers for your products and services. But that should not be our motivation. As business leaders, we should care enough about the world we live in to invest in making people's lives better. That's an obligation we have if we are to simply call ourselves decent human beings.

De Pree is right. There are many kinds of return on investment. And no matter how much your organization invests, no matter what you put in, you and your organization will get back so much more. . . .
Guaranteed.

Small Organization, Big Impact

"But," you may say, "our organization isn't a big hotel chain or an oil company. We have a *small* business with just one or two outlets and only a handful of members. What kind of impact can we have?"

For the answer, let's visit an old Victorian brownstone on Sansom Street in the University City section of Philadelphia. It is the home of the White Dog Cafe, renowned in the City of Brotherly Love and beyond for its five-star cuisine as well as its social conscience. People come from miles around for the wonderful food—and they come again and again to attend a consciousness-raising event or to join a community service project. At least once or twice a week, you can visit the White Dog and hear a talk on U.S. foreign policy or attend a dinner to benefit a civil rights organization or join an Earth Day city tour and picnic.

The White Dog Cafe was born in January 1983 as a coffee and muffin shop on the first floor of the home of founder Judy Wicks. In time, the café took over more and more of the house. Soup and sandwiches were made in the residence kitchen upstairs. Dishes were hand-washed in a sink in the dining room. An outdoor grill was set up in the backyard (which meant that the chef had to wear a parka and boots during the winter months!). In mid-1984, the café was remodeled, and a complete indoor bar-and-grill kitchen was built inside. Over the next few years, the café expanded into two adjoining row houses, allowing the addition of more dining and kitchen areas.

Since then, the White Dog Cafe has been listed by Condé Nast as one of the top fifty American restaurants, and Judy Wicks has appeared on *MacNeil/Lehrer Newshour;* the café has also been written up by the *New York Times, Philadelphia Inquirer, Business Ethics, Ms., Newsweek,* and *Philadelphia* magazine. In 1995, Wicks was awarded the Business Enterprise Trust Award for creative leadership in recognition of her combined business acumen and social conscience.

The food served at the White Dog Cafe is multicultural American, with an emphasis on fresh, organic ingredients and a flair for originality. Wicks insists on serving only humanely grown meat and agricultural products grown in an ecologically sound way. Everything that can be recycled is recycled. Leftover food is collected and given to a hog farmer. Kitchen grease is sent to a company that uses it to produce soap.

The café's interest in promoting community awareness and social consciousness began when a few customers suggested to Wicks that she invite speakers to give breakfast talks. Originally, the idea was to give people something to *mentally* chew over on their way to work. The talks became hugely popular. Customers who couldn't attend the breakfast talks asked for similar events at later hours—an *aha!* moment for owner Wicks. Realizing that these talks could be good for drumming up business on traditionally slow Monday nights, she began the Table Talk series, which she promoted in her quarterly newsletter, *Tales from the White Dog Cafe.* Today, the newsletter promotes events that are going on all through the week. What's more, it regularly devotes space to recognizing customers who are making important contributions to the community.

Some of the programs and events sponsored by the café include:

Community service days. Once a month, café customers and staff team up on volunteer projects in the community, such as renovating houses or building community gardens.

Take a Senior to Brunch. Each Saturday, customers can either bring a senior adult or be matched with a senior patron, and both receive a great meal at half price.

Special annual celebrations. Noche Latina, Native American Thanksgiving Dinner, Dinner in Memory of Dr. Martin Luther King, the Gandhi Birthday Dinner, the Freedom Seder, and other annual events celebrate freedom, justice, and human diversity.

Table Talks. Several times a month, the White Dog Cafe offers a breakfast or dinner with a speaker and group discussion on such issues as children and parents, education, the environment, health care, government policy, socially responsible business ethics, and more.

Storytelling. Every Tuesday night, the café hosts a forum in which people from underrepresented groups in the community—senior citizens, immigrants, homeless people, ex-offenders, and so forth—are invited to share their experiences, followed by an exchange of perspectives and experiences with the audience.

Community tours. Café customers take a guided walking tour of Philadelphia neighborhoods, learning about the issues and needs in those parts of the city. Through these tours, people gain a new sense of connection with the community, plus ideas for ways they can get involved and help.

Child Watch Visitation Program. A local organization, Philadelphia Citizens for Children and Youth, hosts a breakfast with a speaker at the café, then conducts visitors on a guided tour of child and family facilities in the area, such as schools, shelters, parks, and juvenile detention centers. Again, the purpose is to show people how they can get involved and help the children in their community.

Community Wall Murals and Garden Tour. This annual tour focuses on the importance of mural art and garden areas in the inner-city community. It concludes with a luncheon with a guest speaker.

Affordable Housing Tour. Every year, the city's housing director conducts a tour of successful housing projects, focusing on cooperation between citizens, government, and the private sector.

Eco-Tour. This tour gives customers an up-close experience with environmental issues including clean air and water, energy conservation, and recycling.

In addition to hosting or cohosting these many events, the White Dog Cafe contributes one-tenth of all pretax profits to nonprofit causes. These contributions include donations of cash, food, and labor. Organizations that benefit from the café's generosity include Amnesty International, American Friends Service Committee, Business Leaders for Sensible Priorities, the Children's Defense Fund, Habitat for Humanity, the Humane Society, the NAACP Legal Defense Fund, and Witness for Peace.

"When people ask me what I do," says Wicks, "I often reply that I use good food to lure innocent customers into social activism. . . . The White Dog Cafe [is] a place of good food, good cheer, and good will."[7]

Any organization, large or small, can have an impact on the community around it; in fact, it must, in order to demonstrate Relational Performance. When an organization focuses beyond itself, when it gathers its energies and abilities, concentrating them on solving a problem, the relationships within it are strengthened; its code and values are affirmed; trust within it is deepened; and public respect for it grows.

Some people think that a business exists to make money—and we would never deny that. But is that all a business exists to do? That is like saying a human being exists to consume food. Fact is, a human being needs a higher sense of meaning and purpose for living than the next cheeseburger and bag of fries. Food is a means to an end; it's fuel to strengthen us for our *real* task in life, which is to make the world a better home for ourselves and our children and everyone else in the human family. As it is with food, so it is with corporate profits: Profits are a means to an end—not an end in themselves. As Charles Handy observes in *Beyond Certainty,* "To have survived is not, in my view, sufficient justification for a life, either for oneself, or for one's corporate community. To make that life worthwhile one must, I feel, have a purpose beyond oneself."[8]

It is our firm belief that successful organizations make money in order to make a better world. When that is the way we view our organization, then everyone in the community becomes a stakeholder in our enterprise. An organization that has no purpose beyond itself is not healthy. It consumes without giving back. It is a parasite—and a wide-open target for The Thing in the Bushes.

Final question: If your organization were to disappear from the community, would it leave a vacancy? Would it be missed? Would the community feel the loss of all the wonderful acts of service and caring your organization performed?

Or would your organization simply vanish without a ripple, unnoticed and unmourned?

A healthy organization is an organization that *matters* to the community and to the world. Does *your* organization matter?

Developing Code, Performance, and People

EXECUTIVE SUMMARY

A short, practical course on how to (1) develop your code, (2) develop your performance, and (3) develop your people.

Part 1: Develop Your Code

Step 1: Begin with an internal assessment. Conduct a survey with every employee in the organization. Follow up the survey with focus groups to help interpret survey results.

Step 2: Follow your internal assessment with an external assessment. Check out the marketplace and the competition to determine your competitors' strengths and isolate your weaknesses.

Step 3: Take your top twenty-five to thirty leaders off-site for a two-day retreat. Your goal is to identify issues, concerns, threats, ideas, and innovations that could significantly impact business in the future.

217

Step 4: Define your values. Areas of conflicting values are more important than areas of consensus or unanimity. Differences must be faced and dealt with so that the organization can move forward.

Step 5: Define your future. What is your collective vision of the future?

Step 6: Define your mission statement. Mission is an organization's reason for existing.

Step 7: Define your Champagne Moment (vision). A Champagne Moment consists of two parts: (1) a ten- to thirty-year "daring goal" and (2) a clear, bold description of what it will be like to attain that goal. It is a goal worth celebrating.

Step 8: Determine your strategic initiatives. Strategic initiatives are framed by values, mission, Champagne Moments, and desired future. They enable you to reach your desired future.

Step 9: Ask the group, "Is there anything we've missed?" There should be enormous energy and enthusiasm flowing through the group by the end of the retreat. If the energy isn't there, you've probably missed something.

Step 10: Define the next steps. Define who does what, where, and when.

Part 2: Develop Your Performance

What gets measured gets done. Use the LIFE Measurement and Incentive System to develop a business model for your organization. (LIFE is an acronym for Learning and Innovation; Internal Efficiency; Financial Success; and External Indicators.)

Too often, measurement systems fail because we have not taken the time to simply figure out how to take the measurements. After your assessment team has decided what to measure, sit down with the group and determine exactly how each measurement will be made. This includes a method for capturing and reporting data.

Create a baseline measurement for your organization and track your results over time. The data you collect will become the benchmark. Also, an RHO Factor Survey can provide benchmarks against TAG's national database. This "scorecard" can be linked to performance appraisals and compensation for both individuals and management teams.

When you implement LIFE measurements, you know exactly where you stand relative to your business plan. When you define those measurements clearly, the result is an objective way to recognize outstanding performance and pinpoint problem areas.

Part 3: Develop Your People
To provide developmental opportunities for managers and employees, you must organize the structure of your company around processes that maximize Relational Performance. You create a feedback loop of evaluation, measurement, and reporting so that the Relational Performance of your organization can continually grow. As Relational Performance increases, you see increased profitability and decreased turnover.

What makes a successful employee? Regardless of title, tenure, or experience, it is an individual's *competencies* that drive success (see appendix 1). Two key competencies that are especially important to the Relational Performance are (1) the ability to manage conflict well and (2) an enthusiasm for mentoring others.

Superior-performing employees are distinguished from marginal performers by competencies in three categories: values, traits, and motives (what we call *differentiating competencies*). An employee with these competencies goes the extra mile, demonstrates integrity and commitment, and is able to solve complex problems.

The Relational Performance principles provide the tools for renewing and transforming your organization into a highly productive, successful, and healthy organization.

One of this book's authors, Kevin Ford, cut his teeth in the business world selling the early Nike Waffle Trainer running shoe in a sporting goods store. That was back in the days when Nike was exclusively a running shoe company, and before anyone had ever heard of His Airness, Michael Jordan. Nike has come a long way since those days (and so has Kevin, for that matter). But the Nike people have never forgotten where they came from—their story and their code—and that is one of the reasons they have come so far.

When the average person thinks of Nike, they think of the swoosh logo, or the "Just Do It" and "I Can" slogans, or the superstar Nike endorsers like Jordan and Tiger Woods. But if you go to Nike's lush, wooded corporate headquarters in Beaverton, Oregon, and ask the Eniks—that's what the hard-core Nike geeks are called, the ones with the swoosh tattoos on their bodies (Enik is Nike spelled with the E in front, duh!)—they have a somewhat different sense of their own history, a different hagiography. The hallowed heroes of the Eniks are

- the late Bill Bowerman, Oregon track coach and inventor of the waffle-soled shoe;

- Nike founder and CEO Phil Knight, who merged his business acumen with Bowerman's visionary shoe designs to found a sports attire empire; and

- the late, great Steve Prefontaine, whose quest for a better running shoe inspired Bowerman's best shoe-designing efforts.

Prefontaine died in a single-car accident in 1975, never having won an Olympic medal, yet he is more revered within the halls of Nike than even Nike's superstar spokespeople. Pre, as he is known to the thousands of distance runners he inspired, was a brash, blond-haired prodigy who was coached at the University of Oregon by Bowerman. During his all-too-brief career, Pre set many U.S. distance records, competed in the 1972 Munich Olympics, carried on a raucous, rebellious battle with track and field's governing body, and single-handedly transformed an amateur pastime into a professional sport.

One night in 1975, Prefontaine drove away from a party at a friend's house in Eugene. He had only gone a quarter-mile when his sports car flipped over, ending his life at the age of twenty-four. It was a James Dean-like way to die, and it came at a similar point in Pre's career, just as he was ascending and proving his greatness. In death, Prefontaine became the James Dean of the sports world—a hero, a martyr, a saint.

His memorial service was held at Hayward Field, where he had trained so hard for the Olympics. His goal, never achieved but always before him, was to run three miles in 12:36—and that is exactly how long the service was scheduled to last. The clock at the end of the field ticked off the elapsed time of the memorial service, and as the golden moment approached, the crowd fell silent. At exactly 12:36, the clock stopped—and the crowd sent up a cheer, as if Pre had crossed the finish line and was going around once more for a victory lap.

Today, the new hires at Nike undergo the intense nine-day Rookie Training Camp, which includes paying homage at all the Nike holy sites. They are taken to Hayward Field and they run the same track where Bowerman coached and Prefontaine flew. They also visit the hill in

Eugene where Pre's life and career were cut all too short. There a stone marker to his memory reads, "You are missed by so many, and you will never be forgotten." Runners from around the country come to that place, leaving flowers, medals, and ribbons. It is a shrine to a saint— and Nike claims it as part of its heritage.

Rookie Camp is also where the minds of Nike newbies are drenched in the lore of Nike history. They learn about how Coach Bowerman invented the modern running shoe by pouring rubber compounds into his wife's waffle iron to create a cushioned running sole, and about how he experimented with different materials and cushions and designs—anything to give his runners an edge. He calculated that every ounce he could subtract from the weight of a shoe was a total of two hundred fewer pounds a runner would have to lift on his feet in the course of a race. His goal was always a lighter, more comfortable, better-cushioned shoe.

Nike new hires are also indoctrinated in the legend of Phil Knight, a middle-distance runner who was coached by Bowerman in the late 1950s and who teamed with Bowerman in the '60s, founding Nike and becoming the Bill Gates of runningdom. After graduating from Oregon, Knight pursued an MBA at Stanford, where he wrote a master's thesis claiming that low-priced, high-tech athletic shoes from Japan could topple the reigning industry giants such as Adidas.

Then, on a trip to Japan, Knight set out to prove his thesis. He contacted the Onitsuka Tiger shoe company and talked to the bigwigs there about huge untapped opportunities in the United States. When asked the name of the company he represented, he thought fast and made one up: Blue Ribbon Sports. Then he returned to the States, and with five hundred dollars of his own money and an equal contribution from Bowerman, they founded Blue Ribbon Sports. Bowerman came up with the designs and specifications; Tiger made the shoes; and Knight sold them.

In the early '70s, Bowerman and Knight founded Nike (named after the Greek goddess of victory, who is always shown running) and began producing their own shoes. They commissioned a design student, Carolyn Davidson, to design the Nike logo. She came up with the swoosh, for which she was paid thirty-five dollars. Knight quickly realized what an advertising coup it would be to obtain endorsements from world-class athletes, and Bowerman certainly had an "in" with U.S. record-holder Prefontaine. Shod in Nikes, Pre narrowly missed winning a medal in the '72 Olympics. After his death in 1975, Nike signed other stars of sweat, such as John McEnroe and Carl Lewis. Nike even had the foresight to sign Michael Jordan while he was still a college standout at

North Carolina; Air Jordan's continuing loyalty to Nike elevated the company's fortunes throughout his storied career with the Chicago Bulls.

Everything we've just told you about Nike can be recited by every person in the organization. This is not just the history of a company. It is its heritage, its legend, its heroes, its values, its meaning—in short, its *code*.

As Eric Ransdell writes in *Fast Company,*

> Nike has made understanding its heritage an intrinsic part of its corporate culture. Think of this approach as internal branding: The stories that you tell about your past shape your future. Which is why, these days, Nike has a number of senior executives who spend much of their time serving as "corporate storytellers"—explaining the company's heritage to everyone from vice presidents and sales reps to the hourly workers who run the cash registers at Nike's stores.[1]

Nike is an organization rich in code. The Nike legends, which are instilled into the workforce, are not just stories about the history of a company. They have mythic resonance. Nike has had its ups and downs in the marketplace, but it continues to dominate the industry. This dominance can be traced, at least in part, to the fact that Nike is driven by a distinctive culture built upon a distinctive code made up of distinctive heroes, legends, values, mission, and goals. Predictably, Nike's fortunes sagged a bit after the second and final retirement of Michael Jordan from the Bulls, but this latest dip in earnings will inevitably be offset by the company's enduring code, which will attract other winning spokespeople.

Human beings cannot relate to a cold, impersonal corporation, but they will eagerly, enthusiastically commit themselves to a code, a story, an enterprise of mythic proportions. More than any single factor in the life of an organization, it is *code* that drives an organization forward and enables a diverse and heterogeneous collection of egos and personalities to fly in formation toward a single goal.

As Nike training manager Dave Pearson observes,

> Every company has a history. But we have a little bit more than a history. We have a *heritage,* something that's still relevant today. If we connect people to that, chances are they won't view Nike as just another place to work.[2]

Part 1: Develop Your Code

THE PROCESS IS AS IMPORTANT AS THE PREMISE

In this concluding chapter, we are going to tie together all the themes of this book with a short, practical course on laying the foundation for Relational Performance. We are going to show you how to (1) develop your code, (2) develop your performance, and (3) develop your people. At the beginning of this book, we talked about the importance of an organizational code. Now let's look at how to construct a code for your organization.

Code, as we saw in chapter 1, is the core ideology and set of beliefs that we, as an organization, instill in ourselves and proclaim to the world. Our code shapes the culture of our organization and directs our behavior. It is the felt sense of the whole organization that each member carries within. It is a way of thinking, feeling, believing, and behaving—the collective programming of the minds of all members, enabling a diverse collection of individuals to act as one.

At key decision points, our code guides what we do, both as individual members and as an organization. Whenever we are called to select among an array of options, we simply consult our code and respond, *"This* is what we believe in. *This* is our purpose. Therefore I will reject *those* options and select *this* option, because it is the most consistent with who we are and what we believe."

A healthy organization has a consciously crafted code to live by. How, then, do we go about creating a code for our organization? What is the process?

You've probably been part of a strategic planning session in which the boss brings the ten commandments down from the mountain and presents them to his staff. What happens next? Almost invariably, a corporate shrug, a collective yawn—and everyone goes blithely on about their business. No one buys in. That is why we say, *The first rule of code planning is to involve as many people as reasonably possible.* Make sure every step of the process is inclusive.

Second rule: Set the ground rules. You'll need to clarify ground rules upfront. Define who gets to participate. Determine the decision-making method: consensus, unanimity, majority vote, and so forth. Are all participants considered equals? What happens if someone is late or needs to leave early? The process will go much more smoothly if these items are identified upfront. But you can't prepare for everything. In the event that the group hits a bump in the road, call time-out and ask the group if it wants to deal with the bump in the road or stay on task. Always ask for permission when changing the agenda. Here, then, is the code-building process, step by step:

STEP 1. BEGIN WITH AN INTERNAL ASSESSMENT

The first order of business is to conduct a survey with every employee in the organization. Make sure the survey goes beyond the typical employee satisfaction categories and includes many of the principles we've talked about in this book. You can do this yourself or have an outside firm conduct it for your organization. The survey results should help you determine questions for focus groups where you can tease out and interpret those results. Make sure that your focus groups have strong facilitators and that you have heard from each layer or department in the organization. Keep the questions fairly open-ended.

People in management often wonder in advance why they should spend so much time and attention on the opinions and observations of the rank and file, but we have found this to be a crucial step. Employees tend to be closer to the customers and the realities of the marketplace than management is. The people in the trenches often have a grasp of issues that elude those in the home office or the corner office, but people in management often resist this principle (understandably so; we always think our viewpoint is the correct one—that's why it's our viewpoint!).

Another reason we pay attention to the opinions and observations of the rank and file is that these people often feel they have never had a chance to offer their own input. Focus groups of five to seven employees allow for good interaction and enable everyone to feel they have been heard and understood. For the sake of open and relaxed discussion, focus groups should always be conducted at the peer level, not in mixed boss-and-subordinate groups.

To get things rolling, you may want to start with comments and questions about a recent event, such as a new program or initiative. This helps employees begin to open up. Then move to strengths and weaknesses from an external perspective. Ask the employees what they hear from customers. Don't offer much guidance at this point. The less directive you are, the better. They will be itching to get to internal issues, but you will build credibility if you listen honestly and openly to the external issues first. They will then feel safe to move into a discussion about internal issues.

As you begin discussing internal issues, recognize that employees tend to identify technical problems rather than relational network problems. As a result, you will rarely get to The Thing in the Bushes during this opening round of exploration, but that's okay. If The Thing is lurking anywhere near, this initial round of focus groups almost always gives clues to its whereabouts.

STEP 2. FOLLOW UP YOUR INTERNAL ASSESSMENT WITH AN EXTERNAL ASSESSMENT

In other words, check out the marketplace and the competition. This doesn't mean you let your competitors drive what you do. Instead, let *what you do* drive what you do, but also pay attention to changing external forces.

In our experience, it is often helpful to have the members of the organization spend an hour or two role-playing their competitors and how those competitors might strategize ways to put them under. This helps an organization not only to determine the competitor's strengths, but also to isolate its own weaknesses.

Every organization is vulnerable in some way to the threat of external changes: new competitors, changing customer demands and tastes, changing market demographics, technological advances, changing global conditions, and new government regulations. All of these factors have an impact on the way we do business, and organizations must be prepared to adapt to fluid conditions. Role-playing the competitor gets us out of our habitual mindset and enables us to look at the external situation with a fresh perspective.

STEP 3. TAKE YOUR TOP LEADERS OFF-SITE FOR A TWO-DAY RETREAT

In a comfortable, relaxed setting away from the pressures and ringing phones of the business site, people are able to use peripheral thinking abilities that would have been stifled in the office.

Most organizations are good at focused thinking. That is, they are good at dealing with issues that are ever-present and demand immediate attention. But the real competitive advantage comes from learning the practice of peripheral thinking: identifying issues, concerns, threats, ideas, and innovations that lie just beyond the outer edges of our daily lives, but which could significantly impact business in the future. Peripheral thinking doesn't happen when the urgent voices of employees and deadlines are calling for our immediate attention.

Even if your office has luxurious conference facilities on-site, it is best to find a place that is removed—or even remote. Then take your top twenty-five to thirty people there. The mountains, a lakeshore, a seashore—these are places of refreshment and reflection, where peripheral thinking is unleashed and creative juices can flow. Yes, you are there to work, but be sure to plan for lots of breaks, meals, exercise, and so forth to keep minds fresh and spirits alive.

STEP 4. DEFINE YOUR VALUES

Our values determine our purpose as an organization; they shape our vision and guide our decisions. Often, an organization's values have never been clearly understood or consciously delineated—*but that doesn't mean they're not there.* They cannot *not* be there. But if we do not consciously, deliberately define our values as an organization, our unconscious value system will *define us*—and generally not for the better. Our values will ultimately be exposed for all to see as a result of

- the integrity (or lack of same) of the product line;

- the well-being and satisfaction (or lack of same) among our members;

- whether we choose long-term excellence or short-term profits; and

- whether we refuse to accept an assignment unless it is truly in the client's best interests.

In the retreat setting, as you consider and discuss the values of your organization, a number of noncontroversial values and ideals will quickly bob to the surface. There will be little discussion or conflict over these values. Identify them, write them on the flip chart, and move on. But after a while, there will be silences between suggestions. Someone will suggest that a particular idea be added to the list of values, and that idea will meet with resistance. You may find that this is a sore spot with some people—and that these are areas of past conflict. Don't shy away from these issues; allow them to come to the fore where they can be openly discussed. Find out where various leaders in your organization exhibit opposing values, then discuss the conflict openly and calmly. The areas of conflict actually are more important than the easy areas of consensus in examining values.

When we worked with Southern California Edison Federal Credit Union (SCEFCU) in February 2000, we discovered that conflict existed at the management level. Most people in the organization assumed that the conflict was personal in nature, but in the course of our consultation, we discovered that it was really a conflict of values. When we helped the people at SCEFCU realize that they had never really defined their values—and that this lack of definition was the source of the conflict—a collective sigh of relief rippled through the organization.

Values govern decision making. When there is a conflict of values, there will be conflicts over decisions that are made and directions that are taken. Had the people at SCEFCU formulated a values statement? Certainly they had. But when they showed us the values statement they had developed several years earlier, we pointed out to them that the statement was safe, bland, and superficial. The values listed were such noncontroversial chestnuts as honesty, integrity, service, and so forth.

We pointed out that the people needed to dig deeper and think harder. They needed to do more work around areas of values *conflict,* such as leadership styles, employee empowerment philosophy, and the like. Once they did this, the issues were resolved—and so was the conflict.

When we facilitate a discussion about values, we usually break the entire group into smaller ones and ask the smaller groups to reach general consensus—and we define exactly what we mean by that. General consensus is not unanimity, but rather a critical mass of about 70- to 80-percent agreement. Some people don't like the small-group process; they prefer staying in the larger groups. But we've found that those who dislike small groups are the ones who are more vocal in larger settings. Small groups allow everyone to be heard.

We ask each group to select a facilitator and a scribe. This may seem as basic as dirt, but it is imperative that we pay attention to the process; clear ground rules are essential in keeping the group on task. After the groups have worked together and reached consensus, it's the facilitator's job to bring the groups together and identify areas of consensus.

Sometimes consensus is hard to achieve, and that's when facilitators need to be patient. Sure, it's trickier when there is disagreement, but all too often facilitators will avoid areas of conflict and try to paper over differences. This is a mistake. Differences must be highlighted, circled, and underscored. These are the areas that must be faced, discussed, and dealt with, boldly and courageously, so that the organization can move forward.

STEP 5. DEFINE YOUR FUTURE

What is your collective vision of the future? What would you—all of you together—like your organization to look like in five years? What should the future of your organization be in light of what you have already discussed together—in terms of your internal assessment, your external assessment, and your values?

When we facilitate a code-planning retreat, we use what we call the "Back to the Future" exercise. We have the entire group imagine that they are themselves, but five years in the future. The organization has changed and progressed in many positive ways. Now they move back in time five years to our own present time and tell us what the organization is like in the future. We have them describe several areas:

■ *Market profile.* Who is the primary market using the organization's product or service? Describe the demographics of the clientele in as much detail as possible.

■ *Products and services of the future.* They don't exist now, but they will. Consider the impact of the external assessment, changes in technology, consumer demands, competitive pressures, and so forth.

■ *Delivery channels and mechanisms.* How will the products and services be delivered in the future? (Who would've imagined in the late '80s the impact of the Internet on product and service delivery?)

■ *Pricing approach.* Will products and services be priced higher than market levels, lower than market levels, or on par with the market? Will products and services be bundled or priced separately? Will a customer's relationship with the company determine pricing (relationship pricing) or do we ignore relationship in favor of economies of scale?

■ *Marketing approach.* Describe the marketing approach by identifying the primary target clientele, examining their felt needs, identifying best points of contact, discussing how you will establish credibility, determining how you allow them to experience your product or service, and establishing the method you will use to close the deal.

■ *Organizational and internal development.* What new staff do you need? What new skills will your existing staff need? What does the RHO Factor Survey tell you to focus on internally? How healthy are the internal relationships of the organization? What new organizational structures or teams will be in place?

The answers to all of these questions are determined by a process of building group consensus. You will be amazed at how invigorating and energizing it is to create a tangible, concrete shared vision of what the future of your organization *could* look like.

STEP 6. DEFINE YOUR MISSION STATEMENT

This can take place before or after the Back to the Future exercise. A good mission statement should define what we *do*—and what we *don't* do. An organization's mission proceeds directly from its values. Whereas values encompass the principles an organization believes in, mission encompasses the organization's commitment to carry out those values. Mission, in short, is an organization's reason for existing. An awareness of mission gives members a sense of meaning and satisfaction in the performance of their duties, a point where we all can say, "Mission accomplished!"

How do you formulate a mission for your organization? We recommend what we call the "Three Rs of Mission": reason, result, and restriction. A good mission statement defines what the company does in terms of the *reason* for its existence; the *result* we hope to produce; and the *restriction:* the who, where, and when of it happening. *Restriction* means limiting the target, either to a particular region (such as North America), to a particular time frame (such as five or ten years), or to a particular target market (such as teachers). *Result* means that we hope to produce certain results for that restricted constituency (for example, to raise the standard of living or to provide assistance in education).

STEP 7. DEFINE YOUR CHAMPAGNE MOMENT

In chapter 1, we talked about the Champagne Moment, which consists of two parts: (1) a ten- to thirty-year "daring goal" and (2) a clear, bold description of what it will feel like and look like to attain that goal. It is a goal worth celebrating with champagne and confetti—a big, bold, exalted, inspiring goal. That moment of celebration is your Champagne Moment.

A Champagne Moment is daunting, yet compelling: simple enough for everyone in the organization to grasp and articulate; bold enough to be scary. A Champagne Moment is never vague; it is so clear and tangible that everyone in the organization will know and celebrate when they have achieved it.

Some organizations create vision statements, but we prefer that organizations focus their vision around a Champagne Moment. Vision statements tend to be bland and boring, and people often confuse vision statements with mission statements. But there is nothing boring about Champagne Moments. They are big and scary and challenging, but possible to achieve. When you break out the champagne, you know you've arrived.

STEP 8. DETERMINE YOUR STRATEGIC INITIATIVES

Strategic initiatives are framed by values, mission, Champagne Moments, and desired future. Once you have outlined those aspects of your code, you then define your strategic initiatives: the new programs you will initiate during the next two years that will enable you to reach your desired future (a new product line, a new ATM network, a new IS platform, a new series of innovative software releases, a merger and acquisition plan, and so forth). Strategic initiatives are big-picture initiatives. Most importantly, they are *new;* revisions of old programs don't count.

Once you've collectively identified and designed your strategic initiatives, prioritize the top 30 percent. Our experience tells us that the other 70 percent are either irrelevant or will be forced to occur because of the top 30 percent. Let go of the 70 percent in order to create focus on the really important strategic aims of your organization.

STEP 9. "IS THERE ANYTHING ELSE WE'VE MISSED?"

We often find that the group needs a final exercise to bring it all together: a name for the new direction, a strategy statement, or some symbolic representation of the code. Don't assume that just because you've gone through the exercise you now have a clear code. Probe deeply wherever there are differences or areas of conflict or tension. There should be enormous energy and enthusiasm flowing through the group by the end of the retreat (emotional energy and enthusiasm will shine through even the weariness that is inevitable at the end of an intensive session). If the energy isn't there, it's a tale-tell sign that you've missed something.

STEP 10. DEFINE THE NEXT STEPS

Before you leave your retreat—in fact, before leaving any meeting— always identify the next steps to be taken. Define who does what, where, and when.

Once you have defined your code, you are ready to develop your performance.

Part 2: Develop Your Performance

EVERY ORGANIZATION NEEDS A SCORECARD

"The financials look good, Paul," said Kate, the new executive vice president, as she scanned the pages of the business plan. She was a no-nonsense businesswoman with steely hair and eyes to match. "I assume you have some way of quantifying performance."

"Of course we do, Kate," replied Paul, the CEO, seated across the desk from her. He flipped the pages in his own copy of the business plan. "We've defined our performance measurements and . . . ah! Here it is. Page twenty, section seven, 'Performance.'"

"I see," said Kate, finding the boldface heading Paul indicted. She glanced down the column of type. "Have we hit these measurements by our target dates?"

Paul shifted uneasily in his chair. "Target dates? Uh, I think we've hit some of them."

Kate frowned. *"Some* of them, Paul?"

"Well," he gestured dismissively with a nervous smile, "it doesn't really matter. The board doesn't care about those intangibles—just the financials. That's all the regulator really holds us accountable for."

Kate's frown deepened. "Oh?" she inquired.

"Well . . . " Paul began, tugging at his collar. For some reason, his necktie seemed to be tightening around him like a noose. "I mean, sure, they look at management to an extent. But they are really only concerned with the financials."

"So these other measurements are of no consequence whatsoever," said Kate. "This whole section in the business plan that talks about Learning and Innovation, Internal Efficiency, and External Success— that's all a lot of hot air, right?"

"Well . . . " Paul gulped. "I didn't mean . . . "

"Let me ask you this," Kate began sternly, fixing Paul with a laser-hot stare. "Why would those 'intangibles,' as you call them, be included in the business plan if no one really cares about them, hmmm?"

Sound familiar?

All too often, organizations put together business plans that sit on the shelf and collect dust. And even when organizations work the plan, they often fail to measure any results but the financial ones. Why? Because there is typically no means of measuring and holding people accountable for nonfinancial results. So these results are often written off as "intangibles," when they are in fact the most important results of all.

The good news is that these results are measurable. They are tangible. And they are the key to improving the performance of any organization.

What gets measured is what gets done. If you want to build a successful, effective, high-performance organization, you need to be able to keep a performance scorecard—and you must be able to implement changes based on what that scorecard shows. We use just such a performance scorecard. We call it the LIFE Measurement and Incentive System. LIFE is an acronym for

Learning and Innovation;
Internal Efficiency;
Financial Success; and
External Indicators.

After you develop your code, you'll want to tie it down or operationalize it—and that's what the LIFE Measurement System does. As you review the LIFE measurements of your organization, you may realize that you've neglected an entire area in developing the code of your organization. Don't worry about the "hardening of the categories" or that your code is already etched in stone. If you need to, organize another code-building retreat to go back and change it, fix it, amend it.

After you've finalized your organization's LIFE measurements, you'll want to develop goal statements. Each strategic initiative should have a series of goal statements that assign personal responsibility to one person, a measurable output (usually taken from the LIFE measurements), and a deadline date for completion.

Goal statements should then be broken down into action plans—the clearer and more detailed, the better. At TAG, for example, we use Microsoft Project to break down our engagements into fifteen-minute tasks (at the smallest level).

If you are really moving into uncharted areas or if you are developing strategic initiatives that are a total break with the past, you'll want to build financial scenarios to support these new directions. We use linear regression analysis to build a baseline (linear regression analysis is a mathematical forecasting tool that makes projections based on the values of quantified variables). We project trends based on historical data, and this enables us to construct financial assumptions around strategic initiatives, which in turn enable us to create scenarios. We then contrast the scenarios against the baseline to justify our new direction.

After you have completed these steps, make sure you review your current business processes: what practices and procedures need to be changed, what can be improved, what can be eliminated, and so forth. Also, examine your organizational structure. You may want to take this opportunity to change that structure, now that you've identified a new direction. The entire process we've described—code building and defining LIFE measurements—takes about six to nine months in a healthy organization. If your organization accomplishes this process in a shorter period of time, don't assume that it's a good sign; it may mean that your process has been superficial and that something important has been missed. Don't hesitate to retrace your steps until your people have fully dealt with the issues, both manifest and hidden, that confront your organization.

Each step of this process may lead you closer to The Thing in the Bushes. Beware the process that goes too smoothly. If everything goes without a hitch, you're probably missing something. But if problems and resistance arise, then you are probably tracking The Thing right to its lair.

Implementing LIFE Measurements

Why do so many organizations struggle with nonfinancial measurements and accountability? Following are some common reasons. Which of these reasons apply to your organization?

1. Lack of a Well-Defined Business Model

Many organizations aren't really sure what to measure. A strong business model can illustrate what should be measured (how we view the business) and where to start creating change. The Relational Performance Method graphic on the following page illustrates a well-defined business model that incorporates the Relational Performance principles.

We typically view a business from the end point of the model (the organizational structure) because that is where our customers have contact with us. But a well-defined business model gives us an overview of the Relational Performance factors, code, processes, and structure of a business. This enables us to create change at the beginning with the code and an assessment of the organization's culture (the assessment can be made using our organizational assessment tool, the Relationally Healthy Organization [RHO] Factor Survey).

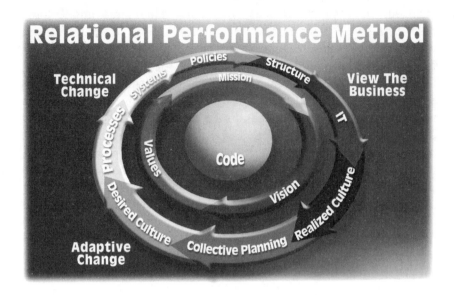

By developing a business model for your organization, you will be able to focus your measurements around the key variables that make up your core business and tell the story of your strategic plan.

2. Underdeveloped Methodologies for Taking Measures

Too often, measurement systems fail because we have not taken the time to simply figure out how we're going to take the measurements. After your assessment team has decided what to measure, sit down with the group and determine exactly how each measurement will be made. This includes the development of a simple, efficient method for capturing and reporting the data. (Your Information Systems department thinks about this stuff all the time. Get them involved.)

3. Insufficient Benchmarks

Because nonfinancial performance measurements are such a new concept, peer data is not readily available. We can all compare our return on investment against other organizations of our size, but what are the benchmarks for how many processes are reengineered annually? You won't find these answers published in a book, so it is critical to develop relationships with vendors, consultants, and other leaders from your industry so that you can ask these critical questions and begin to establish these norms.

In the meantime, begin by establishing a current baseline measurement for your organization. Then, over time, track your results. The data you create will become the benchmark. For many of these categories, the RHO Factor Survey will provide benchmarking against our national database.

4. No Linkage to Performance Evaluation and Compensation Criteria

The balanced scorecard approach must be linked directly to performance appraisals and compensation, or it will probably not work. Many progressive companies have tied performance measurement into the CEO's compensation, with overall achievement of the measurements constituting as much as 50 percent of base pay. Many companies reward the senior management as a team for achieving specified results. In team environments, employees at all levels can be motivated toward achieving organizational performance by linking measurements to team incentives.

5. Professional Resistance

It is not unusual to hear professionals say, "I've been here for twenty years. I don't need any measurements because I know what's going on in my organization." This attitude is perhaps the strongest indicator of imminent disaster. Objective measurements are valuable even for seasoned veterans who are accustomed to going with their gut. Measurements can confirm hunches—and correct misimpressions. If a professional is so certain that his or her instincts are right, then that professional should welcome having those instincts confirmed by objective measurements. While our instincts are often right, none of us can make good decisions without objective data. LIFE measurements give us that data.

Establishing Your LIFE Measurements

There are five essential steps in establishing your LIFE Measurement System. These steps should be taken in sequential order:

1. Define the organizational code. Too often, organizations establish measurements before they have set the overall organizational direction. It is crucial for board members, management, and employees to have a clear sense of where the organization is heading so that eventual measurement will make sense. If your organization has not developed a strategic plan (including a vision statement, values, mission, and specific strategic initiatives), an experienced planning consultant can help facilitate that process.

2. Involve the employees. LIFE measurements provide a great way to create ownership among the staff and help board members link the plan to the things they do in the board meetings. The board and management team can be involved in selecting what categories to measure, but employees should be involved in setting targets. This will create a sense of enthusiasm and support for the strategic direction of the organization by establishing specific expectations. When employees help set the targets—and the dates for achieving the target measurements—they tend to be involved, committed, and motivated.

3. Communicate the measurements. Elsewhere in this book we've talked about the 7-11 Principle, but it doesn't hurt to mention it again! Remember: communication experts observe that the average message must be heard *between seven and eleven times* before it really sinks in. In addition to your vision, mission, values, strategies, and goals, it is crucial to communicate the targets and measurements on a regular basis. Repeat and underscore those targets and measurements in staff meetings, memos, and e-mail. Don't assume that because you've said it once, it will be remembered. Make sure it's remembered by hammering it home.

4. Develop the system. LIFE measurements cannot be simply good ideas. In order to be effective, they must be an integrated part of the organization's systems. Monthly reports should show both the target and the recent history for each measurement. In addition, compensation and incentives should be linked directly to measurements. This will vary significantly by position, but each employee should have an opportunity to impact the measurements.

5. Review the measurements. Review the measurements with your management team. Do those measurements really capture the essence of the strategic plan? If not, what measurements should you change? LIFE measurements should be set for a specified period of time (such as annually), and they should be reviewed and updated. Some measurements will need to be revised to reflect future goals.

SAMPLE LIFE MEASUREMENT AND INCENTIVE SYSTEM

Below is an example of the LIFE System of an Armstrong Group client—a financial institution. This system includes a point system for incentive pay.

LIFE	KEY INDICATOR	MEASUREMENT	POINTS POSSIBLE	POINTS AWARDED
Learning and Innovation	Succession Plan	*Approved by Board	Approval = 1	
	More Depth in Positions	Reorganization & Dept. Assessment Tool Complete	Completed = 1	
	Business Plan Goals Implemented by Each Date	*80%	80% = 1 90% = 2 100% = 3	
Internal Efficiency	Internal Survey	RHO Factor Survey Score in Top 10% of National Database	Top 10% = 2 Top 15% = 1	
	Pay for Performance Throughout Org.	*Developed / Implemented	Developed and Implemented = 2	
	Annual Turnover	25% or Less	25% or Less = 1	
Financial Success	Capital / Asset	*7.5% - 9.0%	7.5% or Lower = 0 7.6% - 8.0% = 1 8.1% - 8.5% = 2 8.6% - 9.0% = 3	
	Loan / Asset	75% - 85%	Within Range = 2	
	ROA	*.75% – 1.0%	Within Range = 2 Over 1.0% = 3	
	Regulator's Score	2 (on a Scale of 1-5)	2 = 1	
	Fixed Assets / Assets	5% - 6%	Within Range = 1	
External Indicators	Customer Satisfaction	*Survey Developed / Completed	Survey Completed = 2	
	Product Usage Per General Account	4	2.75+ = 1 3.0+ = 2	
	Electronic Delivery Usage as % of Total	35%	25% or Greater = 1	
Subtotal				
*Subtracted Points				
Total Points				

Any measurement that falls short of the expected measurement (incomplete project, lower percentage, or lesser performance) will result in one point docked per measurement. In the unlikely event of a negative total point value, the total point score will equal zero.

LIFE Incentives

LIFE measurements should be used as indicators and measurements for your organization's incentive program. All employees and stakeholders benefit from the achievement of the measurements. The CEO should report LIFE measurements to the board and to the management team on a quarterly basis. Incentives should be awarded on an annual basis at the end of the calendar year. Before incentives are awarded, the board should sign off on any incentive given to the CEO. The CEO signs off on vice presidents or managers.

In the second year of this cycle, points are still awarded for any measurements completed in the previous year, provided the measurement hasn't slipped. Incentives are written in stone. Do not award them unless the LIFE measurements have been clearly attained. From time to time, measurement systems will need to be updated and reviewed.

The following table determines the incentive due to each employee at the end of the calendar year:

POSITION	TOTAL POINTS FROM LIFE SCORECARD	MULTIPLICATION FACTOR	PERCENTAGE OF BASE SALARY
CEO	_____ points	(_____ X 1.0)	_____ percent
Vice Presidents	_____ points	(_____ X .64)	_____ percent
Managers	_____ points	(_____ X .64)	_____ percent
Example: *M. Reyes*	*19 points*	*(19 x .64)*	*12.16 percent*

This financial institution scored nineteen points in its first year of LIFE measurements. Vice President Maria Reyes' incentive that year was calculated by multiplying the LIFE score (in her organization's case, 19) by .64, the multiplication factor set for the vice presidential level in her shop. Her incentive was 12.16 percent of her base salary. For the first time, Reyes and her colleagues were able to see precisely how they were doing against specific performance measures. End-of-year bonuses that once seemed to be decided on a whim were suddenly transformed into predictable incentive dollars based on objective measures.

When you implement LIFE measurements, you know exactly where you stand relative to your business plan. When you define those measurements clearly, the result is an objective way to recognize outstanding performance and pinpoint specific areas that are falling behind. By linking incentives to LIFE measurements, your organization will dramatically boost pride, sense of ownership, motivation, and team spirit throughout the management level, which adds up to a fine-tuned, high-performance organization.

New initiatives, new organizational structures, and new ways of thinking about your organization will naturally demand new skills and new habits for your members. That is why we have saved "Develop Your People" for last.

Part 3: Develop Your People

PERFORMULA—THE SYSTEM FOR SUCCESS

We use the RHO Factor Survey to determine the relational health of an organization. Then, as we saw earlier in this chapter, we also facilitate the development of an organizational code—a process that usually takes several months. The development of an organizational code includes focus-group research among employees and an intensive two- or three-day retreat with the organization's leadership team. The code is then reinforced through a software package we have developed called Performula, a streamlined and completely automated performance appraisal/coaching/compensation program designed to reinforce the Relational Performance principles in your organization and develop the relationally healthy habits of your people. You'll want to find a process that works best for your organization, but perhaps you can learn from the one that we use.

You can't change your organizational culture without providing developmental opportunities for your managers and employees. Once your code is reinforced by Performula and by people development, you redesign the processes in your organization to support the new relationally healthy culture. The last step in creating change is to reorganize the structure of your organization around processes that maximize Relational Performance. In this way, you create a feedback loop of evaluation, measurement, and reporting so that the Relational Performance of your organization can continue to grow. As Relational Performance increases, you see increases in profits, growth, and quality while simultaneously reducing unwanted turnover.

Bob Wacker spent twenty-five years in the Human Resource Division at Walt Disney World, rising from a professional staff representative to vice president in Human Resources. In his role, Bob was heavily involved in virtually every major workforce decision as his company grew from some three hundred "cast members" to over forty thousand. He was a key element in one of the most successful HR operations in the world. He is also president of RJW Consulting, Inc., and a consulting affiliate with TAG. Bob says,

> It has always been my belief that businesses which dominate their industries over the long term balance their financial, marketing, and human resources to the fullest. That is why the concept of Relational Performance is so solid. It really does make the difference.

Bob was one of the driving forces behind the development of the Performula software. He instituted a similar program very successfully at Disney and has seen such approaches work well at other leading corporations, including Glaxo Wellcome, Texas Instruments, Frito-Lay, Transamerica, Honeywell, and others.

The secret to Performula's success is that, in designing it, we looked at each company and asked the question: what makes a successful employee? Regardless of title, tenure, or experience, we wanted to know the competencies that drove success, not only at the individual level, but also at the organizational level. Some marginal employees do their jobs well, but superior performers impact organizational performance. Bob suggested that we look for competencies within five broad categories: knowledge, skills, values, traits, and motives.

For example, the skill of "opening an account" is an essential competency for a teller at Norwest Bank. The skill of "Visual Basic programming" is an essential competency for a programmer at IBM. But those skills are a dime a dozen, and we all know that knowledge and skills don't make a great employee. We've all seen employees who do their jobs well (knowledge and skills), but drive their team members crazy in the process, causing unwanted turnover or discord in their departments. Any organization can fill slots with bodies—including bodies of people who know their jobs and perform their tasks—yet many organizations that do so never seem to move forward.

In our study of successful companies, we noticed that superior-performing employees are distinguished from marginal performers by three factors: values, motives, and traits. An employee who possesses competencies within these three factors is an employee who lives out the principles of Relational Performance at the individual level. Because these three factors spell the difference between mediocrity and superior performance, we call them *differentiating competencies*. These competencies provide more overall value to the organization. It is among the differentiating competencies that we find employees who go the extra mile, who are thoroughly honest in their interactions, who demonstrate a high level of commitment to the organization, and who solve complex problems.

The initial beta test of Performula at SCEFCU in 1997 led Dennis Huber, CEO, to say,

> In the early stages of Performula, our organization is already experiencing positive cultural transformation. It's thrilling to hear employees talk more about how they can be a part of the organizational team, how they can better interrelate to others, and how they can really make a difference. The program has given specific definition to so-called "soft skills," which often make the biggest difference in the long-term success of our organization.

Key Competencies for Developing People

Developing the people of your organization begins with this fundamental question: "What kind of person do we want around here?" In other words, what are the competencies required by your organization to sustain and reinforce its code and maintain its performance? (See chapter 2 for a complete discussion of competencies.) Human resources decisions must be made on the basis of competencies such as traits, values, and motives, not just task-oriented skills or areas of knowledge.

As you hire for competencies, you begin to develop a culture around competencies — and that helps to produce a healthy organization. Skills have nothing to do with the relational health of an individual or an organization; competencies (such as "desires continuous improvement" or "empowers others" or "shows empathy") have *everything* to do with relational health. You can always train people for skills, but attitude is either there or it's not.

As we near the end of this book, there are two key competencies we want to focus on that are crucial to developing your people:

1. THE ABILITY TO MANAGE CONFLICT WELL

Conflict resides in every organization. Conflict isn't good or bad—it just *is*. Where Relational Performance is strong, people know how to conduct themselves in conflict situations so that a win-win outcome results. Here are the keys to managing conflict in a healthy way:

- Always face conflict squarely. Don't avoid conflict or paper differences over. Instead, face it with a determination to resolve it.

- Affirm your commitment to the other person. Let the other person know that the relationship means more to you than the issues.

- Come prepared to listen and learn. Be open to the possibility of being persuaded by the other person's perceptions and facts.

- Never attack.

- Never judge the other person's motives. Don't assume the worst; imagine the best. Give that person the benefit of the doubt.

- Be specific—don't generalize. Say, "I was troubled by the remark you made in the meeting," not "You're always so abrasive!"

- Always affirm in public, correct in private.

- If your conversation reaches an impasse, or if tempers flare, consider withdrawing for a cooling-off period, and agree to meet another time to try to deal with the issues more constructively. Underscore your commitment to the relationship.

- Whatever the other person says or does, stay in the Blue Zone (see chapter 5).

2. AN ENTHUSIASM FOR MENTORING OTHERS

The capacity to be a mentor is a crucial competency for Relational Performance. As management guru Peter Drucker once observed, "At the heart of everything I have done has been the thought of [empowering] others, getting the roadblocks out of the way, out of their thinking and their systems, to enable them to become all that they can be."[3] Spoken like a true mentor. Here are the keys to developing the competency of being a mentor to others in your organization:

- Always seek out and affirm the potential in other people.

- Find positive ways to encourage the people around you to continually improve and make positive changes.

- Share your knowledge and experience with others.

- Cultivate good listening habits. Practice patience, nonverbal feedback (eye communication, nodding, and so forth), and reflecting back what you heard the person say so that he or she knows you have heard and understood. Listen to understand. Many people are quick to give advice before listening, and they often miss the emotions and pain others feel. People need a good listener more than they need an advice dispenser.

- Always be aware of your influence on others. Whatever you want the people around you to become, you must be.

- Encourage personal development through feedback. One-on-one conversations, encouraging e-mails and notes, public recognition, rewards, and tactful constructive criticism are feedback tools that encourage growth and development.

- Tolerate mistakes. Mentors know that even failure has instructive value. Instead of reprimanding, encourage people to do better next time.

- Invest your time. You can't expect to invest in another person's growth and development without putting in the hours. When you invest time, you build relationships—and mentoring is first and foremost a function of relationships.

- Let the people around you know they matter. Let them know they are valued. As your people grow and develop, so will your organization.

Sturman Industries Revisited

As we close, let's take one last look at Sturman Industries, the engineering and manufacturing firm we visited in chapter 1, a Colorado-based company that is so relationally healthy, its RHO Factor Survey nearly shot off the charts. One of the reasons Sturman has such good Relational Performance is that founders Carol and Eddie Sturman have learned that relational health is more important than skills in hiring people and building an organization.

"We almost lost our Relational Performance a few years ago," Eddie told us.

> We had one employee who was technically very skilled, an extremely talented person. But he wasn't relationally healthy, and he became very toxic to our environment. Cynicism and dissatisfaction spread like gangrene throughout our organization. We challenged this guy and gave him every opportunity to change. He was not interested in change. He was looking out for himself before the needs of the company—and his attitude could have destroyed us.

> This was a hard lesson for me. I don't like to lose anyone. And nobody ever wants to leave us. Our turnover rate is less than 1 percent. But in this case, I had to be firm for the good of the company. Eventually, I moved this guy out and helped him find another job.

> It's easy to convince yourself to hire someone who has the right technical skills, even if they don't fit the culture. But I've learned my lesson. We use group-interviewing processes now. In fact, most candidates spend an entire day interviewing with no less than twenty people.

Carol Sturman, the company president, agrees that healthy relationships are the key to running a healthy business. She explains,

When we have visitors to our facility, we tell our employees to take them for a hike, to take them to dinner, to spend informal time with them, just having fun. We want our people to build relationships. Relationally healthy partnerships are critical to a Relational Performance company.

Part of building good relationships is going the extra mile for people—and our employees willingly do that. A client once called Dan Pederson, one of our outstanding employees, at home one night. It was late, and the client desperately needed a part. Well, Dan went into the office at 1 A.M., got the part, then drove to the airport. He waited until the airport opened and put the part on the first flight out. That's not something a big company will do, but we do it at Sturman because we care about relationships.

Eddie agrees.

The reason we care so much about relationships is that we genuinely care about our people—and they know it. They know they are not just valued for their skills or their contribution to the bottom line. They are valued as whole human beings—body, soul, and spirit. I mean that quite honestly: the emotional and spiritual well-being of our people is very important to us.

How is that caring demonstrated? Eddie gives an example:

Last Christmas, we had a party that was very moving. One of our machinists is Norm Steinbeiser, who is not only extremely talented at his job, but he is also a great teacher and mentor. Before he came to Sturman, he worked at a company that stifled talent and innovation. Norm is a bright, creative guy who loves people, but they wouldn't allow him to be himself at that other company. They had him in an emotional and spiritual straightjacket. He was dying every day on that job.

When Norm came to Sturman, he was amazed. He just couldn't believe that we would actually *encourage* him to be a mentor and a teacher, that we would actually *encourage*

innovation. He was amazed that we gave him all that freedom. Well, at the Christmas party, Norm's wife stood up,
unannounced. The group grew silent when they saw her
tears. She said, "I want to thank you. I want to thank you
for giving me my husband back." I've gotta tell you, we all
got a little teary-eyed at that point.

During our visit to Sturman, we were introduced to a young engineer
named Joaquin Velazquez. In 1990, Joaquin came to the United States
from Mexico as an illegal alien. He went back home and returned legally
to Los Angeles in 1993. There he met Steve Massey, an engineer with
Sturman (this was when the company was still based in Camarillo, up
the coast from L.A.). Joaquin couldn't speak English at the time, but
Steve offered to go to school with him and help him along. Joaquin
recalls,

I learned English quickly, and then I became interested in
science. I took computer and math classes. I told Steve that
my dream, ever since I was a kid, was to become an engineer. He coached me, helped me pick the right classes for a
future in engineering, and introduced me to Carol and
Eddie. We talked over lunch, and Carol and Eddie told me
that Sturman Industries is dedicated to helping people
achieve their dreams.

I asked them if I could work for them for a month for free.
"If I don't do well," I said, "I'll leave and you'll owe me
nothing. If I do well, you'll hire me." Well, they wouldn't let
me work for free, but they let me work on a trial basis.
Now I'm a full-fledged employee. I've learned electronics,
testing, and electromagnetic coils, and I've continued working on my engineering degree. This is a great place, and I
have a great life. I work about forty hours a week and I
take an hour every day to run and exercise. My wife also
works here, and she loves it. You have freedom to learn
and grow. The only limits are the limits you put on yourself.

That is a powerful statement about what it is like to work in a
healthy organization. People like Joaquin are the reason we have written this book. We want to see more people enjoying their work, living

productive and satisfied lives, and working in healthy organizations like Sturman. We want to see more people like Steve Massey who represent the values of a healthy organization by doing things like giving a life-changing hand to an immigrant who doesn't even speak the language. We want to see more employees like Dan Pederson who are willing to go the extra mile for the sake of a healthy relationship with a client. We want to see more people like Norm Steinbeiser who are set free from a suffocating corporate straightjacket and now enjoy the freedom to innovate, to mentor, and to enjoy their work and life. And we want to see more entrepreneurs and business leaders like Eddie and Carol Sturman who are building successful corporations out of equal parts business wizardry, ethical principles, and human compassion.

We've shown you the benchmark of all Relational Performance benchmarks. We've given you the principles and processes to transform your own organization through Relational Performance. If we can be of further help, just drop us a line, send us an e-mail, or give us a call. (The contact numbers and addresses are in the back of this book.) We'd be happy to talk to you.

Meanwhile, you have the tools; you have the knowledge; you have the motivation. Your organization is ripe for renewal and transformation. Just imagine the awesome possibilities within your people, just poised and waiting to be unleashed. The future belongs to organizations like yours. If you can envision it, you can make it real.

There's a Champagne Moment in your future!

APPENDIX 1: COMPETENCIES

Each of these competencies has been defined and linked to the "anchors," or specific behaviors, that enable you to distinguish those competencies in the members of your organization. This list was based on extensive research, including focus groups and surveys. Use it as a guide for developing your people.

COMPETENCY:	**KNOWS AND DRIVES THE MISSION AND VISION OF THE ORGANIZATION**
Definition:	*Understands the future picture of the organization and knows the process to achieve it*
Anchors:	1. Communicates the strategic vision and expectations to subordinates/team
	2. Recognizes opportunities that can assist in moving toward the strategic vision
	3. Participates in goal setting for the organization; participates in and manages goal achievement
	4. Contributes to, and actively participates in, the organization's strategic process and initiative implementation

COMPETENCY:	**IS MOTIVATED BY RESULTS AND OUTCOMES**
Definition:	*Is inspired and challenged by the completion of goals and positive outcomes*
Anchors:	1. Consistently meets mutually approved deadlines
	2. Demonstrates an appreciation for planning and goal setting
	3. Uses past success to inspire new success
	4. Demonstrates satisfaction in goal attainment

COMPETENCY:	**VALUES GOALS**
Definition:	*Appreciates and adheres to the timely completion of an objective*

Anchors: 1. Demonstrates an appreciation for the necessity of setting and having goals
            2. Uses goals as tools to achieve results
            3. Demonstrates an appreciation and respect for deadlines
            4. Effectively establishes action-plan steps to achieve goals

COMPETENCY: KNOWS THE CULTURE OF THE ORGANIZATION
Definition: *Understands the organization's environment and knows the process to support it*
Anchors: 1. Demonstrates an understanding of the organization's philosophy, mission, strategic vision, and business plan
            2. Shows an understanding of team decision making, communication methods, and participation
            3. Demonstrates an understanding of the organizational structure and interdepartmental relationships
            4. Displays knowledge of how to improve processes and procedures that result in a more efficient operation

COMPETENCY: EMBODIES WHAT THE ORGANIZATION IS ALL ABOUT
Definition: *Demonstrates an understanding of own role as it relates to organizational culture*
Anchors: 1. Demonstrates a clear understanding of the importance of own role in the organization's mission
            2. Displays knowledge of how own job tasks help accomplish organizational strategy
            3. Actions consistently reflect the values of the organization
            4. Helps to focus others on the organization's vision

COMPETENCY: IS A GOOD LEADER
Definition: *Instinctively steps forward to improve the performance of the organization by attracting people to follow her or him through guiding, coaching, directing, influencing, and empowering the human resources of the organization*
Anchors: 1. Initiates action, motivates others, and inspires people to follow the objectives of the organization

2. Sets a good example and exemplifies the vision and values of the organization through actions and decisions
3. Coaches, encourages, and assists others to utilize and improve their talents
4. Willingly addresses negative behavior and coaches to a positive outcome

COMPETENCY: **IS A GOOD TEACHER**
Definition: *Derives satisfaction from inspiring and motivating others to learn and excel through sharing and transferring knowledge*
Anchors:
1. Guides others to reach solutions
2. Willingly shares information
3. Is actively sought out by others as a resource for knowledge and motivation
4. Persistent in ensuring employees' understanding and knowledge

COMPETENCY: **IS A VISIONARY**
Definition: *Is stimulated by the possibilities and anticipation of the future and knows how to bring together the resources and elements to anticipate customer (client, member, patient) needs in order to organize, develop, and build a cohesive picture*
Anchors:
1. Finds resources and defines clear steps to make the future a reality
2. Uncovers all options and possibilities (including nontraditional solutions) relating to the objective
3. Demonstrates the ability to think and act on the strategic/scenario planning level
4. Takes seemingly unrelated information and makes a cohesive picture

COMPETENCY: **IS A MENTOR TO OTHERS**
Definition: *Fosters a relationship of development and positive change with others through concern, empathy, knowledge, inspiration, advice, and active participation*
Anchors:
1. Recognizes and develops an individual's potential; coaches and encourages others to make positive change

2. Approaches employees with an open mind and sensitivity toward the individual
3. Possesses an expertise that inspires others, and willingly shares knowledge and experience
4. Has a presence that makes others want to emulate him or her

COMPETENCY: **KNOWS HOW TO CREATE A PROPER CULTURE FOR THE ORGANIZATION**

Definition: *Knows what elements are needed to shape and exemplify behavior to build an environment that is consistent with the organization's values, beliefs, vision, and mission*

Anchors:
1. Demonstrates an understanding of the processes in each area of responsibility and how to relate to others in the work environment
2. Understands the needs of the organization and develops a profile for hiring. Identifies individuals who fit the organization's profile and takes appropriate action
3. Creates an environment through coaching that motivates employees to embrace change and continuous improvement
4. Establishes and clarifies service and problem-solving expectations

COMPETENCY: **DESIRES TO TAKE INITIATIVE**

Definition: *Identifies needs, "takes the bull by the horns," and follows through*

Anchors:
1. Steps in to assist when necessary and readily participates
2. Foresees needs and takes action to fulfill them
3. Ensures completion and follow-up when necessary
4. Demonstrates a take-charge attitude

COMPETENCY: **DESIRES AND COACHES CONTINUOUS IMPROVEMENT**

Definition: *Continually strives for excellence and quality in all tasks. Desires, coaches, and drives better results on an ongoing basis*

Anchors:
1. Looks for ways to streamline processes for efficiency
2. Consistently reviews results of efforts and initiates changes to improve

3. Consistently recognizes and rewards positive behavior
4. Encourages others to stretch beyond current standards and abilities

COMPETENCY: **EMPOWERS OTHERS**
Definition: *Gives up micromanaging by enabling others to achieve desired results*
Anchors:
1. Provides knowledge and resources to enable others to solve problems
2. Provides encouragement and feedback
3. Encourages risk taking
4. Manages results rather than processes

COMPETENCY: **COMMUNICATES EFFECTIVELY**
Definition: *Effectively discerns and applies a variety of appropriate communication methods to varying situations in order to understand and be understood*
Anchors:
1. Demonstrates effective writing skills and has a command of the English language
2. Adjusts personality style and/or communication medium to communicate most effectively to different audiences
3. Actively listens, asks open-ended questions, and genuinely hears what the other person is saying
4. Uses appropriate communication tools dependent upon the situation

COMPETENCY: **FREELY EXPRESSES IDEAS AND OPINIONS IN A PROFESSIONAL MANNER**
Definition: *Demonstrates the ability to communicate her or his point of view in a way that is respectful of others*
Anchors:
1. Openly provides information in group discussions
2. Knows how to express opinions and ideas in ways that are respectful of others
3. Knows when and how to listen
4. Offers useful advice

COMPETENCY: **ABLE TO MANAGE CONFLICT**
Definition: *When conflicts arise, is able to conduct self in a way that results in win-win outcomes for those involved*

Anchors: 1. Willingly faces conflicts with a desire to resolve them
2. Listens in a way that helps others feel understood
3. Reduces tension in situations before it escalates
4. Uses tact in handling difficult people

COMPETENCY: **SHOWS EMPATHY**
Definition: *Demonstrates an ability to understand and care about others*
Anchors: 1. Responds to another's feelings in a way that demonstrates interest and concern
2. Identifies nonverbal cues (for example, body language, tone of voice) to understand another's feelings
3. Encourages openness with active listening
4. Demonstrates sensitivity to others in a variety of situations

COMPETENCY: **WELCOMES DIFFERENT STYLES OF COMMUNICATION**
Definition: *Able to allow for a broad range of communication styles based on people's differences*
Anchors: 1. Demonstrates an understanding that individual differences result in different perceptions
2. Actively learns how others view things
3. Will consider many perspectives when making decisions
4. Makes use of a variety of communication styles

COMPETENCY: **MAKES CERTAIN OWN COMMUNICATION TO OTHERS IS UNDERSTOOD**
Definition: *Is proactive in assuring that own communication is received and understood*
Anchors: 1. Pursues responses to communication in a timely fashion
2. Asks questions to see if others understand what he or she says
3. Encourages others to ask for clarification about unclear communication
4. Is patient in responding to others' questions about her or his communication

COMPETENCY: **IS PROFESSIONAL**

Definition: *Projects confidence, a quality image, and business etiquette*

Anchors:
1. Establishes credibility with customers (clients, members, patients), supervisors, and subordinates
2. Displays refinement, character, and objectivity in action taken
3. Is polished and poised in appearance and action
4. Corresponds through letters, e-mails, and/or reports in a way that reflects the image of the organization

COMPETENCY: **DESIRES AND VALUES KNOWLEDGE AND LEARNING**

Definition: *Endeavors to satisfy his or her thirst for personal development to improve self and the organization. Willingness to retain and apply information and instruction for self-improvement*

Anchors:
1. Completes individual training plan
2. Willingly shares knowledge and experience with others
3. Takes specific steps to achieve maximum potential personally and professionally
4. Seeks, retains, and applies new information to job

COMPETENCY: **HAS A POSITIVE ATTITUDE**

Definition: *Projects the confidence that anything is possible and sees the positive opportunities inherent in situations*

Anchors:
1. Exudes positive body language and energy
2. Is optimistic (glass is half full) and consistently looks on the bright side
3. Works around obstacles by turning problems into challenges or opportunities
4. Builds on others' ideas and doesn't shoot them down

COMPETENCY: **DESIRES TO BE EMPOWERED**

Definition: *Is inspired by the authority and independence to take action or make decisions*

Anchors:
1. Welcomes opportunities to work independently and is confident in self to make decisions
2. Demonstrates ability to make decisions with minimal direction

3. Is not afraid to take initiative to act upon decisions
4. Demonstrates motivation to act on behalf of the organization

COMPETENCY:	**IS MOTIVATED BY EXCELLENCE**
Definition:	*Is driven to go above and beyond to achieve exceptional results for self and the organization and demonstrates performance that surpasses the standard established*
Anchors:	1. Looks for new opportunities to grow the organization
	2. Upholds and continually improves the reputation of the organization
	3. Looks for benchmarking opportunities and strives to be like the benchmarks
	4. Takes complaints seriously, corrects them, and solves underlying causes to prevent recurrence

COMPETENCY:	**VALUES QUALITY IN PERFORMANCE**
Definition:	*Believes in working toward the best, is conscientious, and exemplifies pride of workmanship*
Anchors:	1. Is accurate in completing customer (client, member, patient) requests (transitions orders, and so on)
	2. Follows through on customer (client, member, patient) requests in a timely manner and shows a strong work ethic
	3. Viewed by others as someone who does quality work
	4. Provides service above and beyond what is expected from a customer (client, member, patient) or coworker

COMPETENCY:	**DESIRES CONTINUOUS IMPROVEMENT**
Definition:	*Continually strives for excellence and quality in all tasks. Desires and drives better results on an ongoing basis*
Anchors:	1. Demonstrates thoroughness and organization
	2. Looks for ways to streamline processes for efficiency
	3. Viewed by others as consistently striving for quality above and beyond what is expected
	4. Consistently reviews results of efforts and initiates changes to improve

COMPETENCY: **IS ABLE TO HANDLE MULTIPLE TASKS**

Definition: *Consistently manages and completes several functions of work*

Anchors:
1. Demonstrates organizational skills (sets, obtains, and manages objectives)
2. Utilizes time-management skills to continually establish and evaluate daily priorities
3. Utilizes internal and external resources (for example, project management tools) to enhance work performance
4. Demonstrates a sense of urgency to complete tasks; meets approved deadlines

COMPETENCY: **KNOWS SPECIFIC JOB TASKS**

Definition: *Understands all of the particular duties, assignments, processes, and procedures necessary to fulfill responsibilities*

Anchors:
1. Compiles appropriate information to complete job tasks
2. Understands and follows the procedures necessary to complete job tasks
3. Follows specific policies necessary to perform job tasks
4. Stays current and helps support promotional initiatives

COMPETENCY: **VALUES ACCOUNTABILITY**

Definition: *Believes in taking ownership and responsibility for individual actions without providing excuses*

Anchors:
1. Accepts assigned responsibilities and stands by decisions made
2. Accepts responsibility for actions without taking it personally
3. Avoids pointing blame or "passing the buck"
4. Offers solutions and takes action through empowerment

COMPETENCY: **VALUES DETAILS**

Definition: *Strongly believes in accuracy and specifics*

Anchors:
1. Demonstrates an understanding and respect for precision and accuracy to achieve targeted results

2. Understands the value of "getting it right" the first time and consistently produces work with minimal errors
3. Seeks all necessary information to make good decisions
4. Minimizes errors through use of set procedures

COMPETENCY: **KNOWS SPECIFIC ORGANIZATIONAL OPERATIONS**
Definition: *Understands the organization's products, services, policies, standards, and procedures, with expertise (technical, communication, and departmental) necessary to perform daily tasks*
Anchors:
1. Demonstrates an understanding of the features and benefits of all products and services
2. Attends promotional and technical training
3. Follows policies as they pertain to products and procedures
4. Demonstrates an understanding of the general functions of all areas of the organization and uses the proper resources to find answers

COMPETENCY: **CREATES A PROFESSIONAL ENVIRONMENT**
Definition: *Demonstrates an ability to help others stay focused*
Anchors:
1. Responds to criticism in a professional manner
2. Is accessible to coworkers and customers (clients, members, patients)
3. Is supportive of coworkers' lives outside the office
4. Keeps a clear distinction between work and personal issues

COMPETENCY: **SEES THE BIG PICTURE**
Definition: *Has the ability to evaluate the wider scope of an individual issue or action and how it relates to the whole organization, and places a greater importance on the overall organization's welfare than on own role*
Anchors:
1. Visualizes long-term direction
2. Understands the relationship between various areas of the organization and integrates decisions with all these areas

3. Recognizes opportunities, products, and services that can assist in moving the organization toward its objectives
4. Recognizes the effect of external trends on the organization

COMPETENCY: **DEMONSTRATES COGNITIVE SKILLS**
Definition: *Has the ability to process information in order to form effective conclusions and judgments based on individual situations*
Anchors:
1. Listens effectively and asks appropriate questions when something is not clear
2. Makes flexible and informed decisions using analytical and/or logical processes
3. Learns from past experiences and education to make decisions for individual situations
4. Draws from appropriate organizational resources to find resolution to issues

COMPETENCY: **IS A CREATIVE ANALYTICAL THINKER**
Definition: *Takes an out-of-the-box approach in synthesizing information into a desired outcome*
Anchors:
1. Looks at all sides of an issue, gathers information, and reaches individual conclusions
2. Shows flexibility in approach, new ideas, information, and problem solving
3. Uses a nontraditional approach to achieve a vision or a goal and verifies the out-of-the-box approach through research
4. Demonstrates the tenacity to seek an answer for everything no matter what the limitations

COMPETENCY: **IS A GOOD DECISION MAKER**
Definition: *Achieves positive results and solutions to situations through a cognitive process*
Anchors:
1. Considers and weighs all available facts and understands the "big picture"
2. Is an analytical thinker who can bring together diverse opinions

3. Understands and establishes a desired end result
4. Is competent and confident in reaching appropriate decisions

COMPETENCY:	IDENTIFIES ORGANIZATIONAL PATTERNS OR PROCESSES THAT ARE UNPRODUCTIVE
Definition:	*Demonstrates an ability to always ask the question "Can we do this better?"*
Anchors:	1. Appropriately questions the effectiveness or efficiency of current work processes

2. Makes recommendations for process improvement
3. Engages others in out-of-the-box thinking to solve problems
4. Is able to identify relationship problems or emotional problems when they interfere with productivity

COMPETENCY:	IS FLEXIBLE
Definition:	*Is able to adjust to new or different circumstances through alternative ways of thinking and doing things*
Anchors:	1. Looks at different points of view, brainstorms open-mindedly, and accepts others' input

2. Maintains own opinions while considering others' opinions (knows when to appropriately maintain own opinion when in the minority)
3. Demonstrates willingness to work with alternative solutions, situations, and ideas
4. Validates others' views by affirmations

COMPETENCY:	DESIRES A CHALLENGE
Definition:	*Is stimulated by the opportunity to combine knowledge, skills, and resources to meet objectives requiring special effort*
Anchors:	1. Recognizes a need for improvement, sees problems as opportunities or challenges, and provides options for solutions

2. Takes initiative to turn a negative situation around and faces resistance with a win-win approach
3. Follows through to reach desired results
4. Readily participates in figuring out complex issues

COMPETENCY: **IS ABLE TO THINK ON OWN FEET**

Definition: *Has the ability to make sound decisions quickly and confidently, given new information or challenges*

Anchors:
1. Requires little or no supervision in making decisions
2. Is comfortable, calm, and confident in ability to deal with things as they are presented, even under pressure
3. Demonstrates a sense of urgency to complete tasks and meet approved deadlines
4. Is flexible to change decision when the situation demands it

COMPETENCY: **VALUES INNOVATION**

Definition: *Demonstrates the importance of change by encouraging risk taking*

Anchors:
1. Willingly asks others how to improve something
2. Is enthusiastic toward ideas shared by others
3. Freely shares new ideas for change
4. Offers suggestions when others seek improvement

COMPETENCY: **KNOWS THE COMPETITION**

Definition: *Knows the products and services offered by the competition in order to position the organization's products and services as superior*

Anchors:
1. Demonstrates an understanding of who the competition is, including benefits and features
2. Shows knowledge of the products, services, pricing, and marketing efforts of competitors
3. Effectively brings in new business by asking probing questions about competitor products and services in order to educate the customer (client, member, patient) and discover differentiating factors
4. Demonstrates knowledge of promotional efforts made by competitive organizations and uses information to formulate a competitive offer

COMPETENCY: **DEMONSTRATES CROSS-FUNCTIONALITY**

Definition: *Is willing to apply his or her knowledge and skills to different jobs*

Anchors:
1. Demonstrates a willingness to learn job functions that are distinct from the original job responsibility

2. Volunteers to learn or perform different functions within the organization
3. Encourages others to learn different job functions within the organization
4. Participates in training other employees

COMPETENCY: **IS DEPENDABLE**

Definition: *Believes in and has the characteristics of unfailing reliability and trustworthiness*

Anchors:
1. Has a good attendance record
2. Is responsible in use of breaks and lunchtime, and is reliably punctual
3. Follows through on assignments given, gets the job done, and consistently meets expectations and deadlines
4. Avoids making and taking personal phone calls

COMPETENCY: **DEMONSTRATES AND VALUES PRODUCTIVITY**

Definition: *Believes in contributing significant results in his or her performance through the efficient use of time*

Anchors:
1. Uses time-management skills to establish, organize, and prioritize activities
2. Meets established standards
3. Provides suggestions to improve the efficiency of performing job tasks
4. Produces measurable results

COMPETENCY: **DEMONSTRATES INTEGRITY**

Definition: *Takes personal responsibility to protect the viability of the organization through statements and actions that are trustworthy, honest, and credible*

Anchors:
1. Demonstrates open, direct communication
2. Is viewed, and pursued, as a reliable source by others
3. Makes a commitment and follows through
4. Is trusted to do the right thing

COMPETENCY: **IS A TEAM PLAYER**

Definition: *Demonstrates the belief that working with others, welcoming contributions from others, positively participating, and enjoying the resulting synergy will achieve the best results*

Anchors: 1. Does her or his fair share and carries own workload
2. Puts the team first and self second (consistently offers to help and shows a willingness to change for the greater good)
3. Actively participates in (or leads) group meetings and/or committees and gains consensus in decision making
4. Accepts constructive criticism

COMPETENCY: **BUILDS ORGANIZATIONAL TRUST**
Definition: *Demonstrates pride in the organization and understands that his or her behavior is a reflection on the organization*
Anchors: 1. Keeps personal and organizational confidences when appropriate
2. Speaks only in professional terms about other employees
3. When evaluating others, gives feedback based on objective criteria in a timely, professional manner
4. Keeps others in organization informed of relevant data

COMPETENCY: **DESIRES AND VALUES SERVING OTHERS**
Definition: *Compelled to assist others to improve knowledge and performance in any way possible*
Anchors: 1. Regularly shares and contributes expertise, knowledge, and information
2. Makes time available to assist others
3. Recognizes critical business or individual needs and responds with appropriate assistance in a timely manner
4. Helps others help themselves

COMPETENCY: **KNOWS CUSTOMER/EMPLOYEE NEEDS**
Definition: *Can identify and discern external/internal customer/employee unique needs through utilizing appropriate resources and questions*
Anchors: 1. Listens carefully and comprehensively to external/internal customer/employee needs and clarifies them

2. Evaluates external/internal customer/employee needs and suggests products and services to meet them
3. Asks open-ended questions to uncover additional needs or information
4. Fulfills external/internal customer/employee needs by utilizing all available communication methods and internal/external resources, when appropriate

COMPETENCY: **IS MOTIVATED BY SATISFYING EXTERNAL/INTERNAL CUSTOMER/EMPLOYEE**

Definition: *Is driven by fulfilling and exceeding external/internal customer/employee needs and expectations*

Anchors:
1. Shows enthusiasm in serving the external/internal customer/employee
2. Analyzes external/internal customer/employee needs to recommend the best end result; digs for a creative solution
3. Provides resolution to external/internal customer/employee complaints in a professional and timely manner
4. Knows, understands, and applies the vision of the organization to his or her job

COMPETENCY: **DEMONSTRATES SERVICE SKILLS TO EXTERNAL/INTERNAL CUSTOMER/EMPLOYEE**

Definition: *Has the ability to exemplify consistent service standards set by the organization*

Anchors:
1. Performs established telephone etiquette and handles interruptions professionally
2. Follows the dress code
3. Delivers prompt, friendly, and courteous service to external/internal customer/employee
4. Successfully turns a problem or complaint into a positive outcome

COMPETENCY: **DEMONSTRATES SALES SKILLS**

Definition: *Has the ability to exemplify consistent sales practices as set by the organization*

Anchors:
1. Satisfactorily completes sales training program

2. Establishes good rapport with customers (clients, members, patients) by greeting them, acknowledging them, and responding to their requests effectively
3. Uncovers customer (client, member, patient) needs and cross-sells appropriate services
4. Effectively asks for the business and closes the sale

COMPETENCY: **DEMONSTRATES AND COACHES SERVICE SKILLS**
Definition: *Has the ability to exemplify and coach consistent service standards set by the organization*
Anchors:
1. Coaches others to perform established telephone etiquette and handle interruptions professionally
2. Coaches others to follow the dress code
3. Coaches others to deliver prompt, friendly, and courteous service to internal/external customers (clients, members, patients)
4. Coaches others to successfully turn a problem or complaint into a positive outcome

COMPETENCY: **KNOWS FACTORS IMPACTING THE ORGANIZATION'S INDUSTRY**
Definition: *Has the ability to understand and interpret environmental factors and forecast their effect on the organization*
Anchors:
1. Demonstrates an understanding of the competition by product
2. Applies the impact of environmental trends to the plans of the organization
3. Researches and analyzes economic information that impacts the organization
4. Asks probing questions about competitor products and services, and discovers differentiating factors in order to educate the staff

COMPETENCY: **VALUES THE SALES CULTURE**
Definition: *Demonstrates an understanding of the importance of promoting the organization*
Anchors:
1. Is supportive of the organization's promotion initiatives
2. Is enthusiastic about promoting the organization

3. Offers positive suggestions and ideas that may improve promoting
4. Understands that her or his behavior outside the organization is a form of promoting

COMPETENCY: **DEMONSTRATES ADMINISTRATIVE SKILLS**
Definition: *Has the ability to perform multiple daily tasks through the use of appropriate or professionally driven resources, technological tools, and general academic knowledge*
Anchors:
1. Demonstrates proficiency and continual improvement in computer skills and online systems
2. Draws upon education, peers, external resources, and experience to perform job duties above and beyond established standards
3. Identifies, accesses, and uses resources to coordinate all aspects of the job
4. Uses time-management skills to establish priorities and meet deadlines

COMPETENCY: **DEMONSTRATES BASIC SYSTEMS SKILLS**
Definition: *Can understand, develop, and utilize systems to increase the effectiveness and efficiency of the organization*
Anchors:
1. Competent in the PC and software skills needed for the job
2. Competent in the in-house core data processing system needed for the job
3. Competent in use of office equipment needed for the job
4. Follows established operational processes

COMPETENCY: **KNOWS HOW TO DEVELOP NEW PRODUCTS AND SERVICES**
Definition: *Has the ability to analyze, organize, and apply information necessary to create and engineer new products and services based on changing customer (client, member, patient) needs*
Anchors:
1. Demonstrates a knowledge of the competition and competitive factors

2. Gathers and quantifies requests and feedback to understand and recognize the needs of the customer (client, member, patient) or employees
3. Analyzes information and develops an implementation plan
4. Provides research through the use of a variety of resources

APPENDIX 2: ORGANIZATIONS MENTIONED IN THIS BOOK

The stories we tell in this book are true case histories. In most cases, we have used the actual names of organizations and individuals. In a few cases, we have disguised the identity of organizations and individuals (including changing some inconsequential details of the story) in order to respect their privacy. We have tried to make it clear in the text which are actual names and which are fictitious names. For the sake of clarity and accuracy, the following is a list of the companies and individuals we have profiled (both actual names and fictitious names), listed in alphabetical order.

Actual Organizations and Individuals

American Express Financial Advisors (Prologue)
Amerman, John (chapter 2)
Blackboard, Inc. (chapter 1)
Bell Atlantic (chapter 9)
Cahill, Doug (chapter 3)
Cardiovascular Group of Northern Virginia (chapter 8)
Carlzon, Jan (chapter 7)
DiCicco, Tony (chapter 2)
Disney, Walt (chapter 1)
Dutch Shell (chapters 1 and 9)
Fel-Pro (chapter 9)
Ford Motor Company (chapters 1, 2, and 8)
Gymboree Corporation (chapter 2)
Hubka, Rachel (chapter 3)
IBEW Plus Credit Union (chapter 2)
Kelleher, Herb (chapter 1)
Marriott International (chapter 9)
Mattel Toys (chapter 2)
McKay Nursery Company (chapter 9)

Merck & Company (chapter 9)
Nike (Epilogue)
North, Carol (chapter 1)
Olin (chapter 3)
Park Meridian Bank (chapters 2 and 9)
Rhodes, Charles "Rocky," of MyCFO (chapter 2)
Scandinavian Airlines (chapter 7)
Southern California Edison Federal Credit Union (Epilogue)
Southwest Airlines (chapters 1 and 2)
Silicon Graphics, Inc. (chapter 2)
Starbucks Corporation (chapters 8 and 9)
Stewart Bus Company (chapter 3)
Sturman Industries (chapters 1, 2, and Epilogue)
Sturman, Eddie and Carol (chapters 1, 2, and Epilogue)
U.S. Army Corps of Engineers Trans-Atlantic Center (chapter 5)
Vermont National Bank (chapter 9)
Westinghouse Steam Turbine Division (chapter 7)
Westinghouse Synthetic Fuels Division (chapter 7)
Wicks, Judy (chapter 9)
Williams, Pat (chapter 4)
White Dog Cafe (chapter 9)
Zeneca Ag Products (chapter 3)

Fictitious Names

Greenlake Savings Bank (chapter 3)
Hughes, Patrick (chapter 5)
Jenkins, Heloise (chapter 2)
Larsen, Don (chapter 3)
Metrolink magazine (chapter 4)
National Association of Occupational and Environmental Physicians
    (chapter 2)
Oliver, McKenna & Smith (Prologue)
Snoozewell Mattress Company (chapter 6)
Sleepytime Spring Company (chapter 6)
Washburn, Emily (chapter 7)
ZIP (chapter 5)

Appendix 3: Culture Type Indicator (CTI)

Please Understand . . . Organizations Have Personalities, Too!

Have you ever taken one of those work preference tests? They can be extremely helpful in understanding your preferred work environments, tasks, motivating factors, and interactions with others. The Myers-Briggs Type Indicator, Predictive Index, the DISC assessment, and so forth help us understand each other and work together better. But did you know that an organization has a personality as well? That's right, work preferences and personalities aren't limited to individuals. In our research at TAG, we have discovered that every organization has its own unique personality and that understanding this personality, or culture type, is critical to organizational success. Understanding your culture type will help you hire the right "fit," train to produce desired outcomes, and manage conflict much more effectively.

For example, innovative companies tend not to be efficient. Think of 3M. Eighty percent of its products never make it to market. Ad agencies persistently miss deadlines. Songwriters, artists, and writers often spend weeks or months without producing anything substantial. Creativity and efficiency are at opposite ends of the spectrum. A creative culture type often means that choices around efficiency must be secondary.

Likewise, efficient businesses tend not to be very creative. When was the last time you were served a creative or unusual dish at a fast food restaurant? How many times do you think a surgeon has said, "Let's insert the scalpel from a different place today?" An efficiency culture type usually means that when push comes to shove, efficiency is more important than creativity.

Unfortunately, most organizations haven't taken the time to understand their own culture type. At TAG, we developed an instrument called the TAG CTI (Culture Type Indicator) to help organizations understand their culture type. The TAG CTI measures employee perceptions regarding the culture of your organization in four primary quadrants: authority, strategy, social groupings, and motivational orientation (see below). Each of these quadrants is represented by a continuum.

AUTHORITY	STRATEGY
Vertical/Horizontal	Innovative/Efficient
SOCIAL GROUPINGS	MOTIVATIONAL ORIENTATION
Solo/Team	Journey/Destination

The authority quadrant deals with questions of the sharing or holding of decision making, power, control, and the distance between layers in the organization. The strategy quadrant relates to issues of strategic direction and daily operations. It relates to competitive advantage and the development of products and services. The social groupings quadrant speaks of the interactions of people within the organization: is teamwork critical, or is it okay for people to act as solo agents? The motivation quadrant relates to the ultimate purpose or mission of the organization: is it primarily bottom-line oriented, or is its existence more related to ongoing processes?

The TAG Culture Type Indicator (CTI) Sample

In the charts on the next pages, please select the statement that most accurately reflects your opinion of your organization as it is presently. You may only select one statement for each pair of statements by placing a check mark next to the statement that you believe is most accurate in reflecting the current beliefs in your organization. This is provided as a self-scoring sample for you to assess your organizational type.

AUTHORITY QUADRANT

	VERTICAL	✔	HORIZONTAL	✔
1	There is a rightful place and order in our organization.		There is a lot of flexibility in our organization.	
2	We have some very strong leaders who make most of the key decisions.		Most people in this organization are involved in key decisions.	
3	Most people in this organization follow directions well.		Most people in this organization figure out their own way to accomplish a task.	
4	Chain of command is very important around here.		Teamwork is very important around here.	
5	Our leaders have a lot more responsibility on their shoulders than other employees.		Most staff generally share the responsibility of the organization.	
6	Our organization has many levels of authority from the top to the bottom.		Our organization has very few levels of authority.	
7	Our leaders expect staff only to approach them with really significant issues.		Our leaders solicit and utilize employees' ideas.	
8	Most staff have a clear understanding of what they can and can't do around here.		Most staff push the edge of the envelope and are empowered to make decisions.	
9	Our organization has job descriptions that fairly accurately reflect a person's duties.		Our organization has job descriptions that rarely reflect a person's duties.	
10	A good way to describe our organization is "vertical and hierarchical."		A good way to describe our organization is "horizontal and flat."	
TOTAL				

Total the number of check marks for the
left column and the right column.

If you scored high on the left column: Vertical Authority (examples: military, assembly lines, courts).

Vertical authority works best in organizations where quick decisions from the top need to be disseminated throughout the ranks as quickly as possible with very little questioning or deviation. This works well in environments where tasks rarely change.

There is a rightful place and order in your organization, where a few very strong leaders make most of the key decisions. Most people in your organization follow directions well.

Chain of command is very important, and leaders tend to carry the majority of the responsibilities. Your organization is multilayered, with key leaders sitting at the top.

Most staff members have a clear understanding of what they can and can't do. Job descriptions are probably fairly detailed and accurate in governing employee roles and responsibilities.

Potential downsides include the lack of subordinate ownership or buy-in to decisions. Subordinates will be motivated to climb the ladder. If they can't climb the ladder, they may either leave the organization or become overly compliant. Change in your organization can be impeded due to bureaucracy.

If you scored high on the right column: Horizontal Authority (examples: start-up companies, high-tech firms, partnerships).

Horizontal authority works best in organizations where employees need to buy in or "own" new ideas, processes, products, or services. It is most useful in organizations that require constant flexibility and adaptation to changing external conditions.

There is a lot of flexibility and teamwork in your organization. Most staff members are involved in key decisions, and then they each tend to figure out their own way to accomplish a task. Responsibility is fairly evenly distributed across minimal layers. Leaders are visibly involved with the staff. Job descriptions tend to be erroneous, because most employees find themselves taking on different roles and tasks almost on a daily basis.

The potential downside to horizontal authority revolves around stability. The constant flux of this kind of organization will make it difficult for leaders to make definitive decisions and expect them to be uniformly adopted by all. Employees will be used to the consensus decision-making model. This could actually hinder speed and organizational flexibility for short-term changes.

STRATEGY QUADRANT

	INNOVATIVE	✓	EFFICIENT	✓
11	Our daily routine can be very unstructured.		Our daily routine is governed by well-documented processes and procedures.	
12	We are usually pretty laid back around here.		We are usually very focused around here.	
13	Mistakes are all part of the game in our organization.		Mistakes are closely monitored and kept to a minimum.	
14	It's okay to pave your own path around here.		It's important to follow procedures closely around here.	
15	Creativity is very important.		Efficiency is very important.	
16	We strive for innovation.		We strive for improvement.	
17	It is important to develop new products, services, or programs.		It is important to ensure quality standards on existing products, services, or programs.	
18	We are on the cutting edge in our industry.		We are appropriately conservative in our industry.	
19	Tasks tend to change very frequently.		Tasks usually tend to stay consistent.	
20	We do what it takes to succeed, regardless of the expense.		We strive to reduce expenses in order to succeed.	
TOTAL				

Total the number of check marks for the
left column and the right column.

If you scored high on the left column: Innovative Strategy (examples: ad agencies, fine restaurants, software developers).

If your organization scored high on this quadrant, it means that you probably rely on staying ahead of the curve in new products, services, and delivery channels as a means to accomplishing your goals. This works well when efficiency is not hugely important. A high score could indicate that your organization is in a start-up mode, is in the midst of a major transition, or relies heavily on innovation.

Chaos is a normal part of your daily routine, and mistakes are tolerated as part of the game. Employees think it's okay to pave their own path, as long as they are being creative. You generally think it's important to develop new products, services, or programs to stay on the cutting edge in your industry. Tasks tend to change very frequently, and success is more important than cutting costs.

You may have a difficult time with stabilizing processes and procedures. New initiatives will routinely keep expenses fairly high. Unless you are incredibly successful, talented staff may look for newer and better opportunities along the way. Turnover will be high unless talent and performance are truly rewarded.

If you scored high on the right column: Efficient Strategy (examples: operating rooms, air traffic controllers, fast food restaurants).

If your organization scored high on the efficiency scale, you are more concerned with quality, speed, and efficiency to produce the results you are looking for. Your organization has a tendency to standardize as much as it possibly can. Efficiency is incredibly important in organizations where mistakes can be costly (or even deadly), such as air traffic control, banking, and health care. A high score in this area may also indicate a company that has been around for a while and has had time to stabilize processes (sometimes even in innovative environments).

Your daily routine is governed by processes and procedures that rarely change. Stress levels can be fairly high if potential mistakes are unacceptable. It is important to follow procedures precisely in order to be efficient. Once an employee learns a task, the task rarely changes, but the process may be continually improved.

Efficiency can be boring for creative employees. It is important to allow them to suggest improvements to processes and procedures. Efficiency may inhibit the organization's ability to develop new products and services. A focus on efficiency may also create a lack of forward thinking.

SOCIAL GROUPINGS QUADRANT

	SOLO	✓	TEAM	✓
21	Our organization is a loosely knit group of individuals.		Our organization is a team where individuals have interactive roles.	
22	People are free to make decisions on their own.		People make decisions in consensus with others.	
23	Achievement is valued most by people in this organization.		Relationships are valued most by people in this organization.	
24	Most people in our organization work independently.		Most people in our organization regularly work with others.	
25	If our organization were a sport, it would be an individual sport such as golf, tennis, running, or swimming.		If our organization were a sport, it would be a team sport such as basketball, soccer, baseball, or football.	
26	Being your own person is very important around here.		Being a team player is very important around here.	
27	My success in this organization depends primarily on my own performance.		My success in this organization depends primarily on my team's performance.	
28	Our organization requires a low number of meetings.		Our organization requires a high number of meetings.	
29	If I left this organization, my departure wouldn't negatively impact others.		If I left this organization, it would create a burden for others.	
30	When a problem arises I can generally solve it myself.		When a problem arises it generally takes the team to solve it.	
TOTAL				

Total the number of check marks for the
left column and the right column.

If you scored high on the left column: Solo Association (examples: insurance agencies, real estate agencies, independent distributors).

A high score here is indicative of organizations where collaboration is not important. Insurance agencies, product distributors, sales associations, medical practices, and so forth tend to score high in this area. People affiliate to offset expenses and perhaps to share community, but collaboration is not really important.

Your organization is a loosely knit group of uniquely talented individuals where people are free to make decisions on their own. Each person is fairly achievement and performance oriented. Individuals would prefer to work on their own, rather than to be subject to a higher authority. There is little dependence on each other.

The downside to this kind of organization is most apparent when collaboration really is necessary. Often organizations act in a solo capacity, but would be better off developing cross-functional approaches to problem solving. The solo association is most detrimental in large organizations where departments act in isolation for no justifiable reason.

If you scored high on the right column: Team Collaboration (examples: consulting firms, public relations agencies, publishing houses).

Team collaboration indicates a high need for thinking synergistically and systemically. Teams allow for the eradication of individual weaknesses. The whole is greater than the sum of the parts. This is especially important in businesses where individuals simply can't perform as well on their own.

Your organization sees itself as a team where every individual has a unique role, and people are looking for a place to belong. Decisions must be made in consensus with others, and people depend on each other for the success of the organization. Peer accountability tends to be high, and turnover adversely impacts the organization.

Team environments can be inefficient and may slow down talented individuals. The "lowest common denominator" effect can thwart the organization's success, especially when teamwork is not critical. Teams can also become enmeshed; the organization starts looking more like a dysfunctional family than a business. It is critical to distinguish between "team" and "family" as a social construct. A business should never represent itself as a family.

MOTIVATION QUADRANT

	DESTINATION	✓	JOURNEY	✓
31	In our organization, work is more important than outside life.		In our organization, outside life is more important than work.	
32	Performance is most critical in our organization.		Relationships are most critical in our organization.	
33	Financial success is the bottom line.		Service is the bottom line.	
34	We expect to produce results very quickly around here.		We know it will take time for results to emerge.	
35	We need to work quickly.		We can take our time.	
36	If we don't produce results, we will fail our mission.		If we don't make a difference in people's lives, we will fail our mission.	
37	In our organization, talent is critical.		In our organization, sensitivity is critical.	
38	Where our organization is headed is more important than where we are.		Where we are is more important than where we are heading.	
39	Our meetings are more characterized by decision making than social interactions.		Our meetings are more characterized by social interactions than decision making.	
40	Our organization values "the destination."		Our organization values "the journey."	
TOTAL				

Total the number of check marks for the
left column and the right column.

If you scored high on the left column: Destination Driven (examples: banks and credit unions, manufacturing companies, publicly held companies).

A high score here indicates a bottom-line orientation for your organization. Results, performance, and measurements are critical. Failure to meet objectives may result in the dissolution of your business. This is especially important when passive investors are involved and expect a return on investments.

People in your organization really enjoy work. It is important to produce results very quickly and to work very quickly. You have a pretty clear picture of where you want your organization to go, and meetings are characterized by decisions, accountability, and deadlines.

Destination-driven organizations can neglect people and ignore "the process," ultimately leading to their demise. While the bottom line is crucial, be sure to pay attention to how you get there. The end doesn't always justify the means.

If you scored high on the right column: Journey Oriented (examples: churches, counseling centers, social agencies).

If you scored high on this scale, then you likely work for an organization that cares more about the daily process than the bottom-line results. Your people tend to see work as necessary to survival, but it is not an orienting value. Relationships are critical in your organization. Results can be obscured by the process over a long period of time. There's not much need to rush, and it's very important to make a difference in what you do. You enjoy being together in your meetings, which are characterized by lots of socializing.

Journey-oriented organizations may have a difficult time with deadlines and accountabilities. Be sure to distinguish between the results and the process. You may find yourself on a treadmill with no apparent way to know when you've arrived.

The Bottom Line

Often there is a discrepancy between the perceived place on the continuum and the behaviors associated with that perception. This is an organizational dissonance, and it needs to be handled as a core organizational development issue. For example, an organization may place a high value on "team" as represented on the continuum, but behaviors communicate a "solo" approach. The incongruent message creates organizational confusion and often results in a blind spot that hinders productivity at the most fundamental levels.

As you think about the four quadrants ask yourself:

■ Which side of the continuum do we want to be on?
■ If outsiders were looking in, which side would they see?
■ Is there incongruence between perception and reality?
■ Are our managers and employees on the same side?
■ Do certain divisions need to be on a different side than the others?
■ Have we clearly defined these expectations so that our staff can make split-second judgments?
■ Are these values represented in our hiring, training, development, reward, recognition, promotion, and firing decisions?
■ Do these values help us make the right strategic and tactical decisions?

Notes

Prologue: The Thing in the Bushes

1. Jennifer Salopek, "Train Your Brain," *Training and Development,* October 1998, electronically retrieved from http://www.astd.org/CMS/templates/index.html?template_id=1&articleid=20211.

1: Break the Code

1. Kevin and Jackie Freiberg, *Nuts!* (New York: Broadway Books, 1996), p. 36.
2. Freiberg, p. 37.
3. Quoted by James C. Collins and Jerry I. Porras, *Built to Last: Successful Habits of Visionary Companies* (New York: HarperBusiness, 1997), p. 48.
4. Quoted by James C. Collins and Jerry I. Porras, "Building Your Company's Vision," *Harvard Business Review,* September 1, 1996, electronically retrieved at http://www.elibrary.com.
5. Collins and Porras.
6. Electronically retrieved at http://www.discovery.com/area/someone/someone971013/answer.html.
7. Electronically retrieved at http://lava.larc.nasa.gov/ABSTRACTS/LV-1998-00007.html.
8. Thomas Watson Jr., *A Business and Its Beliefs* (New York: McGraw-Hill, 1963), p. 5.

2: Encourage Personal Excellence

1. Tom Morris, "How Much Is Enough?" *Fast Company,* July-August 1999.
2. "Downshifting Yourself," *Industry Week,* May 20, 1996, p. 126.
3. Faye Rice and Rahul Jacob, "Managing: Champions of Communication," *Fortune,* 3 June 1991, p. 111.

3: Unleash Leadership in Everyone

1. Joel Garreau, "Point Men for the Revolution: Can the Marines survive a shift from hierarchies to networks," *The Washington Post,* 6 March 1999, p. A1.
2. Thomas A. Stewart and Ricardo Sookdeo, "Cover Story: How to Lead a Revolution," *Fortune,* November 28, 1994, p. 48; Rick Mullin, "A New Culture for Zeneca Ag Products," *Chemical Week,* June 7, 1995, p. 40.
3. Michael E. McGill and John W. Slocum Jr., "A Little Leadership, Please?" *Organizational Dynamics,* January 1, 1998, electronically retrieved at www.elibrary.com.
4. Stewart and Sookdeo.
5. Leighton Ford, *Transforming Leadership* (Downer's Grove, IL: InterVarsity, 1993), p. 251.

4: Practice Relational Network Thinking

1. Pat Williams, *Ahead of the Game* (Grand Rapids: Baker, 1999), pp. 196-197.

6: Nurture Effective Communication

1. Cited by Deborah Tannen, "The Power of Talk: Who Gets Heard and Why," *Harvard Business Review*, 1 September 1995, pp. 138ff; electronically retrieved from www.elibrary.com.

7: Balance Trust and Cynicism

1. Marc Breslow, "Michael Moore to GM: Show Some Respect!" *Dollars & Sense,* September 19, 1998, p. 9.
2. Brian S. Akre, "Yokich: 'No trust . . . whatsoever' between GM and United Auto Workers," AP Online, June 26, 1998.
3. Mike Lopresti, "Coach K & Duke Really Back," Gannett News Service, February 17, 1997, p. S12.
4. *USA Today*, March 11, 1999, p. 2C.
5. Letters, *Sports Illustrated,* April 13, 1992, p. 6.
6. Thomas Teal, "The Human Side of Management," *Harvard Business Review,* 1 November 1996, pp. 35ff.

8: Proactively Manage Change

1. As quoted by Scott Kirsner, "Collision Course," *Fast Company,* 1 February 2000, p. 118.

9: Focus Beyond Yourself

1. Story electronically retrieved at http://www.globalideasbank.org/wbi/WBI-85.HTML.
2. Frank Vogl, "Business Ethics: More and more, industries must incorporate social issues in management for success," *The Earth Times,* August 7, 1998, p. 9; Michael Harrison, "We looked in the mirror and we didn't like what we saw," *Independent,* April 22, 1998, p. 19.
3. Electronically retrieved at http://www.mgeneral.com/3-now/97-now/041097db.htm.
4. Rosabeth Moss Kanter, "From Spare Change to Real Change: The Social Sector as Beta Site for Business Innovation," *Harvard Business Review,* May 1, 1999, pp. 122ff.
5. Kanter.
6. Kanter, p. 127.
7. Electronically retrieved at http://www.whitedog.com.
8. Charles Handy, *Beyond Certainty* (Boston: Harvard Business School Press, 1998), p. 75.

Epilogue: Developing Code, Performance, and People

1. Eric Ransdell, "The Nike Story? Just Tell It!" *Fast Company,* 1 February 2000, p. 44.
2. Ransdell.
3. Quoted in "Leadership Coaching: Lessons from the Dean," *The Strategist,* the newsletter of Nice Enterprises, Inc., February 1998, Vol. 15, No. 2, electronically retrieved at http://www.trynice.com.

ABOUT THE AUTHORS

KEVIN G. FORD

Kevin Ford is the president of TAG, a management consulting firm in Fairfax, Virginia, with offices in Pittsburgh, Denver, Phoenix, and Detroit. He is the chairman of Performula Development Company and a senior consultant with the Joy Leadership Center. Kevin was the Senior Facilitator for the Redesign of the U.S. Army, commissioned by the Office of the Chief of Staff.

Kevin's focus is in organizational development, performance management, and strategic planning. He was the pioneer of PERFORMULA™, a completely automated, competency-based performance management system. The software program is now being released to businesses around the country.

He is also a coauthor of the nationally acclaimed RHO Factor Survey, an organizational assessment instrument featured by the American Academy of Management. Kevin has spoken publicly to thousands of people around the world and has been quoted extensively in the press. He is in constant demand as a facilitator and speaker for various corporations and organizations.

He is currently working with Ken Blanchard, George Gallup Jr., Charles Handy, Pete Coors, Truett Cathey, Steve Reinemund, and several other world-renowned business leaders to study the inner life of leadership.

JAMES P. OSTERHAUS, PH.D.

DR. JAMES P. OSTERHAUS is a senior consultant for TAG. He is also a counseling psychologist and has helped a variety of organizations and families bring about relational health. Dr. Osterhaus holds a Ph.D. in counseling psychology from American University and has degrees in counseling from Virginia Polytechnic Institute and Catholic University. He is the author of *Family Tales, Questions Couples Ask,* and *Bonds of Iron.*

He was commissioned by the Office of the Vice President to study reorganizational issues in the federal government. He is a popular facilitator and speaker for businesses throughout North America and is in constant demand as an Executive Coach.

ABOUT TAG

TAG is a management consulting firm in Fairfax, Virginia, with offices in Pittsburgh, Denver, Phoenix, and Detroit. TAG has worked with clients around the nation, including the Federal Aviation Administration, Kaiser Permanente, Merrill Lynch, the Dana Corporation, and Blackboard, Inc. TAG's experience is unparalleled. Its partners and consultants include the former vice president of human resources at Walt Disney World, management faculty from the Georgetown School of Business, the creative genius behind the Pizza! Pizza! and Got Milk? campaigns, the winner of the 1993 Smithsonian Technology Award, and a commission from the Office of the Vice President of the United States to study organizational development issues in the federal government.

To contact TAG, call 1-877-TAGLINE or visit their website at www.877tagline.com. Kevin Ford can be reached by e-mail at *kford@877tagline.com*. James Osterhaus can be reached at *josterhaus@877tagline.com*.

Ford, Kevin Graham   HD58.9
The thing in   F699t

Ford, Kevin Graham
AUTHOR
The thing in the bushes   HD58.9
TITLE   F699t
13600

	2001
DATE DUE	BORROWER'S NAME